D1478783

THE BALINESE PEOPLE

THE BALINESE PEOPLE

A REINVESTIGATION
OF CHARACTER

GORDON D. JENSEN
LUH KETUT SURYANI

KUALA LUMPUR
OXFORD UNIVERSITY PRESS
OXFORD SINGAPORE NEW YORK

Oxford University Press

Oxford New York Toronto
Delhi Bombay Calcutta Madras Karachi
Kuala Lumpur Singapore Hong Kong Tokyo
Nairobi Dar es Salaam Cape Town
Melbourne Auckland Madrid

and associated companies in
Berlin Ibadan

Oxford is a trade mark of Oxford University Press

Published in the United States
by Oxford University Press, New York

© Oxford University Press 1992
First published 1992
Second impression 1993

British Library Cataloguing in Publication Data

Jensen, Gordon D.
The Balinese people: a reinvestigation of character.
I. Title II. Suryani, Luh Ketut
959.86

ISBN 0-19-588557-0

Library of Congress Cataloging-in-Publication Data

Jensen, Gordon D.
The Balinese people: a reinvestigation of character/Gordon D. Jensen,
Luh Ketut Suryani.
p. cm.
Includes bibliographical references and index.
ISBN 0-19-588577-0:
1. Balinese (Indonesian people)—Psychology. 2. Balinese
(Indonesian people)—Mental health.   3. Balinese (Indonesian
people)—Social life and customs.   4. Personality and culture—
Indonesia—Bali Island.   5. Bali Island (Indonesia)—Social life
and customs.   6. Bateson, Gregory.   7. Mead, Margaret, 1901–1978.
I. Suryani, Luh Ketut, 1944– .   II. Title.
DS632.B25J46 1992
305.89 922-dc20
91-36772
CIP

Printed by Kyodo Printing Co. (S) Pte. Ltd., Singapore
Published by Oxford University Press,
19–25, Jalan Kuchai Lama, 58200 Kuala Lumpur, Malaysia

To the Balinese people

Acknowledgements

WE gratefully acknowledge the help of many who have given of themselves and their time to provide us with help, inspiration, and information for our studies and writing.

Dr Tjokorda Alit K. Adnjana, lecturer in Pharmacology, Udayana University, Suryani's husband, accompanied us on many trips to the field, conducted interviews, took photographs, co-authored our papers on palm wine drinking and acute psychosis, and assisted in the word processing of manuscripts. Because he grew up in a household of the royal family of Klungkung, he was a source of information about that subculture and could offer comparisons with the plains villages where he has lived for 20 years. He was a constant source of support. He and Suryani welcomed Jensen to their home during most of his visits to Bali.

Made Kaler, secretary to Bateson and Mead in 1936–8, granted us interviews. Karba, a major subject of their studies and films, gave us a number of interviews in Bayung Gede. Others who assisted us in various ways included: Dr A. A. M. Djelantik, former dean, Udayana University, School of Medicine, lecturer in Sekolah Tinggi Seni Indonesia (STSI), and head of Walter Spies Foundation; Professor Hildred Geertz, Department of Anthropology, Princeton University; Meutia Farida Swasono, medical anthropologist, University of Indonesia, Jakarta; Professor George Devos and Elizabeth Collins, Ph.D. candidate, Department of Anthropology, University of California, Berkeley; and Professor Arnold Meadow, Department of Psychiatry, University of California, Davis. The studies were funded in part by a grant from the University of California, Pacific Rim Faculty Exchange Program.

We are indebted and extend heartfelt thanks to the people and village heads of Bayung Gede, to hundreds of Balinese villagers, several traditional healers, Hindu priests, government officials, and educators who gave freely and generously of their time and themselves. We thank our families for their assistance in many ways; and finally, we give offerings to the gods of Bali, who played a prominent role in the success of our ventures.

Davis, California   GORDON D. JENSEN
Denpasar, Bali   LUH KETUT SURYANI
April 1991

Contents

Plates

14 A Balinese Hindu temple in the mountainous area of Bedugul.

15 A gate to the sacred part of a Balinese Hindu temple.

16 The shrines of gods and ancestors at households in the plains are distinctly different from those at Bayung Gede. Each shrine is constructed of wood, brick, and a thatched roof.

17 A placenta is buried in the ground beneath this shrine at a household in a plains village. The placenta is the physical manifestation of one of the four 'sibling spirits' of the newborn (see Plate 40).

18 A clan praying together at a yearly family ceremony.

19 Two young women praying and being blessed at the temple belonging to their clan (*dadia*). The priest is sprinkling holy water from a bamboo utensil.

20 Offerings for the gods being borne by women in their finest clothes at a yearly ceremony in the village of Timbrah.

21 Food offerings, brought by women for a village ceremony in the plains, are placed on a platform in a temple pavilion (*bale*).

22 Young girls who will sing at the trance ceremony awaiting the procession through the village of Timbrah.

23 All dressed up awaiting a village ceremonial parade at Butabulan.

24 A *topeng* dancer with a *gamelan* orchestra in the background in the city of Ubud. The mask and elaborate costume are traditional for this dance.

25 Several priests, in trance, dancing at the yearly ceremony of a clan in Denpasar.

26 A high priest conducting ceremonies for a family at Klungkung.

27 Priests in trance at a clan ceremony.

28 The puppet master (*dalang*) of the shadow play (*wayang kulit*) sitting (on the left) behind the flame which backlights the screen. A four-man orchestra is on the right. The village children gather in the rear area to watch and listen. Most villagers sit in front of the screen to watch the shadows of the puppets and listen to the lengthy, animated, humorous monologue of the puppet master.

29 Mt. Batur, the sacred mountain to the villagers of Bayung Gede. It is an active volcano.

30 A view of Bayung Gede. It appears much the same as in the photograph by Bateson 50 years ago.

31 The main intersection of roads at Bayung Gede.

32   A side-street in Bayung Gede with walls surrounding household compounds. This photograph is identical with one taken by Bateson 50 years ago.

33   The kitchen and parents' sleeping quarters in a household compound in Bayung Gede. The architectural style is the same as that shown in Bateson's photographs 50 years ago.

34   Household shrines of the gods in Bayung Gede. These are made of woven bamboo placed on tree branches stuck in the ground which grow and produce leaves. Contrast these with those in the plains (see Plate 16).

35   A teenager sitting in the children's building in a household at Bayung Gede. The picture of a traditional Balinese woman is placed side by side with a modern 'pin-up girl'.

36   A child 'nurse' and baby at Bayung Gede. The Balinese child is carried for most of the first three years of life.

37   A young father of Bayung Gede holds his ailing infant.

38   A woman with goitre, common in this geographic area of Bayung Gede.

39   Karba's 80-year-old uncle at Bayung Gede. Although stooped, he still works actively.

40   Two placentas placed in coconut shells hang in a tree at Bayung Gede. This custom is peculiar to this village and is different from the custom in the plains (see Plate 17). However, the spiritual meaning attached to the placenta is uniform throughout Bali.

41   Offerings at the village temple in Bayung Gede.

42   A warrior dance (*baris*) at a village ceremony in Bayung Gede. The costumes are identical to those photographed by Bateson in 1938.

43   Karba, who was Margaret Mead's favourite subject in Bayung Gede, posing with the authors 52 years later. He became a village priest in 1987.

44   The emotions displayed here contradict Bateson and Mead's statements that the Balinese are emotionally withdrawn.

45   A husband and his wife in Bayung Gede posing uncomfortably for the authors. They display *lek*, which is embarrassment in the face of high-status persons.

46   A young woman placing an offering containing food and flowers for the evil spirits which dwell near the ground. The

wall of the family compound is in the background. The offerings (*mebanten*) in the tray balanced on her left hand will be placed at numerous locations known to be frequented by spirits.

47 The trunk of one banyan tree (a holy tree held in awe) near a small temple at Saba. The tourist standing near the centre indicates the size of the tree.

48 Rangda, the witch, in trance, being assisted by a man on each side during a ceremony at Kesiman.

49 A mischievous and playful *barong*, surrounded by accompanying villagers, moving through the village during the ceremonial days of Galungan. The villagers collect donations of money to be used in support of the local town administrative unit (*banjar*).

50 A *barong* mask.

51 A man in the plains grooming his fighting cock. The Balinese are seldom alone and generally spend time together in small groups such as this.

52 Men wrapping a razor-sharp blade around the leg of a cock in preparation for a cock-fight. This cock-fight preceded the village mass trance ceremony at Kesiman and is a symbolic spilling of blood to appease the evil spirits. Cock-fights are also occasions for betting and sport.

53 A *gamelan* orchestra playing at a clan ceremony.

54 A man self-stabbing himself with a kris at Kesiman during the annual ceremony of Kuningan. The surrounding men monitor him and will remove the kris from his hands when they deem it appropriate, usually after 20–30 seconds of self-stabbing. This represents a climactic event in dances involving Rangda, and in some ceremonies.

55 Emotional expressiveness shown by children in Bayung Gede. They do not exhibit the schizoid behaviour Bateson and Mead stated were characteristic of the Balinese.

56 Women preparing rice cakes for a family ceremony in Gumicik.

57 Men attentively observing a temple ceremony. Rice placed on the forehead and temple shows that they have prayed.

58 A traditional healer (*balian*) discussing his methods of treatment with the authors. He is intently engaged in this social interaction.

Chapter 1
Introduction

BATESON and Mead's study of the Balinese 50 years ago[1] and their subsequent publications and films still stand as standard reference works on Balinese personality and culture. In their book *Balinese Character: A Photographic Analysis* (1942), they presented an enormous amount of ethnographic data, much of which was illustrated with photographs (756 in all). Together, these emphasized the richness and complexity of ceremonies, dances, and events of everyday life that made up the culture. Their views of the Balinese have influenced many scholars[2] and have educated countless university students. However, in Bali their work is virtually unknown by native anthropologists. Those who have heard of it have either not read it or cannot understand it because of the writing style and format.

The authors' readings about Balinese culture included Bateson and Mead's publications. They found relatively few inaccuracies in the descriptive data in *Balinese Character*: some of minor and some of greater significance. However, based on their knowledge, experience, and observations, they were at considerable disagreement with Bateson and Mead's conclusions about Balinese character and disagreed with most of their interpretations of the culture. The Balinese today are far different from their portrayal. Had the Balinese changed so extensively over those 50 years or were Bateson and Mead basically wrong? The authors were inspired to undertake more detailed appraisals of Bateson and Mead's work, including systematic studies designed to evaluate their interpretations and conclusions.

In 1985, the authors first began their collaboration with a study of physical and mental health (Suryani et al., 1988) in a village in the mountainous Kintamani area, about 5 kilometres from Bayung Gede,[3] the primary village studied by Bateson and Mead.[4] In connection with this study, Jensen developed a broader interest in Balinese culture, particularly its psychosocial aspects. Suryani already had a long-standing interest in Balinese culture and had published several papers dealing with culture-bound syndromes and relationships between mental disorders and culture, particularly as these are important for clinical work. The authors' observations and studies for this work continued through 1990.

It should be noted that *Balinese Character* was authored by Bateson and Mead. However, the introduction and the portion of the book titled 'Balinese Character', including the conclusion (pp. 1–48), were signed by Mead alone. Bateson was responsible for the photography, contributed to the analysis of the data, and signed the section on notes and captions to the photographs (pp. 49–54). The bulk of the book and the data presented are contained in the photographs and their captions. The analytic scheme of these data was attributed to Bateson and formed much of the basis for the conclusions of Mead's section. When reference is made to Bateson and Mead or their work, it is in conjunction with the book *Balinese Character*. Quotations from Bateson and/or Mead or page references without author citation are from *Balinese Character* unless otherwise noted. Although partial quotations were selected as illustrative of issues, care was taken to ensure that these were not out of context. It is not possible to determine from the writing of *Balinese Character* if one or both authors were primarily responsible for the conclusions that were under Mead's name. However, ideas and quotations from the jointly authored book have been attributed to Mead when they came from the text she solely authored. When it seemed clear from Mead's writing and Bateson's photographs that they both played a part, both authors are cited.[5]

Bateson and Mead did not define the term 'character' in their book but in partial explanation referred to a common ethos: a thread, a prevalent tone, emotion, and sentiment of the people that, in spite of great diversity, runs through the people of Bali (the culture) (p. xiv).[6] Bateson and Mead (p. 60) stated that 'the basic psychological emphases of Balinese culture are the same both in Bayung Gede and the plains. The treatment of children is the same and the basic ethos is the same.' In their photographs they 'treated the culture of the mountains and the plains as a single psychological unit'. Bateson's original concept of ethos was 'a culturally standardized system of organization of the instincts and emotions of individuals' (1936: 118), abstractions that could be applied to all kinds of behaviour. They regarded character traits as behavioural and/or emotional phenomena. For example, Mead stated that the Balinese are fearful and that it is a culture based on fear; fear has behavioural manifestations and is an emotional phenomenon.

Bateson and Mead's publications and films on Bali were concerned primarily with the psychology of the culture. In this critique, the authors have focused primarily on the emotional, behavioural, psychological, and psychiatric aspects of Bateson and Mead's writings and the culture because this is their primary area of expertise as psychiatrists. Their work here is considered partly ethnography but mostly cross-cultural behavioural science and psychiatry. Since the authors are not anthropologists, they have not analysed Bateson and Mead's work in terms of cultural anthropology. Jensen obtained a background in cultural anthropology as a graduate student in anthropology. Suryani has been studying Balinese culture for the past 13 years, particularly as it pertains to medicine and psychiatry.

Many ethnographers of Balinese culture have made interpretations based on Western concepts and points of view. This has been fraught with many difficulties and misinterpretations for a variety of reasons (Hobart, 1985). For example, the Balinese attach an entirely different significance to cock-fights, compared to Westerners. Western thinking and meaning of language are often inapplicable to Balinese concepts. What has been generally lacking is an internal point of view by a Balinese.[7] This work fills that gap: it represents study by a scientist with lifelong experience of the culture. Suryani's professional position and personal relationships endow her with entrée to the people and many situations, comfortable acceptance by subjects, an intimate 'feel' for the culture, and a cognitive perspective that no foreigner can possess. In comparison with an outsider, a native researcher can better enter into the world of the Balinese as they live it.

Concepts from the field of cognitive anthropology hold that, in essence, 'cognition is culture', and that the behaviour and feelings of a culture are explicable only when placed within the belief system and cognitive set[8] of the culture. Balinese cognitive insights are very different from Western insights and it is difficult, if not impossible in many instances, for Westerners to acquire them. Mead recognized that she was treated and responded to in a peculiar way by the Balinese but she was insensitive to the reasons for this (see Chapter 4, p. 47).[9] In addition to presenting a Balinese perspective, this work represents a collaboration between a native Balinese scientist and a Western scientist, both of whom received training in Western medicine and psychiatry. This enabled joint study of the Western concepts expressed in English by Bateson and Mead. The intricacies, translations, theoretical advantages, and possibilities offered by such a collaboration were proposed by LeVine (1982: 220–4). For this he used the term 'bi-cultural research method' and stated:

The difficulty is that if the translation problem is taken seriously, solving it can become an end in itself, as indeed it is for those anthropologists who aim only to understand the rules and beliefs that constitute another culture and translate them into a language of scientific observation. In studying the personality system, however, we have to go beyond deciphering the cultural code, an essential step, to understand the subjective meanings encoded in the individual's organization of behaviour. The job demands so much of an outside investigator that it may never be carried out in more than a few cultures. The solution I propose is for collaboration between two behavioural scientists, one from the culture being studied and one from outside, in translating the psychological data collected by the indigenous behavioural scientist into a comparable data language, by explicating the contexts that give the individual's behaviour its cultural meanings. (LeVine, 1932: 220.)

In working with a foreign collaborator on the problem of translating the cultural rules for interpreting communication in his own culture, the non-Western behavioural scientist is forced to put into words implicit understandings that he may never have verbalized previously (and which less sophisticated persons of his cultural background cannot express verbally) and to make translations of these words into the European language that communicate into original meanings adequately. (LeVine, 1932: 223.)

The methodology and assumptions of the disciplines of the investigators affect results. Anthropologists' approaches are different from psychiatrists'. The authors' methodology was both similar to and different from that of anthropological fieldwork methodology as described by Mead (Mead and Macgregor, 1951: 189–98). In studying the many activities of daily life and other aspects of culture (e.g., drama and dance), the authors used an ethnographic approach similar to that of Bateson and Mead.

Studies of behaviours and emotions involved in activities such as cock-fights, blessings of offerings, traditional healing, and trance utilized interview techniques similar to those described by LeVine (1932: 305) for study of affective reactions and generally included direct observation of the activities. In interpreting these data, the authors utilized Western psychological and psychiatric theories. Their studies of patients can be regarded as clinical–sociocultural. The latter is an elaboration of the biopsychosocial model (Fink, 1988) by addition of the cultural dimension: attention is given to each of the interrelated parameters of behaviour and emotion. Clinical psychiatric methodology uses more than observed data because behaviour is considered to have multiple determinants, including context and inner experiences of the individual. The authors tried to enter into this inner world of the person to learn what his behaviour means in terms of his inner experience. They did not interpret or assume how the person felt in a situation or try to derive his feelings primarily from observations of his behaviour; on the contrary, they asked the subject how he felt, what he believed, and what the meaning of the experience or situation was for him. Questions were also asked to get the individual's ideas of the rules of the culture, the socially acceptable and unacceptable aspects, and how people reacted to them overtly and covertly (see LeVine, 1932: 305). Bateson and Mead relied heavily on photographs to present data. However, photographs reveal only a split second of behaviour and little of inner experience. Movies and videotapes show more but still are a limited portrayal of the meaning of behaviour.

The authors' method included both systematic and anecdotal observations and interviews[10] with persons in many areas of Bali,[11] including Bayung Gede. Interviews with Balinese were conducted primarily by Suryani in the native language of the individual, either Balinese or Indonesian. The average length of an interview was approximately an hour and some individuals were interviewed repeatedly on separate occasions. Informed consent was obtained for interviews and the use of photographs of persons identified in the book,[12] including Made Kaler, Bateson and Mead's closely associated secretary and translator. The authors made experimentally structured and naturalistic observations of mother–child interactions, the kinds that were key to Bateson and Mead's interpretations and conclusions. These observations were supplemented with videotapes of mothers and children in natural situations in Bayung Gede and other villages in the plains of Bali. Videotaped sequences in which it was clear that the camera was unobtrusive were viewed repeatedly for specific behaviours. More than 1,000 slides of Balinese culture taken by the authors over the past 10 years were studied for this purpose. The photographs for this book were taken by the authors.

The methodologies used varied according to the individual study. Most were field studies using observation and interviews. The authors' topic-oriented studies published elsewhere (e.g., on mental and physical health of the elderly, on acute psychosis, on culture-bound syndromes, and on palm wine drinking) included appropriate sampling procedures, semi-structured interview protocols, objective instruments, standardized criteria for diagnoses, and statistical analysis of data. These studies contributed to their data and knowledge of the culture and psychology of the people throughout the island.

The authors' field studies generally involved considerable time and travel. Suryani's study (1988) of 113 cases of acute psychosis required her to make five half-day visits to the home of each patient to talk with family members about the patient and the community. These visits were made to villages in all geographic districts of Bali over a one-year period. For the study of palm wine drinking (Suryani, Adnjana, and Jensen, 1990), Suryani made weekly visits of one to three days to a village in north Bali over a six-month period. The study of the elderly at a village in the mountainous Kintamani area (Suryani et al., 1988) similarly required Suryani and her assistants to make two half-day visits to each of 40 subjects over a six-month period.

In the course of their research, the authors became familiar with most of the locales, houses, and the palace where Bateson and Mead lived during their study. The house of Walter Spies, the artist who first received them on their visit and recommended that they select Bayung Gede as their village of study, has been converted into the Campuan Hotel near the popular tourist town of Ubud and it still has the impressive, lush, tropical-like environment that Mead (1977: 160) described. Colin McPhee's house[13] in Sayan, also near Ubud, which is set back from the road on the edge of a gorge, is still there and one can rent a room at a 'homestay'[14] just next door, below it, as Jensen did. Each time he passed this house on his way to his own bungalow, he was struck with an awesome feeling that this is the place where Bateson and Mead stayed for two months and experienced the tense incidents of the police interrogating all foreigners and jailing some, including Spies (Howard, 1984).[15] Mead (1977: 192) mentioned the palace at Bangli with its three golden doors, where they rented a pavilion and established their headquarters during the second year of their study and planned to conduct future studies. One can stay there today and rent a room as Jensen did by coincidence. An even more outstanding feature of this palace is an ancient stone carving over and around a golden door which is of Chinese design, brightly painted and a unique example of Chinese influence on the king at that time. This palace also has a building in the grounds that stands out like a sore thumb among the many Balinese pavilions because it is a Dutch design with solid walls and Dutch doors and windows. These buildings illustrate the influence of foreign cultures on this royal household. Bateson and Mead's house in Bayung Gede was located about 200 metres from the centre of the village. It has since been destroyed; an elementary school now stands on its site, but the same families live next door and across the street and these older residents recall Bateson and Mead, particularly Mead.

In summary, the authors were unable to replicate critical data or support the majority of Bateson and Mead's interpretations and conclusions, and found their basic assumptions inherently flawed. Bateson and Mead's study presented an inaccurate and misleading characterization of the Balinese as they are today and as they were at the time of the study 50 years ago.

This book presents data and results of studies which were aimed and designed to evaluate Bateson and Mead's work.[16] In addition to this critique, alternative formulations of psychosocial aspects of

Balinese culture are presented. The aim is to establish a more correct and valid portrayal of the life of the Balinese; what may be called, in the abstract, their character and culture. Unlike many works on cross-cultural psychiatry and cultural anthropology, the research for and writing of this book were done for the benefit of the people of the culture studied, as much as for Westerners.

The Balinese discussed in this book refer to the Balinese Hindu, who make up the overwhelming proportion of the people of Bali, i.e., 93.3 per cent of the population. However, Bali is a culture that has been influenced over the centuries by Hindu, Buddhist, Muslim, Chinese, and Dutch cultures, not to mention the American influence that now comes by way of the popular television programmes such as 'The Bold and the Beautiful', 'Dynasty', and 'The Cosby Show', presented in both Indonesian and English languages. For example, the city of Singaraja, the Dutch centre of government since the mid-nineteenth century, has clear characteristics due to Dutch and Muslim influences that are not evident in other large cities. Therefore, it is to be understood that the term 'Balinese' is a generalization with reservations. However, the authors agree with Bateson and Mead that through the Balinese there run common threads of character.[17]

Bateson and Mead excluded from their discussion the ruling caste (Ksatria), and the culture of north Bali, because these were influenced by foreigners in the preceding 60 years and because the members of these groups placed an 'emphasis upon the individual rather than upon his status' (p. xiv). They were correct about the foreign influence in north Bali because of the Dutch centre of government in Singaraja. However, they were incorrect about the factor of status. In fact, it is the lowest caste, Sudra, throughout the culture that is less concerned about stratification rather than the three higher castes because the lowest caste was not taught the implications of caste by parents, e.g., the special form of language and appropriate gestures used in addressing higher caste people. Only since the advent of public education have all children been taught those aspects of status. The lower caste is different from those above in the degree in which members express emotions such as in disagreements with parents, since they do not have the same customs of deference to parents, older brother, and other people. All Balinese are included in the authors' discussion in this book.

Suryani grew up as a member of the lowest caste in the regions of both north and south Bali[18] and married a man of the Ksatria caste from the last ruling family of Klungkung (in south Bali) and lived in that royal family household for some time. Suryani made in-depth studies of villages in north and south Bali. These experiences gave her an intimate knowledge of these areas and castes.

Of the eight former kingdoms on the small island of Bali, the members of the royal family of Klungkung were universally regarded as having paramount status. Even today the ordinary citizens of Klungkung are still very respectful towards the members of the palace (*puri*). When the last king of Klungkung died in 1965, all Klungkung males, both those residing in Klungkung and those outside the district, spontaneously shaved their heads in mourning. This gesture of respect has, in large measure, been based on the belief in the extraordinary powers of the royal family. Thus, when confronted with a natural disaster or an epidemic the people have always expected the members of the *puri* to visit the area affected and to be able to intervene with the gods for the alleviation of the catastrophe. For the same reason, all the adult members of this *puri* are still addressed as Dewa Agung or Dewa Agung Isteri (your highness, lord/lady, but literally 'an elevated godly being') and the children are called Cokor Dewa in the case of boys and Cokorda Isteri in the case of girls (Suryani, 1984).

In April 1989, a group of 20 Balinese and foreign scholars convened in Denpasar to receive and discuss the results of the authors' studies. The dialogue between the Balinese and foreign discussants with regard to the ways Balinese handle aggression, arguments, and conflicts illustrated a cultural gulf: the Balinese did not respond directly to repeated questions by Westerners about how Balinese experience and resolve conflict. Possibly their pattern of response derived from two factors: (1) the English terms used may have had different meanings for the Balinese, and (2) their avoidance of the issues and denial of conflict may have been consistent with the principal way that the Balinese typically handle these issues themselves, i.e., by suppression (see Chapter 8). The presentation, in both Indonesian and English languages, illustrated the ever-present challenge of valid translation of terms and concepts in this type of cross-cultural work.

In the process of studying and discovering many points of disagreement with Bateson and Mead, the authors often felt trepidation and tension at the prospect of a critique which would expose major errors. Both Bateson and Mead are regarded as highly important figures in the recent history of science: Mead as an anthropologist and Bateson as a basic behavioural scientist in studies of the mind, communication, and schizophrenia, as well as anthropology. The authors often wish both of them were alive and thus have the opportunity to respond to the findings in this book.

The process of researching for and writing of this book is, curiously, not unlike the cremation ceremony of Bali:[19] digging up the remains of a person long since buried, carefully cleaning the skeletal bones, aligning them to approximately the person's form, wrapping them carefully, placing this representation of the person in a tower for transport to the cemetery, making the offerings of respect, torching it, watching it go up in a tower of flames, gathering the remaining ashes from the dying embers, and finally taking them out to sea to cast them to the waters from which their soul will arise, and then perhaps encounter them in their reincarnated form. To the Balinese, cremation is both an end and a beginning of new life.

The authors had no professional relationship with Mead, nor did they ever meet her personally. They know of her only through her writings, her voice on films, her biographers, her autobiography, association with colleagues who had worked with her and/or knew her personally, and some of her students. Jensen did have professional contact with Bateson at the time when Bateson was studying communication in dolphins and Jensen's career was centred on research in primate social behaviour.

1. Bateson and Mead began the field study in 1936 and completed it in 1939.

2. Included are C. Geertz, 1966; Bock, 1988; Mrazek, 1983; Ketter, 1983; Eissler, 1944; Estabrook, 1942; Lewin, 1945; Gill and Brenman, 1961. C. Geertz commented in 1990 that he believed it was Mead's best work.

3. The spellings of most names and words have changed over the years. The pronunciations are unchanged. Bayung Gede is pronounced by-ung ge-day.

4. One has to admire and cannot help but be impressed with Bateson and Mead's pioneering spirit, especially when one visits Bayung Gede where life is obviously hard, dirty, and relatively unhealthy. Travel in those days was much more laborious than today. In Bayung Gede there were no electric lights, no toilets, and no running water; the streets were dusty and mud was everywhere in the rainy season. Bateson and Mead braved a physically taxing environment, especially for a foreigner, and withstood the physically and emotionally draining effects of a bout of malaria contracted in New Guinea. They treated these hardships not at all or only casually in their writings. Such was the life then for many ethnographers in the field and so it is today for much fieldwork.

5. According to H. Geertz (personal communication): 'A careful study of Gregory Bateson's other writings, before, during the work on Bali, and subsequently, shows that he made important intellectual contributions to the Bali Research. I have examined the field notes of Bateson and Mead in detail, and it is clear from the field notes of Bateson and Mead that this was completely collaborative work. In regard to the writing of *Balinese Character* itself, Bateson wrote all of the explanatory and interpretive material concerning the photographs, based on their joint analysis of all of their materials. It was on the basis of this analysis of photographic evidence that Mead wrote the introduction and conclusion for the book, not the reverse. This analysis, in the structure of its argument and in the manner in which evidence is marshalled shows clearly logical reasoning. Mead's other writings do not show this sort of theoretical precision, while Bateson's do.'

6. In a characterization of the Japanese, T. S. Lebra (1976: 1) utilized the term 'ethos' to mean both 'the thematic distinctiveness and the entirety of the Japanese cultural matrix'. For example, he emphasized the overwhelming impression from the literature that the Japanese are extremely sensitive to and concerned about social interaction and relationships, a behaviour pattern he called 'social preoccupation'.

7. There are now several publications in English on Balinese art by native Balinese scholars. See Djelantik (1986) and Bandem and deBoer (1981).

8. 'Cognitive set' is defined here as knowledge, categories, and patterns of thinking that direct a person's perception, thinking, and feeling in one way or another.

9. For an example of how Western and Balinese interpret and treat stimuli and events differently, see McPhee's (1946) description of peculiar sights (Chapter 6).

10. Instruments of reliability of observations are a challenge for future studies.

11. This included studies in all of the eight districts of Bali, in the mountain and plains areas in both north and south Bali.

12. Made Kaler from Denpasar and Karba from Bayung Gede were informed of the purposes of the interviews and kindly gave the authors permission to quote them.

13. McPhee, a musicologist, wrote about this house in *A House in Bali* (1946). According to ethnographer Hildred Geertz, the community of Westerners 'may have influenced Bateson unduly' (Howard, 1984: 191).

14. The local term for a small family-run group of rooms or apartments.

15. During a brief period in 1939 the government was concerned about homosexuality, particularly with regard to foreigners.

16. The authors have focused on Bateson and Mead's conclusions and those interpretations that are most significant for understanding Balinese character. Many of the errors and misinterpretations identified but which are of lesser significance for personality and character have not been cited. Such a fine tooth-comb appraisal would double the size of the task and detract from the main issues.

17. Mead and Bateson (p. xv) elaborated: 'There is no apparent difference in the character structure of the people in villages where trance is shared by all and those in villages where no one ever goes into trance; people in villages where every other woman is believed to be a witch and those in villages where no one is believed to be a witch. In most of the cultures of which we have systematic knowledge such matters are intricately and inextricably part of the personality of every participant member of the culture, but in Bali the same attitude of mind, the same system of posture and gesture, seem able to operate with these great contrasts in content with virtually no alteration in form. So also for climatic contrasts, and contrasts in wealth and poverty: the mountain people are dirtier, slower, and more suspicious than the plains people; the poor are more frightened than the rich; but the differences are in degree only; the same types of dirtiness, of suspicion, and anxiety are common at all levels.'

18. It was in south Bali that Bateson and Mead had the most experience.

19. For photographic illustrations and descriptions, see Bateson and Mead (pp. 232–55).

Chapter 2
Bali and Balinese Background

IN order to develop an understanding of Balinese culture and character, one needs some orientation to the country and its people. For this purpose, a sketch of the geography and demographics of the island is presented, and principles of the Balinese Hindu religion, social system, concepts of illness, and ceremonies are briefly summarized. The latter topics will be elaborated upon in the greater part of the book.

The island of Bali is geographically located about 8 degrees south of the equator and about 18 degrees north of the western end of Australia. It is a relatively small island, one of thousands that make up the archipelago of Indonesia, little known as the fifth largest nation in the world. Bali is 5 633 square kilometres, about twice as long as it is wide. A range of high volcanic mountains divides it into northern and southern portions. For the Balinese Hindu, the mountains are the palaces of the gods. The highest mountain, Mt. Agung (2 900 metres), located in Karangasem district, is sacred to the Balinese Hindus; on its slope stands the oldest and biggest temple in Bali, the mother temple (Pura Besakih).

Bali is a province of Indonesia; its capital is the city of Denpasar. There are eight districts (*kabupaten*) in Bali,[1] and the villages (*desa*) are made up of one or more (depending upon village size) organizational units called *banjar*. The total number of *banjar* is about 4,200. They are governing groups and are the basis of much of the communal life of the society. *Banjar* are a major institution in the community. They are a link with the central government and pass on their directives and information on issues such as family planning and health education, but most importantly, they serve the customs of religion. Like the family, they are of critical importance in everyday life. Traditional *banjar*—those that follow the traditional rules and customs, meetings, laws, and ceremonials—also deal with work, dances, music, and other arts. Modern *banjar*, usually in the urban areas, are not so strict in attendance rules of members and may have fewer community functions than the traditional *banjar* in the rural areas. The *banjar* meeting hall, centrally located in each village, is an open pavilion, serving as a local clubhouse and gathering place, day and night. A television set provides entertainment.

Members of the *banjar* are obliged to help one another perform a number of duties, especially those relating to religious ceremonies, such as the burial of a citizen of the *banjar*, and the construction and maintenance of buildings necessary for functions of the *banjar*. These are obligatory activities for *banjar* members and take precedence over their regular jobs and duties, whether they are employed by state institutions or private enterprise. A man may need to leave work without notice and without pay for days to weeks in order to work for his *banjar*.

One function of the *banjar* is to interpret the written and unwritten laws of the country and the *banjar* in order to ensure the security and peace of the *desa* and to uphold the honour and good name of *banjar* and *desa*. When problems arise, the mechanisms of the *banjar*, not lawyers, settle disputes and mete out punishment. For example, if a *banjar* member infringes on the decorum of the community, breaks its rules, or fails in his duties for the *banjar*, a sacred oath-taking ceremony (*mecor*) witnessed by the men of the *banjar* is held to decide guilt or innocence. It is understood by all that if the decision is in error and fails to punish the guilty, the gods will do so. A guilty person is sanctioned, fined, or if convicted of a very serious offence, isolated from the community. The latter punishment is indeed severe because it means that no one in the community will talk with him/her (*puik*), or help him/her to perform religious ceremonies and the person so punished may not take part in the activities of the *banjar*. An awareness of these sanctions motivates the people to strive faithfully to execute all their *banjar* duties and follow the village rules which are clearly known to all.

In the 1930s a *banjar* at night was described by McPhee (1946: 20–1):

At night the men's clubhouse became the social center. It was a long hut of bamboo and palm-thatch, with a raised floor of earth that had dried hard as a rock. Here the gamelan that belonged to the music club of the younger men in the village was kept. In the daytime you seldom passed without hearing from within the soft chime of gongs or metal keys as some child, sitting in the cool darkness of the empty hut, improvised and learnt for himself how to play. But after dark the hut was a luminous center surrounded by a blaze of little lamps. Outside the saleswomen had set down their tables of sweets and betel, while the members of the club gathered inside to practice. Now was the time to go through the music they already knew, for the sheer pleasure of it, or work over the difficult parts of some new composition they were just learning. . . . Late into the community night they played. From the house I could hear them going over phrase after phrase, correcting, improving, until the music began to flow of its own accord.

Today *gamelan* clubs practise often at many *banjar* while a few villagers sit around the edge chatting and watching. *Banjar* activities can draw large crowds and the atmosphere may resemble that around temples at times of festivals, especially in the evenings, when many food carts and stalls of food and other items surround the edges of the temple or line narrow, lantern-lit dirt streets filled with crowds taking breaks from an ongoing drama or dance performance.

Social Systems That Bind

Four social systems bind the Balinese together: the clan system (*dadia*), the stratification system (*kasta*), the community system (*banjar*), and the interest and working group system (*seka*).

The *dadia* system encompasses the combined extended families and all their ancestors. In this relationship, family members periodically band together in one place in ceremonies for the worship of God: at the house shrine (*sanggah*) for the immediate family or at the temple for the extended family (*pura*). At these ceremonies, they express feelings of devotion and respect for elders, e.g., at the ceremony of death (*nyumbah*), where food offered to the ancestors can be eaten (*nyurud*). These activities also strengthen the family bond.

The family, ancestors, and community are tightly enmeshed and interdependent. No one, except the vagrant or schizophrenic, can function without being part of all three. Every Balinese Hindu is imbued with them from birth and this early imprinting (to use an analogy from the field of ethology), with regular and frequent reinforcement, lasts throughout this life and the lives thereafter.

The divisions of caste, originally of Hindu origin, were based on their functions in the community: Brahmana, the highest caste (comprising high priests), were responsible for religious ceremonies; Ksatria (comprising kings, rulers, and their families, including the leader of the irrigation system or head of a village) had key roles in government; Wesia were involved in business and activities involving public welfare; and Sudra[2] were farmers and performed tasks for the other castes. There has never been an untouchable or outcast group as in Hindu India. Beginning around the 1920s, some members of the lowest caste, Sudra, objected to social implications of the caste terminology and changed it to Catur Warna or Catur Wangsa (meaning 'four colours'); they also changed Sudra to Jaba. In Bali, caste is determined by inheritance but it is no longer significant for individual functions in society or occupations. Today caste is functional only for social status and inheritance. The roles of priests in ceremonies are carried out not only by the high priest, but also by priests from any of the lower castes and most priests are from the lowest caste. In practice, many people of the Jaba caste regard priests from their caste as having high status, similar to the high priest from the Brahmana.

Each community is made up of many groups, each group consisting of individuals who come together for co-operative activities involving specific interests. Such groups are called clubs or *seka*. Each is named after its specific activity. There are working groups, such as *seka manyi* for harvesting rice, and *seka semal* for chasing squirrels that damage coconut trees, *seka mamula* for planting rice, and *seka numbeg* for cultivating; and there are groups which pursue an interest in the arts and even palm wine drinking such as *seka gong gamelan* (orchestra), *seka drama* (theatre), *seka barong* responsible for the care and dances of the *barong, seka kecak* (a dance), and *seka tuak* (palm wine). Young people, e.g., adolescents not yet married, are also members of their own special group called *seka truna-truni*. Equality and co-operation of members are the first rules of clubs.

The irrigation system (*subak*) (Covarrubias, 1937), based on religion, is presided over by the high priest and goddess of rice. Representatives from villages affected by the regional irrigation systems control the distribution of irrigation water that flows from the mountains to the sea and make decisions about planting crops. These complex networks of streams, canals, and ditches, so essential to life, bind large portions of the island together. Allocation of water is up to the *subak*. Villages hold elaborate ceremonies in honour of the rice goddess for protecting the rice planting, making crops flourish, and ensuring that rice storage houses in individual homes are full. The last-mentioned custom has decreased since the introduction of the new strains of rice which are not suitable for long-term storage, as was the old traditional rice. Irrigation systems encompass multiple communities and are an expression of long-standing intercommunity collaborative action.

The population of Bali in 1989 was 2,644,127, with about equal numbers of males and females. This represents less than 2 per cent of the total population of Indonesia, but Bali is the destination of more than 50 per cent of the tourists visiting Indonesia. Bali has experienced considerable population growth since the 1930s when its population was only one million. More recently, growth has slowed down in the period 1971–80, the average growth per year being 1.69 per cent.

One might well wonder how an island that has so little land and where population density is one of the highest in the world could assimilate so many new inhabitants and provide housing space to a population that more than doubled in 40 years. Amazingly, Bali does not appear crowded to the resident or the visitor because of its endless vistas of rice fields, with a water-buffalo here and there, and miles of road through sparsely populated areas, even around the populous capital city of Denpasar. Bayung Gede in 1991 looks as it did in Bateson's photographs 50 years ago, and its population has only increased from about 500 to 750. Suryani remembers, as a child 45 years ago, hearing her father tell of encountering tigers in the forest near their home in north Bali. Today, not a single tiger is left in Bali and much of previously forested land has been cleared for farming.

Most of the main roads in Bali are two-lane and clogged by trucks, minibuses, cars, motor cycles, bicycles and food carts during the day and especially during festival times, which are frequent. After dark, these traffic jams disappear and streets are strikingly quiet. A cremation ceremony or village ceremony can take precedence over main thoroughfare traffic, causing an entire main highway through Denpasar to be closed off for half a day. One-horse buggy taxis (*dokar*) still abound in Denpasar and other large cities. These are more expensive than the public or private minibuses, but they have the advantage of taking you to the door. They are privately owned and can carry up to 4–5 adults or crowd in about 8 children.

Ninety-three and three-tenths per cent of the Balinese are Hindu. About 5 per cent are Muslim and the remainder are Buddhist, Protestant, and Catholic. Occupations include farmers (animal husbandry, forestry, and fishery), 50.74 per cent; government officers and public services, 15.33 per cent; tradesmen, hotel staff, and restaurant employees, 14.52 per cent; industrial workers, 9.84 per cent, and builders, 4.82 per cent.

Per capita income is relatively low in Bali, currently averaging the equivalent of less than US$300.00 per year. However, poverty is not evident in the way that it is in developing countries such as India, Mexico, and Brazil. There are very few beggars or homeless even in the capital city of Denpasar and fewer in the countryside. There are no shanty towns. Even the poorest can afford or manage to obtain clothes, shelter, and food. In some villages, Western-type medical care is marginal. However, public health clinics exist even in the remote areas. Looking at lifestyle and earnings from a Balinese perspective, the authors disagree with Wikan (1987: 356) that the Balinese may be among the world's poorest people.

Bali has no seasons in terms of temperature or growing, only a rainy season from December through March and a dry season. During the rainy season it seems much hotter because of higher humidity. In the mountain areas it rains more than on the plains and at the shores. Water is no problem (except in the desolate western part of the island); it flows through the rice paddies, and in the streams, rivers, and ditches that run alongside the roads in which the people bath themselves and their cows daily. These streams always appear dirty because they pick up soil along the way and are sometimes used for refuse. Viral hepatitis is endemic and carried in the irrigation and bathing streams. Malaria is rare but still endemic in the northern part of the island. However, it is quite common on the neighbouring island of Lombok.

Of course, food is a critical aspect of life in Bali. People of all ages tend to be thin, and obesity is very unusual. No one goes hungry because of the low cost of food, the availability of natural fruit, family support and sharing, and the food served at the frequent festivals. Rice is a staple (two or three times a day), but vegetables, meat (beef, pork, and chicken), and seafood (less in the mountains) are also consumed. The food is spicy and often hot with chopped peppers. Spice Islands, a historical name for Indonesia, was not a misnomer. There are other special flavourings:

In the air was a powerful, complex smell, acrid and pungent, of burnt feathers, fish, and frying coconut oil. I was to find this a daily smell, punctual and inevitable as the morning smell of coffee at home. It came chiefly from *sra*, a paste of shrimps that had once been ground, dried, mixed with sea-water, then buried for months to ferment. It was used in almost everything, fried first to develop the aroma. It was unbelievably putrid. An amount the size of a pea was more than enough to flavor a dish. It gave a racy, briny tang to the food, and I soon found myself craving it as an animal craves salt. Her sweets were even stranger. For lunch would end perhaps with corn and grated coconut mixed with a syrup of palm-sugar, soggy little balls of rice-paste treacherously filled with more syrup, or a sliced pineapple to be eaten with salt, red pepper and garlic. (McPhee, 1946: 17.)

Each village has its market-place and some of the larger ones are attended by people from several villages in the area. One can buy all sorts of food and things: dried fish, live chickens, snacks, refreshments, imported items for homes, kitchen articles, incense, perfume oil from fresh blossoms, thongs, toys, woven mats, and hats. It is a place to meet, gossip, and socialize, or just to while away time in a busy festive atmosphere.

Early books and travel publications on Bali (e.g., Krause, 1988; Powell, 1930) pictured and described the island at the beginning of this century as a paradise boasting lush tropical landscape and graceful people, with an unreal emphasis on lovely young women bathing nude under falling water. The former is still very much in evidence but the latter is less common. Although Bali is much more populated now than it was a half century ago, it remains incredibly scenic with vistas of terraced rice paddies, reflecting a myriad of colours from deep green to brown, and mirroring mountains, clouds, and palm trees, set against backdrops of palms, bamboo groves, and an occasional house with a grass roof. A rice harvest is usually going on somewhere because of non-synchronous planting and rice is harvested in the labour-intensive way by local groups of people, predominantly women, cutting the rice plants by hand, and carrying them on their heads to another spot for threshing against a board. The view from Colin McPhee and Jane Belo's house in Sayan, where Bateson and Mead stayed in 1939, overlooks a most spectacular valley of terraced rice paddies with a river coursing below. The valley appears much the same as that described by McPhee in his delightful book, *A House in Bali* (1946), which also recounted the problems evil spirits caused to his house, a graphic portrayal of the beliefs and religion of Bali.

Ceremonies

Religious ceremonies, which are integral to the thinking and attitudes of the Balinese, continue as frequently and as strongly as ever and remain relatively unchanged over the years in spite of modernization trends. Children are excused from school and adults from work in order to participate.

The Balinese regularly perform a multitude of ceremonies which occupy a relatively large portion of their time and effort, consume a significant portion of their savings, and have deep significance for life. A number of scholars have described many in detail (Belo, 1953; Covarrubias, 1937; Boon, 1977; Hooykaas, 1977; and Moerdowo, 1973). Ceremonies usually involve the extended family, one's own *banjar*, or the entire *desa*. Some ceremonies, such as Panca Wali Krama at the mother temple, involve all of Bali: during one month in every 10 years, cars, trucks, and buses bring people of all ages to pray and make offerings. Almost all ceremonies involve the participation of many people. Generally, both men and women take part and their roles are separate. For example, women make the *banten* and other offerings, and help prepare and serve food; men organize and arrange the procedure for the ceremony, attend to the construction of all effigies and special buildings for the occasion, make costumes for the dances, arrange and repair orchestral instruments, and manage the logistical problems which must be dealt with in order to ensure success.

Most ceremonies and dances take place in and around the temple structures, as is strikingly evident to visitors to Bali. There are more than 10,000 temples in Bali, which serve a variety of purposes, including family, state, rice fields, and the sea. The village temples are large enough to accommodate most of the community at a single ceremony. Temples are walled-in open-air areas containing several small pavilions and shrines.

Persons of all status, including the poorest families, participate in community festivals and temple ceremonies. This is true of the four villages in south Bali and the two in north Bali in which the studies for this book were carried out. The authors' findings contradict statements by Wikan (1987), based on her studies of several villages in north Bali, that aesthetic festivals were for the wealthy.[3]

An important group of ceremonies observed by the Balinese relate to the individual's life cycle (*manusa yadnya*). Each milestone in this cycle is marked by a ceremony, the purpose of which is to expiate past wrong deeds and thereby achieve greater perfection in this, and the future, life. Such ceremonies are conducted at birth, at the separation and burial of the placenta, at seven days of age, at one month, at one month and seven days, at three months, at six months, and at the birthday celebrations every six months thereafter (*otonan*), according to the Balinese calendar.[4] Other milestone ceremonies occur at the loss of deciduous teeth, menarche, and adolescence (e.g., tooth filing, now a token filing procedure to bring the upper teeth into a straight line in order to diminish the six evil qualities of human nature: anger, desire, greed, jealousy, irresoluteness, and intoxication), at marriage, and at death (e.g., cremation, *ngaben*; twelve days thereafter, *ngrorasin*; and unification with God, *ngukur, mligia*). An elective milestone in life is the preparation (culminating in a ceremony called *pawintenan*) to become a holy person, who vows celibacy and is instructed in a certain diet (e.g., vegetarian) and other rituals in order to remove bad thinking and better serve God and the gods. A holy person carries out religious duties individually and has a chance to become a priest who ministers at Hindu ceremonies, and serves and assists the people in religious ceremonies.

There are many general ceremonies related to time according to the Balinese calendar (e.g., Galungan, Kuningan). In a six-month period there are at least five Tumpek ceremonies: Landep, Uduh, Uye (*kandang*), Kuningan, and Wayang. The purpose of Tumpek Landep is to give thanks for all material things made from metal; Tumpek Uduh, for plants; Tumpek Uye (*kandang*), for animals; Tumpek Wayang, for puppets; and Tumpek Kuningan, for the well-being of the world and its contents. In addition there is the full moon ceremony (Purnama), and the 'dark moon' ceremony (Tilem); Kajeng Kliwon ceremonies occur every 15 days, a potentially fearful time because on this day evil spirits abound and persons with bad intentions may easily be possessed and, in turn, disturb or harm others. Special offerings are given for the demons: rice in five different colours formed in the shape of a human, a slice of onion and ginger, and a little piece of pork with a drop of fresh blood, offered on the ground at the middle gate of the house. Persons with mental illness generally date the onset of their symptoms to that day.

The ceremony of Nyepi marks the new year, according to the Balinese Isaka calendar, and occurs approximately every 364 days, usually in March. At Nyepi all fires are extinguished, both literally in the real world and figuratively in hearts that are malevolent. By participating in this day of silence, the Balinese hope to restore inner peace. The day preceding Nyepi is even more important. There are 'exorcistic' rituals of great power which are made more serious by Balinese notions that for the past months there have been many more dangerous demons roaming the villages and causing illnesses, crop failures, and other disasters. The Balinese perform the *mecaru* ceremony with offerings and sacrifices (such as a chicken, duck, or cow) to placate the demon deities (Buta and Kala), and the *ngrupuk* ceremony to placate all evil spirits which surround their homes, family, and members of their *banjar* and their *desa* so that they will leave and peace will again prevail.

The ceremonies of Galungan (every 210 days) and Kuningan (the tenth day after Galungan) are major events celebrating mankind's victory of good over evil (i.e., the repudiation of bad deeds and feelings) such as thievery, violence, anger, and jealousy. On these festive occasions there are many colourful ceremonies throughout the island which are easy for the visitor to encounter and attend because they are marked by crowds around roadside temples and by processions of brightly clothed people in local costumes, the women carrying tall offerings on their heads, accompanied by *barong* and *gong* orchestras, all walking along the road on their way to the temples.

The ceremony of Saraswati is to thank the goddess of knowledge; Pagerwesi, to make offerings to God for providing welfare and giving happiness to the world and all its contents; and Siwalatri, to give thanks to Siwa, one manifestation of God, for dissolution of sins, such as being angry at a parent or failing to make an offering to the gods.

Offerings to the gods are a part of every ceremony. They usually contain flowers and betel-nut arranged in a small tray made of woven young palm leaf (*banten*) along with incense smoke (*dupa*), and holy water (*tirta*), accompanied by a high priest's *mantera* (i.e., holy chanting to call the gods). Other offerings for ceremonies include not only *banten*, but also aesthetically arranged baskets or stacks of fruit, egg, chicken, or duck, which are usually carried to the temple by women.[5]

In addition to the general community-wide and individual ceremonies, there are many local ceremonies such as those at home, at *banjar*, at an anniversary of the construction or repair of a local temple, and even at a specific temple on the grounds of the mother temple at Besakih.

Mead's colourful writing[6] gives a flavour of the people on ceremonial days:

But at the New Year, these same roads are empty, stretching up and down the frequent hills, between terraced fields holding green rice, to another district when the rice is golden, on to a third where the rice is so young that the flooded beds seem filled mostly with reflections from the sky. The air on every other day of the year is filled with sound, high staccato voices shouting the clipped ambiguous words of familiar speech or artificially prolonging the syllables of polite address, quips of passers-by to the vendor girls who make a professional art of repartee, babies squalling on hips of their child nurses; and over and above and behind all these human sounds, the air on other days carries music from practicing orchestras, from an individual idly tapping a single metallophone, from children with jew's-harps, and from whirring musical windmills set on narrow standards high against the sky. On feast days, the roads are crowded with processions of people in silks and brocades, walking in easily broken lines behind their orchestras and their gods; gods represented by temporary minute images seated in small sedan chairs; gods represented by images made of leaves and flowers; gods which are masks or bits of old relics. With the processions mingle groups of people grimed from work, hurrying lightly beneath heavy loads; and theatrical troupes, their paint and fine costumes tucked away in little bundles, trudge wearily behind the two-man mask, the patron dragon (Barong) who walks quietly with covered face.

To this may be added the heady images of a roadside procession: a group of 30 men or so in chorus singing long melodious chords, interspersed with a band of body-resonating giant gongs, throbbing drums, and cymbals; a small forest of coloured tassel-rimmed parasols high above the crowds; long lines of women carrying intricately arranged offerings stacked on their heads, a few of whom appear to go spontaneously into trance as they are possessed by the gods while still miraculously maintaining the balance of the offerings on their heads; people sitting on the temple grounds raising their hands in prayer as the priest casts holy water over them; crowds of people milling about in the gathering darkness, lit only by lantern and moonlight; all seemingly happening at once, raising the emotions to a heightened and sustained level.

Trance rituals and ceremonies play a significant and enduring role in dealing with evil spirits and witchcraft (Belo, 1960). According to Belo, almost the whole populace in some villages go into trance at certain ceremonies. However, there are individuals who do not experience trance. Trance states in ritual and dance are socially approved, facilitated, and controlled. Trance is a normal or paranormal state, as is hypnosis; both are altered states of consciousness. McPhee, an observer of the 1930s trance phenomena that exist today in the same manner, vividly described one such occurrence (1946: 47):

While, from the shadows, there came the sound of animated music from the *gamelan*, a group of women stepped forth to dance the *gabor*, the presentation of offerings of wine, oil, incense. Their shoulders were bare, their breasts bound with woven scarves, and in their hair were crowded orchids, jasmine, gardenias. I recognized Nyoman's two wives among them as they danced, seriously, tranquil, as though in their sleep. In and out of the shrines they wove, disappearing in the shadows, emerging into the moonlight, until at last they paused before the altars, where a priestess stood, to fan the essence of the offerings in the direction of the gods.

It was close to dawn when, in the now almost deserted courtyard, the priestess fell once more in trance. In a hoarse, exhausted voice she announced the presence of the god. It was the god now speaking. There was a pause. The god called attention to the poor condition of the temple. It was in need of repair. Another pause. The priest now asked advice about certain village affairs. What must the offerings be for the next feast? Back and forth the voices went, until at last the priestess grew silent and would talk no more. In the dim light of early morning she woke, looked dazedly around, and we knew the gods had left.

Principal Hindu–Dharma Beliefs in Bali

The Balinese Hindu religion, which is of critical importance to an understanding of the Balinese (Geertz and Geertz, 1975), is unique. It has roots in India but was developed largely in Java, and it has been influenced by Buddhism, by the original Balinese (aboriginal) culture, and by Balinese pre-Hindu animistic and ancestral cults. The five principal beliefs (*panca srada*) are: (1) the existence of a Supreme God (Sang Hyang Widi Wasa); (2) the existence of an eternal soul (*atman*); (3) the conviction that every deed has rewards (*karma pala*); (4) reincarnation (*punarbawa*); and (5) an eventual unity with God (*moksa*).

Punarbawa is rebirth into the world which is repeated until one attains the perfect life, at which point it ends because one is unified with God. *Punarbawa* is not only a belief but a prominent aspect of daily life. The Balinese believe that the events of a person's current life are caused, in part and often, by deeds in a previous life. One's current life is oriented to expiate past undesirable deeds and work towards a better future life.

In order for families to know what their reborn infant is like, they take him to a spiritual specialist (*balian matuun*) to find out which ancestor's soul is in the child and the nature of that personality. As Mead put it, the body is the clothing for the soul. The *balian* becomes possessed by the soul of the ancestor, which tells the family what it needs in order to carry out its new life, e.g., promises that were not fulfilled in a previous life, such as giving a puppet performance, offering a roasted pig to expiate a sin, and protecting against greed or a bad personality. The purpose of this visit is to strengthen the family's hope that their infant's present life will be a success.

The people of Bali believe that it is bad to be born on certain days. For example, a particular Saturday, Wuku Wayang by the Balinese calendar, is considered inauspicious and a person born on this day is destined to suffer from emotional distress and cause trouble to others. To counteract the consequences of this unfortunate situation, the Balinese perform a special ceremony of atonement in the hope that the gods will confer good fortune on the child and ensure that the unfortunate birthday circumstance will not adversely affect his future development.

The Sibling Spirits

Four spiritual forces which interact to form part of the personality are called the 'four siblings' (Kanda Mpat) (Connor, 1982). The physical manifestations of them at birth are blood, amniotic fluid, placenta, and the vernix caseosa, the soft cheesy-like material that covers the newborn's skin. The placenta is treated with care, buried in the household compound, and given ceremonies at one, three, and six months. After the six-month ceremony, the character of the 'siblings' unify to become two spirits of the soul: Kala and Dewa. The spirit Kala is responsible for a person's bad thoughts, emotions, and deeds; if a person is angry it is believed that Kala has influenced him. Good emotions, thoughts, and deeds are attributed to the other spirit, Dewa: when one is calm, Dewa is in the ascendant. These spirits continue to influence the soul throughout life, and they have the power to help a person at work and guard him against his enemies. They are given offerings by that person, who may fall ill if he neglects his duties to the sibling. At death a person's soul (*atman*) becomes unified with God or appears again through reincarnation, and the sibling spirits return to their source (i.e., water, fire, air, and soil).

Factors in Balance and Concepts of Illness

The Balinese believe that three factors are crucial to a person's well-being, happiness, and health: (1) the microcosmos (*buana alit*), which is made up of individual persons; (2) the macrocosmos (*buana agung*), which comprises the universe; and (3) the supreme God (Sang Hyang Widi Wasa). In their daily lives, at home, in the market, or at the office (parts of the macrocosmos), the Balinese strive to keep the three factors in equilibrium, a concept called *tri hita karana*. All living or working places have small temples to enable the people to make offerings and pray. One could even pray for safe automobile travel by calling on God to preserve the balance of vehicles on the street (the macrocosmos), so that a collision will be avoided and one's soul[7] will not be jeopardized.

The practice of harmony and balance from the Balinese Hindu principles (*tri hita karana*) results in not showing too much vigour of emotional expression of any type and relates to the concept of a centre for all things. *Kaja* (towards the mountain) leads towards the sacred; *kelod* (towards the sea) leads to demons or evil; and the middle world, secular and without special forces, is where the people live. Similarly, the village is located between the temple and the haunted graveyard. The house is located between the house shrine and the refuse pit (Bandem and deBoer, 1981). There is a middle colour made by mixing all colours, called *brumbum*, which is the symbol of the god Siwa. Centre, harmony, and balance are unconsciously striven for in many aspects of thought, emotion, and behaviour in daily living.

The microcosmos (the soul) also interacts with the sibling spirits. To the authors' knowledge, the three factors (microcosmos, macrocosmos, and God) and their balance are more influential in daily life than are the sibling spirits. Peace is attained by doing good deeds and by maintaining balance. Balance determines the person's well-being and imbalance causes mental symptoms such as anxiety or depression, mental disorders, and physical illness.

The Balinese believe that one's soul is involved in illness and that they will become vulnerable to illness if the three factors are not in equilibrium.[8] They believe that both natural factors (e.g., fractures and infections) and supernatural factors (e.g., evil spirits, mistakes in ceremonies, and sins of ancestors) cause illnesses.

They regard the traditional healer (*balian*) as being able to understand and treat problems arising from both supernatural and natural causes and thus able to restore equilibrium of the three factors. They believe doctors are able to treat only diseases caused by natural factors. For this reason, if a family member has a mental disorder, the Balinese generally go first to the *balian*. Whether the family goes to a *balian* or a doctor, or both, family members also attend ceremonies to help ensure balance and equilibrium of the family and individual (Connor, 1984). Traditional healers are of several different types (Connor, 1982) and use a variety of techniques, including trance (of the healer and/or the client), white magic (to counteract black magic), smoke treatment, holy water, medicinal concoctions, meditation, massage, and amulets.[9]

The authors have observed a number of *balian* treating clients, friends, relatives, and their own selves. The healer with whom they are most familiar practises in Bangli and has been involved in collaborative studies with psychiatrists at the Bangli mental hospital. He runs a busy practice in his home with a stream of clients coming each evening. They present him with a variety of complaints, both physical and psychological. For each client, he chants prayers to God, blesses the offerings brought by the patient, and goes into a trance state in which he receives power to heal from God. The patient prays to be cured. In therapy he puts a drop of oil on the top of the client's head and blows on it as he looks down into the head to make a diagnosis: when he sees coloured smoke, he knows that there is an evil spirit present and its location in the body. The *balian* then touches the patient in a variety of ways, generally while the client's family members are in attendance, and he may inform the client of the nature of the problem, i.e., natural or supernatural in cause and of the diagnosis, such as 'Bali illness'. The authors have observed clients experience excruciating pain when this *balian* touches their arm or knee at the points where the evil spirit or black magic is located.[10] The *balian* repeatedly touches these areas and breathes strongly on his hand or arm while holding the client's extremity, which is his way of exercising the power of the possessed god, to remove the black magic which was the cause of the client's chronic symptoms and thereby effect a cure.

All Balinese believe in the black magic theory of illness causation. Follow–up interviews with a Balinese physician client confirmed that he was relieved of the chronic headaches for which he sought treatment. Another colleague, a young American woman, presented herself for treatment of an abdominal mass. However, he diagnosed a 'weakness' caused by evil spirits and proceeded to treat her for that. She later revealed that she had a severe recurrent problem of weakness and malaise brought on by ingesting sugar in any form. It began when she was in Indonesia 10 years ago and could not be diagnosed by Western medical examinations. Much to her astonishment and gratification, the problem disappeared after the *balian* treatment and did not recur in subsequent months.

The smoke treatment, used for physical and mental disorders, consists of the client sitting for about 30 minutes in a closed small tent made of woven palm leaf mats with a smouldering sandalwood fire at his feet (Leimena and Thong, 1983). This is a method to rid the body of black magic or evil spirits.

The authors witnessed another common traditional healing technique when a friend requested help to locate a *balian* for treatment of a painful tooth and swollen jaw. This time they went to Sanur, a beach area near Denpasar which is famous for its strong spiritual power (*sakti*). This shore area is lined with many tourist hotels. A *balian* was located by asking men who were sprucing up a local *banjar*. The *balian*, a thin old man, dressed in a sarong, appeared after about a 15-minute wait. After he was told of the nature of the complaint he proceeded with measured care to pour a few spoonfuls of holy water from a full glass into an empty glass which he then carefully blew into with several breaths and handed to the client to drink. This is the power to get rid of black magic and prevent recurrence. This procedure was repeated several times and abruptly he indicated that the treatment was finished.[11] His fee was whatever the person wanted to pay: in this case, a little less than two US dollars. Two hours afterwards, the patient noted a lessening of the pain, and four hours later, the pain had completely disappeared and the swelling seemed to have subsided as well, a gratifying solution to a problem that had distressed her for the previous four days.[12]

The procedure of a *balian* described by Belo (1960: 23–4) in the 1930s resembles that encountered today:

On one occasion when I was at her house a man came in with two followers bearing presents and the necessary offering. They came before her as she sat on the little porch of her house, made obeisance, and addressed her by her title as trance practitioner, Koelit. She accepted the gifts—rice, vegetables, dried fish, and fruit which was out of season. The offering contained a coconut, eggs, and money—Chinese cash. She asked what they wanted to consult her about and sat quietly chewing betel for a time. Then she rose and went to the bathing spout at the back of her house, washed her hands and face, and let the water spatter a bit on her torso. She combed back her hair and plucked a red hibiscus from the hedge, placing it on the top of her head.

Then she came back and seated herself on the raised platform on the porch of her house. She sat cross-legged as a man does and rested her hands on her thighs. After only a few minutes, sitting quietly with her eyes closed, she suddenly raised her arms and clapped her thighs, her customary sign that the god has entered into her. She lifted her arms and performed a few movements of the dance. Her eyes, open now, were staring, and her entire attitude was usual to her in a trance. She uttered many unintelligible sounds and finally, becoming more articulate, referred to the question of the medicine. After this she was silent again, only making dance movements. Then she announced the prescription: a newly laid egg from a black hen, followed by drinking seven times water mixed with certain leaves. A few more dance movements, and she clapped her hands over her head, coming out of trance, and made three times the gesture of reference to the god. She continued talking then, in her normal personality, asking the visitors if they had understood. Then she began to chew betel again and sat chatting informally with them as the conversation became general.

The authors' observations of successful treatments by *balian* on a number of occasions leave no doubt about their clever abilities to diagnose, their seemingly psychic abilities, and their power to heal. The range of disorders for which they are successful is wide but not unlimited. They treat disorders caused by natural causes, including fractures and infections, as well as those which Western physicians would regard as primarily psychogenic or psychiatrists would regard as mental disorders. *Balian* are often able to recognize mental and physical illnesses outside their scope of care and may refer the clients to practitioners of Western medicine.

The *balian* observed by the authors have in common great confidence in their methods of treatment and often a calming hypnotic-like presence. The family is often present to witness all or part of the treatment, and they and the client typically trust and believe in the *balian*, and their faith is strengthened if he/she is able to discern the problem correctly and the treatment is effective. If not, they will consult other *balian* until their problem is solved.

Whereas trance states in *balian* are normal phenomena, trance states may also represent mental disorders. Suryani (1984) described a culture-bound disorder, *bebainan*, which is a trance condition (Appendix 1). An outbreak of trance disorder (*kasurupan*) in a group of schoolchildren was also described (Appendix 2). Such disorders are treated successfully by either *balian* or Western psychiatrists and sometimes by both.

In summary, Bali is a relatively small, scenic island in the very large archipelago of Indonesia, highly agrarian, with a strong tourist industry. Ninety-three per cent of the 2.5 million population are of the Balinese Hindu faith. The Balinese Hindu religion permeates all facets of Balinese life, including emotional expression, and is key to the cognitive sets of the people. Three factors are basic to health: the microcosmos or soul; the macrocosmos or universe; and the supreme God. The Balinese strive to keep the three factors in balance because lack of balance can cause illness or problems for the individual or community. The concept of balance is also of great importance for feelings of peace. Traditional healers treat illness by restoring balance.

1. Jembrana, Tabanan, Badung, Gianyar, Klungkung, Bangli, Karangasem, and Buleleng. These correspond geographically with the former kingdoms (*kerajaan*).

2. Bateson and Mead called the lowest caste 'casteless'. This interpretation may have stemmed from a misunderstanding of terms.

3. This could be a matter of misreading the terms 'aesthetic festival' (Wikan, 1988: 356) and 'wealthy'. Certainly elaborate and expensive cremations are limited to the wealthy but all persons of the community may attend these and all partake in common, frequent, very colourful, and often elaborate ceremonials and festivals of the villages.

4. The Balinese calendar systems are complex and follow three systems: one is the international calendar; one Balinese system uses a calendar of 35 days in each

month, and every six months, 210 days; and the other Balinese system uses 30 days for one month according to the moon (one year has 12 months). Days of the 35-day Balinese calendar are named differently according to cycles or sequences of 10 days. For example, 3, 5, and 7 days are named sequentially. Pasah, Beteng, and Kajeng are a sequence of three days. A sequence of 5 days is named Umanis, Pahing, Pon, Wage, and Kliwon. Appointments of days for ceremonies and daily activities are arranged according to some combinations. For example, Kajeng Kliwon which comes every 15 days (3 times 5 days) is a day when the evil spirit may be destructive, so offerings will be made. They have a name for every 7 days, Wuku; in six months there are 30 Wuku. In every month, the Saturday Kliwon (7 times 5 days) is called Tumpek. This is an important day for ceremonies. For further information, see Covarrubias (1937: 282, 315) and Eiseman (1989: 172–92).

   5. For a detailed description of offerings, see Bateson and Mead (1942: 260–1).

   6. Barnouw (1985: 101) cited Mead's writing in *Growing up in New Guinea* (1930a), as the fullest expression of her 'unusual gifts—imagination, acute observation, and literacy flair'.

   7. The Balinese soul is to the human what the motor is to the car; it propels it. In Bali mental activity, including thinking, emotions, behaviour, and personality are determined by the soul and all physical activity are functions of the soul. By contrast, Westerners regard mental activity as primarily functions of the psyche or cerebral processes, such as intellect and cognition. Many Balinese would not agree with this way of presenting the relation of the soul (*atman*) and body. This formulation is a highly Westernized version which has appeared in Bali only in the last 30 years and has become popular only in the past 15 years (Parisada Hindu Dharma). The Western notion of the difference between body and soul (mind) is not really a traditional Balinese assumption. It is rejected by most Hindu and Buddhist thinkers over the ages, from which much of Bali's religious ritual, imagery, and canons of belief have risen.

   8. Bateson (1982: 120) specified balance as evident in a number of aspects of Balinese ethos, including art, and in acts of physical elevation, such as a little girl trance dancer held on a man's shoulders.

   9. Traditional healers, including shaman, across different cultures have many techniques in common (Kleinman, 1980).

   10. Touching the body at acupressure points can be very painful and this is an alternative explanation of this touch of the *balian*.

   11. This method of healing has been imported from Java within the past 15 years. It is very popular in Bali today, but is recognized as Javanese.

   12. This account is purely anecdotal and the authors had no follow-up information. It is conceivable that the pain and swelling would have subsided without the treatment. However, the result is rather typical of accounts given by patients treated by *balian*.

Chapter 3
The Village of Bayung Gede: Flawed
Basic Assumptions

BATESON and Mead 'assumed that Bali had a cultural base upon which various intrusive elements have been progressively grafted over the centuries, and that a more rewarding approach would be to study this base first' (p. xiii). They stated that they selected Bayung Gede as the village for their primary study because it lacked most of the conspicuous elements of 'intrusive cultures'. They stated that Bayung Gede was ceremonially bare, even when compared with other mountain villages, and that it had a minimum of the 'over-elaboration of art and ceremonialism which is such a marked characteristic of Balinese culture' (p. xiii). They assumed that it represented the cultural base of Bali.

In addition, because they noted that goitre was common in Bayung Gede, they assumed that thyroid deficiency was the cause of the entire population being 'markedly slow in both intellectual response and in speed of bodily movement' (p. xiii). They felt that this factor and the 'schematically simplified' cultural emphasis enabled them to understand the base of Balinese culture, which in turn would help them understand the more complex forms of culture which they had encountered in the plains villages (i.e., the non-mountainous areas).

The validity of these assumptions is questionable or nil. This conclusion is based on the authors' observations at Bayung Gede, including interviews with inhabitants, two local priests, Made Kaler (Bateson and Mead's assistant and secretary during the two years of the study), and Professor Moerdowo (a scholar of Balinese culture, who is especially knowledgeable about the aboriginal villages of Bali). The authors also drew on their medical training and expertise.

Interviews with Made Kaler

Made Kaler was interviewed in January and April 1989 at his home in Denpasar. He is one of the few living individuals who were associated with either Bateson or Mead and their study in Bali. He was with them almost continually during the two years of their stay.

Made Kaler spoke with lasting amazement and admiration about Bateson and Mead's energy and their long hours of daily work on observations and data. He said they inspired him to lead a life of hard work. He is credited with having founded the first elementary school which taught the English language in Bali, an institution that subsequently became a university. He retired 20 years ago from his life-long career as an educator. At the age of 78 he was wiry, alert, energetic, and intellectually keen, and he was still actively managing an inn he owns, which is connected with his home. He showed no evidence of memory problems. He greeted the authors cordially and spoke openly and enthusiastically. His comprehension and fluency in English were relatively facile but most of the interviews with him were conducted in his native languages, Balinese and Indonesian.

He regarded Bayung Gede as culturally different from the plains villages but similar in most respects to a number of other villages in the same general mountain area about which he was knowledgeable. He did not say that the people of Bayung Gede were slow in intellectual response but admitted they had a limited ability to communicate about themselves and were unable to explain the reasons for or meaning of aspects of their culture. At that time none of the villagers were formally educated.

Kaler said that the villagers of Bayung Gede had difficulty in understanding Mead because she was 'not fluent' in the language of Bayung Gede, which was Balinese in the 1930s, as it is primarily today.[1] Villagers of Bayung Gede speak a stratified language, using higher levels well, unlike the inhabitants of some mountain villages who are unable to do this. Mead never mentioned translators except in a letter written home in which she said Kaler translated anything Balinese (and Dutch and Malay) that he was given (Howard, 1984); in her publications she always referred to him as a secretary. His assistance was undoubtedly one reason she spoke of him as a godsend. Only a person raised in Bali could master the complex Balinese language, with its multiple levels of discourse and diversity. Kaler's translations of Balinese into English were of the 'Dutch English' he knew and not American English. Bateson and Mead's translation from Dutch English into the American idiom would present an opportunity for further distortion[2], particularly in aspects of psychology. It is easy to understand how words of emotion such as fear (*takut*), and worry (*takut*), and shame (*lek*)[3] could be misinterpreted in the translation process. Mead pointed out that translation is a classic stumbling block for ethnology (p. xi).

Effects of Illness on Behaviour

It was observed that many of the children of Bayung Gede manifested infections of various types, including rhinitis, purulent otitis, bronchitis, skin disease (i.e., scabies and pyoderma), and many appeared clinically ill from ascariasis (round worm infestation). Kaler commented that sickness was even more prevalent in Bayung Gede at the time of the study.[4] In Bali, symptomatic ascariasis afflicts primarily infants and children up to the ages of about 6–10 years; in 1989, about 80 per cent of this age group was affected by the disease. It is manifested by a characteristic apathetic facies, malnutrition, often a protruding abdomen, and behavioural changes of irritability and lethargy (Cerf, 1981). Bateson and Mead were apparently unaware of the general chronic ill health of the children. Possibly this factor accounted for their impression that the children were slow in response and movement. It is apparent from their photos and films that most of the infants and young children were ill.[5] However, neither physical illness nor slowness is apparent in the adults in their films.

Bateson and Mead also reported a relatively frequent occurrence of goitre (15 per cent) in the adults of Bayung Gede, which led them erroneously to believe that the entire population manifested hypothyroidism, with consequent slowness of intellectual response and movement. Goitre was endemic in the Kintamani area in the era of the original study and there was still a relatively high prevalence in 1989. However, clinical hypothyroidism is generally not present in goitre conditions. Furthermore, it is not possible that a majority of inhabitants in a goitre area would suffer from hypothyroidism (Hoffenberg, 1986). It is true that symptomatic hypothyroidism can result in lethargy and depression with accompanying slowness, but it is unlikely that more than a small number of people could be so affected. For Bayung Gede, the authors observed about 10 adults with goitre who did not show signs of hypothyroidism. Bateson and Mead's lack of medical training would account for their failure to recognize chronic illness in children and misinterpret the consequences of goitre.

Mead wrote that her nursing of Karba (her favourite child at Bayung Gede) through fevers of teething saved him from an early death, which had claimed all his brothers and sisters (Mead and MacGregor, 1951). Her statement exemplifies her limited understanding of pathophysiology at that time[6] but may also reflect a sense of personal heroism, as well as being an expression of maternal inclinations, since she desired to become pregnant during her stay in Bali (Howard, 1984).

Bayung Gede and the Base Culture Concept

The authors' studies and information indicate that Bayung Gede is not a base culture of Bali but, instead, represents a mixture of aboriginal and Balinese Hindu culture of the plains as it existed in the 1930s and as it existed in 1989. It is also unique in some ways. These considerations are relevant to the degree in which it is reasonable to generalize Bateson and Mead's findings and apply them to other mountain villages and to Bali as a whole.

In the 1930s Bayung Gede was, and can still be considered in 1989, a relatively isolated mountain village. Most Balinese have never heard of it. It is 3 kilometres off the main road that crosses the island—then well travelled by both Balinese and foreigners—and that has been a trade route across Bali for centuries. At the time of Bateson and Mead's study, a dirt path, difficult to traverse in the rainy season, led to the village; it became a narrow paved road in 1983. Although, at the time of the study, no tourists had visited the village, the people were aware of the Dutch and were often visited by itinerant groups of Balinese dancers, musicians, and entertainers. Vagrants passed through and other villagers came for cock-fights. People from other villages also immigrated to Bayung Gede; one man, 60 years of age, informed the authors that he had come to the village as a small child and lived there ever since. Furthermore, villagers had regular and frequent social contact at the busy general market-place at Kintamani, only 4 kilometres away. Five kilometres away is a very large temple at Batur, which is second in importance only to the mother temple of Besakih; priests representing distant villages sometimes came to attend ceremonies at Batur and at Bayung Gede.

Several features of the buildings, temples, roads, and cemeteries and their arrangements attest to both Balinese Hindu and aboriginal influences. These also provide a contrast with the two well-studied aboriginal villages in Bali, Tenganan and Trunyan.[7] Trunyan, which is visible from Kintamani, is a relatively isolated village close to Bayung Gede. It is in a valley on the shore of Lake Batur at the foot of Mt. Batur, which rises up sharply, Fuji-like, and acts as a backdrop to Kintamani. The inhabitants of Trunyan look upon Mt. Batur, the highest mountain in the vicinity, as their sacred mountain, rather than Mt. Agung, the sacred one of the Balinese Hindus.

Bateson and Mead gave the following reasons why they felt Bayung Gede was little influenced by Hindu tradition: (1) the villagers lacked Hindu names for gods; (2) they did not practise cremation; (3) they did not place importance on the relationship of colour to the direction of offerings; (4) they did not have castes; (5) they had no taboo against eating beef; and (6) they had no relationship with a Brahmana priestly household (p. xiii). Only two of these assertions are correct.

It is not true that the villagers of Bayung Gede do not use Hindu names for the gods. Like all Balinese Hindus, they make offerings to and hold ceremonies for three Hindu gods: Betara Sri, the goddess of rice; Betara Wisnu, the god who takes care of the world; and Betara Surya, the sun god. The villagers also pray to the Hindu God, Sang Hyang Widi Wasa. However the villagers do not use Trimurti (the gods Wisnu, Brahma, and Siwa) as is usual for Balinese Hindus.

It is true that the villagers of Bayung Gede do not use coloured cloth banners to designate direction, as in Hindu tradition. For example, red is the symbol of the god, Brahma, who is from the direction of the mountain (*kaja*). Black is the symbol of Wisnu from the direction of the sea (*kelod*) (Covarrubias, 1937).

Bateson and Mead were incorrect about the Brahmana priest (*pedanda*). According to the present priests (*pemangku*) of Bayung Gede, Brahmana priests have always enjoyed ties with the people and temples of Bayung Gede and are invited to important temple ceremonies.

Bateson and Mead erred in their interpretation that the lack of evidence of cremation indicated an absence of Balinese Hindu influence on burial. The term 'cremation' refers only to the burning of the corpse. Most Balinese, and particularly those of Bayung Gede, refer to the death and burial ceremony in general as *ngaben*. To the majority of Balinese, *ngaben* means returning the corpse to its original state (i.e., soil, water, fire, and air) and includes the burning of the corpse. In Bayung Gede and some other mountain villages which are influenced by Hinduism, the term carries the same meaning, although it does not include the corpse-burning aspect. In Bayung Gede the burial ceremonies are simpler than, and different from, those in the plains, which are not only elaborate, festive, time-consuming, and expensive, but involve using a tower (*wadah*) for the corpse and burning the entire corpse or its bones. At Bayung Gede offerings are made at home and at the temple, and the ceremonies have the same spiritual meanings as those in the plains. In Bayung Gede, the corpse is carried to a special area in a field outside the village where it is washed (in the plains they wash the corpse at home). As in the plains, many people attend this ceremony and the atmosphere is festive. After washing the corpse, adolescent males carry it to the cemetery and bury it. Small objects are stuck in the grave to allow egress of the soul. In striking contrast, in the aboriginal village of Trunyan, little influenced by Hinduism, there is no burial; the body is set out in the forest to deteriorate and be eaten by animals.

Although the custom of including beef at offerings is peculiar to Bayung Gede, the matter of no taboo against eating beef does not signify an absence of Balinese Hindu influence, as Bateson and Mead believed. Generally, the taboo against eating beef is not widespread throughout Bali. In olden times the highest caste (priests) did have a taboo against eating beef but the vast majority of the population observe this practice only sporadically, depending on family custom in the plains and mountain villages. Balinese who avoid eating beef do so because it is their family custom (e.g. they may believe that eating beef will make them sick) and not because it is an Indian Hindu religious custom.

Contrary to Bateson and Mead's statement that the people of Bayung Gede lack membership in any caste (p. 256), there is a caste in Bayung Gede; all of the people come from the lowest caste, Jaba, formerly called Sudra, because they are poor peasants.[8] There are no residents of a higher caste. The people were well aware of differences in proper language for addressing persons of a higher caste and status from outside the village.[9]

Although Bayung Gede is seldom visited by tourists, it has gained fame among students of culture as a result of Bateson and Mead's detailed and original work 50 years ago, and it certainly merits further study. Data about Bayung Gede which bear on Bateson and Mead's findings and provide additional data about the village are presented below.

Some aspects of Bayung Gede houses, architecture, customs, and roads are different, if not unique. Traditionally, each household compound has three structures: (1) a kitchen which is also the sleeping place of the parents, the area for delivery of babies, and the place for the corpse when a family member dies; (2) the sleeping place for children, as well as storage place for ceremonial objects; and (3) the storage place for rice. By contrast, in the typical compound of a Balinese Hindu house, there are five to seven separate buildings, including one for grandparents, one to three for ceremonies, and the kitchen used solely for preparing food.

The architecture of the houses in Bayung Gede is unique: the roofs are steeply pitched and covered with split bamboo instead of grass or tile (p. 57), as in the plains. The streets are also laid out differently, being oriented towards Mt. Batur. It is usual for Balinese Hindus to orient the house shrine (*sanggah*) in the direction of Mt. Agung.[10] In Bayung Gede, however, the house shrines are located at the back of the kitchen and oriented in the direction of Mt. Batur. Balinese Hindu house temples are built of stone or wood; in Bayung Gede the temples of God are of a different form and are built of woven bamboo and placed on top of sticks in the ground that take root and leaf. Today these appear identical with those in Bateson's photograph (p. 57).

Bayung Gede has unique cemetery customs that are aboriginal-like. At the cemetery there is a sacred temple that consists of a log stuck in the ground. The villagers do not know its ancient origin. Four very large old trees stand guard by the entrance to this temple suggesting animistic influence. Because the temple is sacred, the authors were not allowed to follow the path leading from the big trees at the entrance but were guided through the jungle-like forest to a spot nearby where the log in its small clearing could be observed. Such monolithic religious objects are also characteristic of Balinese aboriginal villages (Bandem and deBoer, 1981).

At Bayung Gede the placenta is not buried as is the custom in Bali but placed in a coconut shell and hung in a tree at the edge of the village. The residents do not know the meaning of this unique custom but the village priest informed the authors that the placenta has the same spiritual power as one of the 'siblings' in the Balinese Hindu religion (see Chapter 2).

The authors also documented a number of other Bayung Gede customs that are not Balinese Hindu in origin and are unlike those of the plains villages:

1. Only adolescent males may enter the cemetery for burials.

2. Only males who have undergone a special ceremony may take trees from the cemetery forest and then only what they can remove by use of their hands.

3. One temple in the village may be used only by adolescent males and married men who have undergone a purification ceremony.

4. Marriage between first cousins is prohibited. A special area on the edge of the village is reserved for people who have been banished for breaking rules; one woman and her 50-year-old son (whom Mead helped to deliver) have lived there for 50 years because she broke the Bayung Gede taboo against marrying a cousin.

5. Persons who marry outside village members are required to give two cows to the village if they are to be allowed to continue to live there.

6. At marriage the bride and groom must leave their parents' compounds and find a house of their own.

7. Five village headmen (Kabayan), a team of equals, perform both administrative and religious activities for the *banjar*.

Customs showing Balinese Hindu influence in Bayung Gede include: (1) the use of the Balinese calendar; (2) birthday rites and other rites of passage, such as ear piercing; (3) Nyepi, the day of silence; (4) Balinese Hindu temples, priests, ceremonies, and offerings; and (5) the relatively recent *legong* dance forms which are incorporated in the little girl trance dance, the origin of which dates to the pre-Hindu period of Bali (Bandem, 1990), well described by Bateson and Mead (pp. 90–3) and Belo (1960).

Bateson and Mead's characterization of Bayung Gede as 'ceremonially bare' (p. xiii) is grossly misleading. Besides, Bateson and Mead appear to contradict themselves with their statement about the 'very rich development of communal ceremonial in Bayung Gede' (p. 56). Furthermore, a number of the photographs also contradict their statements.[11] The temple ceremonies at Bayung Gede in 1989 were elaborate and as lengthy as those in the plains, and were Balinese Hindu in style.

According to the people of Bayung Gede in 1989, the temple ceremonies have remained the same over the past 50 years. They do not wish to change the ceremonies because they want to conform to the custom of ceremonies that their ancestors had performed for the gods. Change would arise only by direction of the gods in the form of instructions through a trance medium. The only change they acknowledged in current memory was in the content of offerings, e.g., cake, fruit, and vegetables.

An example of an elaborate ceremony at Bayung Gede was the one held on the completion of renovations of the village main temple. The villagers began preparations a week preceding the ceremony, including repairing *gamelan* instruments, making and painting costumes, constructing special structures for offerings and puppet play, and installing colourful decorations of many types. The ceremonial activities lasted a full week. On the climactic day, ceremonies began in the early afternoon and lasted till 2 a.m. About 100 women and some children brought ornately arranged offerings of fruit, rice, flowers, and chicken; food was prepared for the entire village; the *gamelan* orchestra, consisting of about

40 musicians, played for much of the day and for the dances; priests struck the special ceremonial gong intermittently for hours; men rhythmically struck the town's slit *gong*; a parade of about 200 dancers, priests, orchestra, village dignitaries, and other colourfully attired participants marched around the large temple grounds, three times counterclockwise (from right to left because right is the orientation of good for all Balinese); two groups of 16 male dancers and a group of female dancers skilfully performed five lengthy, complex, and intricate sacred dances in the inner temple courtyard, including the Baris Jojor, Baris Tumbak, Baris Perise, Baris Dadap, and Rejang. The *baris* dancers were dressed in distinctive triangular headdresses covered with pieces of shell that quivered and flashed in the light as they moved. Their costumes were multicoloured and retained a fixed pattern over many years because they were believed to have come from their ancestors. Only instructions from the gods could cause a change. In two of these dances, the men carried spears and represented bodyguards (warriors) of visiting deities (Bandem and deBoer, 1981: 20). A 65-year-old man, who remembered Mead giving him rice as a boy, confirmed that these ceremonies had been taking place in Bayung Gede since he was a small child, a number of years before Mead's study.[12] Two weeks later, another similarly elaborate and lengthy ceremony, this one for the goddess of rice, was held. Most of the villagers were present and the mood was festive. The villagers were friendly, gracious, and enjoyed talking with the authors.

Bateson and Mead assumed that the psychology of the people of the plains was similar to that of the mountains, and therefore treated both as one 'psychological unit' (p. 60). These assumptions are questionable. The people of the plains are exposed to many different influences from outside Bali and they have frequent contact with people from outside their own villages. As Bateson and Mead stated, no tourists had ever visited Bayung Gede. The Bayung Gede villagers also travel much less than the plains villagers. Consequently the plains people feel more at ease in a strange place, and they tend to be more comfortable with strangers. Finally, animism is a stronger influence for the people of Bayung Gede and this affects the basis of their thinking.

The above factors caution against assuming that the plains and the mountain villagers have a similar psychology in several important respects (see Chapter 5 for differences in expression of emotions and facial expressiveness). Therefore, the conclusions on the Balinese character in Chapter 9 were not derived from generalizations based on observations of Bayung Gede alone but on similar observations in the plains villages.

In summary, Bateson and Mead wrongly assumed that Bayung Gede, the primary village of their study, represented the 'base culture' of Bali; that it had been little influenced by Hindu, Javanese, Buddhist, or Dutch cultures as had the plains villages. On the contrary, this book has shown that Bayung Gede represents a culture exhibiting aboriginal and Balinese Hindu influences. It is both different from and similar to other mountain villages, and in some ways it is unique. Although Bayung Gede's ceremonies are generally less elaborate than those in the plains, Bateson and Mead's statement about the village being ceremonially bare was a gross misrepresentation. Bateson and Mead's erroneous assumptions about the slowness of intellectual response and movement of the people of Bayung Gede and its cause in hypothyroidism were based on incorrect knowledge of the illness. No evidence could be found of this even among those people suffering from goitre. Bateson and Mead also failed to note the frequent infections, nor did they recognize a prevalent chronic illness (ascariasis) in the children, that would affect their behaviour, possibly making them lethargic and irritable. Chronic illness is evident in their photographs and is still present in inhabitants of the village in 1989. All of these factors may have had a bearing on some of Bateson and Mead's erroneous conclusions discussed in the following chapters.

1. In many plains villages and the cities today, Indonesian is the primary language and Balinese is dropping off.

2. H. Geertz (personal communication), on the other hand, concluded that Bateson and Mead 'could understand Balinese quite well, well enough for them to carry out their research as they understood it to be. I have studied their field notes from the period that they were in Batuan, after they had been in Bali more than a year, and there are many signs that they could talk with Balinese. There are long passages in both their field notes where it is clear that they have been talking with

Balinese and noting down what they have said. Made Kaler was their language teacher, and helped with translation. He wrote out thousands of pages of Balinese statements made to him by the people of Bayung Gede and Batuan. After these were typed up, Bateson and Mead and he would go over them carefully. Bateson wrote between the lines on these transcripts all the words that he had to ask Made Kaler for meanings. There are very few of these on each page, indicating that Bateson and Mead understood most of each text. In addition, the 'translations' that Made Kaler made of these particular words were always very accurate, and often not in English but in other more common Balinese terms. Made Kaler never wrote out translations of these texts. He did serve at times in the first year as an interpreter, but by the time they were in Batuan, he conducted a great deal of independent research of his own, leaving Bateson and Mead to work on their own as well.'

3. *Takut* and *lek* both have two meanings. *Lek* can mean embarrassment, shame, or 'stage fright' as described by C. Geertz (see Chapter 4).

4. In 1989, the children in the mountainous Kintamani area appeared to be generally less healthy than those in the plains villages and the cities.

5. For example, they illustrated their concept of 'unresponsive infants' with infants who, from the authors' inspection of the photos, were ill (p. 204).

6. Teething can be associated with fever but in Western countries it is not a cause of death. It seems likely that Karba had infections for which Mead's care may have been critical.

7. While these two villages are primarily aboriginal in character, they also have some Balinese Hindu influences, and many long-term and important links with the 'outside world' of Bali.

8. Bateson and Mead wrote, 'Three castes, Brahman, Kesatrya, and Vesia, are recognized, the hypogamy is permitted to the males of all three castes, the women so married being progressively raised in status by successive generations of higher caste descendants.' The bulk of the population is spoken of as 'outsiders (*djaba*) lacking membership in these castes'. As pointed out in Chapter 2, Bateson and Mead misinterpreted the caste system. No group has been, or is now, referred to as outsiders.

9. There are detailed regulations distinguishing many levels of status, usually indicated by titles.

10. In some parts of Bali, there is a different orientation, such as the town of Tabanan, which is towards Mt. Gaung Batu Kau.

11. Pages (and photo numbers): 56(4); 64(3, 5); 72(3,5,6,7); 92(1,3,5,7); 255(4).

12. Bateson and Mead (p. 134) published a photograph of a dancer of the Baris Tumbak at Bayung Gede wearing a costume identical to those of today.

Chapter 4
Methodological Problems and Differences with Bateson and Mead

To appraise and reanalyse much of the data of *Balinese Character* is a challenging and problematic task for persons without expertise in Balinese culture, cultural anthropology, medicine, psychology, psychiatry, and psychoanalysis. The style of writing is particularly difficult for Balinese scholars and readers. The style is difficult even for anthropologists and it has been read by relatively few because of its forbidding format. The method of study was primarily ethnographic as that was the practice at that time, but Bateson and Mead had supplemented this with their special method of photographic analysis. Interpretations of data were generally psychoanalytically oriented.

Bias and Preconceived Notions

Bateson and Mead appeared to lack insight into their possible bias. One of the chief reasons they selected Bali for study was a preconceived view of the relationship between culture and schizophrenia (Mead and MacGregor, 1951). Their study was supported in part by a foundation focused on schizophrenia (dementia praecox). Possibly these factors entered into the related misinterpretations of data and inappropriate characterization of Balinese personality as schizoid.[1]

The authors have wondered if Mead had a propensity to fit the data to her theories or preconceived ideas. Freeman (1983) asserted that Mead's depictions of Samoan culture, as set forth in her renowned book *Coming of Age in Samoa* (1928), were motivated by her desire to substantiate a particular cherished doctrine. Barnouw's critique (1985: 108) of Mead's South Seas studies (prior to Bali) cited a pattern of preconceived mental set. Given Bateson and Mead's results for Bali, the authors wondered if a similar process may have been in operation there. For example, Mead's misleading characterization of Bayung Gede as 'ceremonially bare' could have been related to biased assumptions about a base culture of Bayung Gede, one little influenced by the Hindu culture.

Freeman's critique (1983) of Mead's work in Samoa stirred up quite a lot of publicity and multiple refutations by American anthropologists (Brady, 1985; Patience and Smith, 1986; Rappaport, 1986; Feinberg, 1988). Freeman supported his critique with his own data on Samoans and attributed Mead's mistakes to a number of methodological errors but most importantly to a motivation to provide the leading anthropologist, her mentor, Franz Boas, with support for his championed theoretical concept of cultural determinism (i.e., that human behaviour is shaped entirely by culture and not by biological factors).[2] In that era the academic community was engaged in a fierce argument regarding nature versus nurture in the determination of behaviour, personality, and culture, as well as controversy over the issue of eugenics.

Bateson and Mead's conclusions about the Balinese being schizoid and about certain of their child-rearing patterns being predisposed to schizophrenia could be viewed as fitting the doctrine of cultural determinism, i.e., opposed to the prevailing psychiatric view at the time that schizophrenia was a biological and primarily inherited disorder. Years later Bateson followed a related line of reasoning and study to develop his double-bind theory of schizophrenia, a theory that the cause of schizophrenia lies in a certain type of pathologic communication in a patient's family.[3] Currently the weight of scientific evidence favours the theory that biologic and genetic factors are predominant in the cause of schizophrenia.[4]

It is for anthropologists and historians to assess the possible effects of anthropological concepts and theories of the era and the degree to which Mead was influenced by her mentors, Ruth Benedict and Franz Boas. This assessment of Bateson and Mead's work has focused primarily on pragmatic and psychologic issues in relation to their generalizations about Bali.

Possibly the critical impressions Bateson[5] and Mead[6] formed early on in their study stuck with them. In some instances they further supported and elaborated upon these with selective data.[7] It is not unusual for scientists to develop ideas based on pilot data and then proceed to support or disprove them with formal studies. A problem arises if scientists attend only to those data which support their theories and ideas.

The Effects of Foreigners on the Balinese

Bateson and Mead did not understand how they were perceived by the Balinese and appeared to lack sensitivity to their roles. Part of the behaviour they observed was a function of their impact upon their subjects. Mead described her perceived effect as a personal stimulus on the Balinese: she was puzzled by why she was unable to gain rapport with the people of Bayung Gede for months. She was stymied by a reaction which she interpreted as fear: 'Mothers smiled false anxious smiles, babies screamed, and dogs barked' (p. 31). She had not encountered this problem in her earlier field studies. Though she never ventured a reason, she stated that she overcame it by adopting a theatrical style of interaction with babies; in essence, play-acting. This reaction by the villagers is understandable when one considers Mead as a stimulus for the Balinese. When Made Kaler, her assistant at Bayung Gede, was asked why villagers might be afraid of her, he explained that to them she looked some-what like Rangda, the evil witch with which they were so familiar. This was because of her light skin, light hair, eyes, and strange appearance (to them). Most had never seen a white woman before. Denny Thong, an Indonesian psychiatrist in Bali, came to the same conclusion after meeting her personally in the 1970s.[8]

Furthermore, Mead placed herself in the role of doctor by treating minor cuts and infections. Occasionally the villagers attributed impressive cures to her ministrations (Howard, 1984: 197). In their eyes, this made her a *balian*, the only kind of doctor they knew, who is imbued with supernatural powers and who can work magic. Made Kaler attested to the fact that the people referred to her as a *balian*.

The villagers also regarded Bateson and Mead as Europeans, like the Dutch, of whom they were generally afraid and whom they believed to be persons of ultimate power and superiority. Two of their subjects claimed that they and other small children were afraid of them; one said he thought they were Dutch. The Dutch acted superior to all Balinese and were autocratic but benevolent rulers who had a well-known history of forceful and violent conquest of Bali. Dutch people or anyone perceived as Dutch would have evoked fear or worry (*takut*) in the Balinese of that era. Bateson and Mead's foreignness (i.e., Dutch-like characteristics) may have had a very powerful effect on the behaviour of most of the Balinese they observed. It is possible that their appearance affected the Balinese to such an extent that they seemed to Bateson and Mead to be generally lacking in emotion.

Made Kaler reported to the authors that wherever Mead went in Bayung Gede, she attracted a crowd of villagers and that this reaction persisted. This was in spite of the villagers' increasing familiarity with her and her attempts to follow some local and Balinese customs such as eating with her fingers when visiting villagers. Apparently she attempted to make the villagers accept her as far as possible, and the villagers obviously liked her but she remained a curiosity.

Not only were Mead and Bateson in some respects uncomfortable, fearful, worrisome, and strange to the Balinese of that era, but because of their high status they evoked feelings of embarrassment or shame, what is called *lek* by the Balinese. This uncomfortable feeling was well described by C. Geertz (1966) who translated it as 'stage fright'. It may also be manifested by quietness, restrained emotional expression, and often by turning away from the person.

About two months after his arrival in Bali, Bateson was struck by behaviour which, in the authors' interpretation, fits the description of *lek*. He stated, 'The most striking thing about these people is their nervousness—always expecting that someone is going to bite them when they are in some sort of uncultural situation (e.g., in their contact with us). This leads to other appearances—of impenetrable dullness.' (Lipset, 1980: 152.)

At Bayung Gede the authors often observed the gathering crowd during interviews and the people's frequent turning away when the camera was focused on them. Children gathered to watch the interviews but as soon as the camera was directed at them they turned away, hid, or fled, shrieking in excitement, only to return slowly to watch again. The reaction of apparent fear and shyness, sometimes suggestive of a children's game, was noticed to some extent in the plains villages and was more obvious to Jensen than to Suryani because of their differences in skin and hair colour (light versus dark) and because of the element of foreignness. Bateson and Mead published several pictures of children and adults who reacted with fear and discomfort to the cameras and to being in their presence at their house (pp. 186, 146). Made Kaler stated that they were always a little shy of Bateson's cameras.

Mead's and, to some extent, Bateson's combined attributes of Rangda, *balian*, and strange high status 'European' (Dutch), the camera, *nyeh* (tension), and *lek* could all have affected the impressions they gained, and contributed to their interpretations and conclusions about Balinese withdrawal of emotional expression (see Chapter 5).

Method: Innovation and Inadequacies

It is evident from Bateson and Mead's published data that they were generally excellent observers and collectors of data. Although they were careful in observational notes, they made some factual errors which may reflect carelessness. Their recording of data was highly systematic, as illustrated by their method of taking and editing notes (Mead and MacGregor, 1951: 195–7). They used the participant observer technique: they appeared to have gathered data on as many natural aspects of Balinese life as possible, although occasionally they arranged a specific event, such as a dance performance.

Their photographic method was innovative and impressive, although this was never used again by Bateson and little used by other anthropologists.[9] This innovation was a step towards increased objectivity. According to them, the method of the monograph was to 'state intangible relationships among different types of culturally standardized behaviour by placing side by side mutually relevant photographs'. This often meant placing, on one page (plate), a variety of different situations illustrative of the culturally standardized behaviour relevant to a concept (e.g., 'defense of the mouth' or 'parents as witch or dragon'). Some plates illustrated behaviour at discrete cultural events, such as the 210th day birthday celebration, while others showed groupings of related general behaviour, such as play by little girls, or illustrated more general issues, such as rites of passage and stages of child development.

There is no way to know the number of subjects that Bateson and Mead observed exhibiting a particular type of behaviour or trait. For example, how many mothers showed the turning-away behaviour that was central to the interpretations of a lack of climax in the culture and of emotionally withdrawn personalities of the Balinese? Bateson and Mead illustrated the turning-away behaviour with only two mothers: one on page 148 and the other in the film, 'Karba's First Years'. Mead used a total of eight subjects (infants and children) in the subsequent reanalysis of the data for a study of motor development (Mead and Macgregor, 1951) and this appears to be all the subjects that were followed longitudinally.

Several dozen subjects in photos were identified by name. Bateson and Mead's publications and photographs were shown to Karba at Bayung Gede and he asked for a copy of the film about himself, 'Karba's First Years', which neither he nor the villagers had ever seen. Bateson and Mead stated that they saw no reason to conceal identities in their publications and did not obtain informed consent as is now the practice in medical research. One wondered how Bateson and Mead would have felt about having their naked baby pictures and movies identified by name and shown around the world, along with a foreigner's critical interpretation of them and their mothers' behaviour.

During all of their time in Bayung Gede and most of their time in Bali, Bateson and Mead lived together in houses set apart from local families or they stayed in homes with Europeans except for their sojourn with a priest's family in Batuan. This is reasonable, considering they were a husband and wife team. However, if they had lived more closely with Balinese families, they would have had more opportunities to observe intimate daily interactions with nuances of behaviour and some emotions that are more openly expressed in the privacy of a Balinese family.

Questionable Interpretations

Bateson and Mead's overall data, mostly photographic, is impressive and highly informative but generally inadequate for each particular trait or pattern of behaviour (e.g., see p. 68 in their book on awayness and Chapter 5 in this volume). It appears that they sometimes used single cases or very few cases to make generalized interpretations about all Balinese. There are numerous examples of this, including 'the body as a tube' (p. 116), 'the mother: narcissism' (p. 151), 'the father–child relationship' (p. 180); and identification of food with faeces (p. 120). Possibly a practice of generalizing from a few cases accounts for their description of the mother's playing with her baby's penis. Bateson and Mead described a characteristic pattern of the mother suddenly and sharply pulling at her baby's penis (p. 32) as a way of playing with him (p. 131) and getting him to respond. The authors have never observed this behaviour by a mother in the plains or at Bayung Gede. Three mothers at Bayung Gede who were asked about this practice denied ever witnessing such behaviour. Such behaviour, even if it does occur, must be a rare occurrence and not a general practice as presented by Bateson and Mead. Bateson and Mead's observation of this behaviour is not questioned but it is hypothesized that they observed it in a few instances at most and generalized from these, a methodological pitfall.

Often the data do not bear out a given concept, e.g., frustrating 'narcissistic personality' of the mother (p. 151) and 'stimulation and frustration' by the mother (p. 68). The photos and their texts were not always pertinent to the concept or trait they purported to illustrate and many of the crucial interpretations of the photos and films are debatable, e.g., 'borrowed babies' (p. 152). (See also Chapter 5.)

Bateson and Mead's method included relating many sorts of situations to a given concept. However, some misinterpretations resulted in drawing spurious or erroneous relationships. An example is the plate regarding 'autocosmic genital symbolism' (i.e., '. . . some object in the outside world is identified as an extension of one's own body'). They cited a baby as the most important autocosmic symbol (p. 131). Picture 5 (p. 131), a mother squeezing mucous out of her baby's nose, shows in actuality the practice of the time because there was no Kleenex or cloth available for this purpose. In picture 6, the mother is holding her baby for a bath in a position that is not considered unusual in any culture. In picture 3, a child is carrying a cucumber in a baby sling and Bateson and Mead interpreted this as a substitute for a baby doll. It would be impossible to be sure of this unless there were observations indicating that the child treated the cucumber as a doll in other respects. Picture 7, of 'autocosmic genital symbolism', shows a drawing of a mother suckling a big caterpillar. Bateson and Mead interpreted this as a 'traditional punishment in Hell'. It is, in fact, an image from the well-known story of 'Bima Suarga' (Bima is The Other World, or Hell), which is illustrated in the famous royal palace paintings in Klungkung (Kerta Gosa) and frequently in other pictures produced by the Balinese in Klungkung and Batuan. It is the soul of a woman who is being punished because she did not suckle her child enough and let it cry. The Balinese regard the 'Bima Suarga' story as an exhortation to mothers to give good care to their babies lest such a fate befall them.

An example of Bateson and Mead's incorrect illustration of a concept is their interpretation that eating is shameful (pp. 112, 124) because the Balinese turn away from each other while eating. Neither the interpretation nor the observation is correct. The Balinese do not look away or turn away from each other while eating. Furthermore, the pictures do not illustrate shame. The Balinese seldom feel shame while eating. Possibly Bateson and Mead mistranslated the meaning of *lek* as shame in the eating situation. The Balinese may cover their mouths while eating but it is not because of feelings of shame as believed by Bateson and Mead. Rather, it is considered impolite or uneducated not to do so. Children are also taught by their mothers not to eat quickly and noisily (*cupak*).[10] It is correct that the Balinese speak little while eating but it is incorrect to interpret this as shame. The Balinese believe it is impolite to speak while eating. It is proper to focus on eating, to show respect and politeness. If you are impolite (e.g., in eating or dressing), people tell you that you ought to feel ashamed (*lek*).

Most of Bateson and Mead's conclusions do not correspond with the issues presented in their text, nor do most of the generalizations relate directly to their data. Rather, conclusions represented abstractions or synthetic statements about character, derived from their observations and data as a whole (p. xvi).

A serious criticism is that Bateson and Mead drew general conclusions about all Balinese primarily from data obtained from studying a limited and atypical population: the people of Bayung Gede (see Chapter 3). The plains villagers of Bali are far more representative of the overall culture. Bateson and Mead made observations in one plains village (Batuan) but these were in the latter part of their study and the source of a minor proportion of their data on child rearing.

Bateson and Mead supplemented their observations with information gained from talks with Western colleagues in Bali, including Walter Spies, an artist and student of Balinese culture, and Jane Belo and Colin McPhee with whom they stayed in the village of Sayan for two months in 1939 when they returned briefly to Bali. Belo had studied trance and McPhee studied music. Hildred Geertz, anthropologist and scholar of Balinese culture, surmised that these Westerners' prevailing 'myths' about the Balinese may have unduly influenced Mead and Bateson (Howard, 1984: 191). Made Kaler informed us that they relied more on Westerners, particularly the Dutch, than on the Balinese as sources of information; they did not discuss issues with him. Kaler believed that is the reason for their misstatement about his education in Java (Mead, 1972).[11] Possibly a reliance on foreigners' accounts for some of their general errors in interpretation and a number of specific errors in data, such as the statement that Nyepi occurs every 400 days (p. 1) (it takes place about every 364 days), the characteristics of the people of north Bali, and customs in Bayung Gede.

Curiously, Bateson and Mead were apparently unaware of Covarrubias' (1937) work on Bali, which preceded theirs by only three years. Covarrubias worked closely with Walter Spies and also stayed with him at his home in Campuan for short periods as did Bateson and Mead. His book *Island of Bali* contains extensive ethnographic data with many interpretations. Possibly Bateson and Mead ignored his work because he was a musician-artist and not an anthropologist by training.

Limitations of Psychological Concepts

Bateson and Mead's use of psychologic theories for interpretations is subject to major criticism. Most of their interpretations were stated in terms that were ill-defined, did not fit any theory, were weakly supported by data, or were contradictory. An example is their interpretation of a child playing with a ball as a symbolical representation of food and 'the body as a tube'. This is gross psychological speculation (pp. 116, 223). In this connection, the text states that the Balinese classify eating with defecation (p. 116). This was apparently inferred from their observation that the Balinese seek privacy when eating and during defecation (p. 21). Similarly, they asserted that the Balinese identify food with faeces, based on their observation of a dog eating the faeces of a baby (p. 120). Another example of unsupported interpretation is the discussion of Balinese ceremonial use of water: 'Water breaks the corrupting tie, not with dirt, but with having had contact with dirt' (p. 23). They presented no basis for this interpretation. In fact, the Balinese use water to clean their mouths of food particles after eating. Holy water is used to purify oneself but it has no connotation of dirt or contact with dirt. Rather, purification represents a psychological concept of goodness, health, and peace. To cite one more example, Mead described genital touching in a child and concluded that 'his whole body, but especially his genitals, is like a toy or small musical instrument upon which those about him play; they make him toys which tell the same tale and it is not surprising that he develops a body consciousness very different from our own' (p. 26). Bateson and Mead presented no relevant data about toys and there is no way to clearly determine what Mead meant by body consciousness. The unproven assumption appears to be that genital touching of the infant produces a positive attitude towards the genitals later in life.

Bateson and Mead devoted several pages to what they called autocosmic play and symbols (pp. 23–9, 131–6). This term, virtually unknown in psychiatry today, was coined by Erikson (1940: 715–30). It has not survived in psychoanalytic, psychologic, or anthropologic terminology or theory. Mead defined it as a symbolic extension of one's own body in contrast to something apart from the self. She and Batesan hypothesized that the Balinese fantasize images of the relationships of parts of the body to the whole (their body consciousness) and that the parts are separable from the body and can have lives of their own. They thought that this was especially true of images of the penis. The weaknesses of Bateson and Mead's presentations on autocosmic play are the absence of data or evidence for the interpretations and alternative interpretations of data.[12]

Bateson and Mead were operating within the limitations of the relatively primitive state of psychology and psychiatry at that time, and they were imbued with the psychoanalytic concepts of the era, including some fundamental aspects that are now archaic. A major example of the latter was that relatively simple child-rearing patterns could determine basic adult personality and cultural character. They were strongly influenced by Erikson, who used a similar approach in that era (1950).[13]

Bateson and Mead had only superficial and partly erroneous understanding of psychoanalytic theory of the era (Freud, 1953). After two months at Bayung Gede, Mead wrote (Howard, 1984): 'I've got my major clues, I think, on the superego formation and the latency point.' An example of questionable understanding is their discussion of superego formation: '. . . the relationship between child nurse and baby is not of such a kind as would result in introjection of a personalized superego' (p. 212). The implied reasons were that 'the baby is treated mostly not as a person capable of learning by reward and punishment, but simply as more or less awkward bundle'; and 'for the Western type of character structure [i.e., superego], it is surely necessary that there be a great contrast between [ages of] the two persons'. The first reason was unverifiable from the authors' knowledge and observations. The second reason is not held as valid by theorists of psychoanalysis: child nurses as young as 6 years of age can be strong objects of identification and superego formation.

Many of the psychological interpretations lack comprehensibility or are not supportable. Examples are 'the notion that scrambling for money [in association with funerals] is a means of eliminating the unclean' (p. 123) and the 'identification of food with feces' (p. 120). These notions, as Bateson and Mead purported to illustrate in the photos and associated descriptions, are inconsistent with meanings held by the Balinese. For example, the people scrambled for the cash at funerals because they wanted the money to reuse it, either for ceremonies or for purchase of goods. The people do not believe such money has an unclean connotation. This is an illustration of a common methodological failing of Bateson and Mead: the observation was astute but they applied their own interpretation to it without regard to, and probably in ignorance of, the meaning of the behaviour to the Balinese.

The authors found considerable problems in Mead's psycho-analytically oriented interpretation of self-stabbing in the kris dance: a turning of anger on oneself and an expression of repressed sexual orgasm (p. 168). There is little data to support either; as pointed out in Chapter 6, the meaning for the Balinese is entirely different. Bateson and Mead confused 'somnambulistic state' with 'trance' (p. 168). Strictly defined, the terms refer to separate states; somnambulism pertains to a sleep-related state and not to trance or possession (Oesterreich, 1979; APA, 1984).

Further illustrative of questionable understanding of psychoanalytic theory is Mead's comment about Bali in a letter to John Dollard, psychologist: '. . . not an ounce of free intelligence and free libido in the whole culture' (Howard, 1984: 193). This latter statement makes no sense in terms of psychoanalytic libido theory or cognitive theory. Sexual libido is clearly present in the culture. Seductive and sexy dancers (*joged*) and flirtatious folk songs have been a part of Balinese culture for centuries (Bandem and deBoer, 1981: 97, 108). The authors observed indications of libido in a youth in Bayung Gede: a wall of his sleeping room was decorated with pictures of glamourous and sexy women. In Bayung Gede, the villagers separate children from the parents' room sharply at the age of 3, for which they gave no reason but which presumably was to give the parents some privacy. Mead herself wrote of dancers flirting with members of the orchestra during the performance and of 'sexual dramas'. One possible explanation for Mead's comment about the absence of free intelligence and libido is that for Balinese individuals, who have intelligence and libido, as do all human beings according to Freudian theory, the 'outlet' or 'expression' was not 'free' but severely constrained.

In efforts to understand what Mead might conceivably have had in mind regarding libido, the authors considered another possibility. The use of this Western concept implies a view of the individual as separate from society. This is less true in Bali where the individual is an integral part of family, society, and ancestors. They are bound together in this larger system.[14] If Mead conceived of libido (the energy-driving instincts of aggression and sexuality) as bound up in this system (though she did not speak of it as such), she might have thought there was none available for individual expression. Instead, it would be expressed in ceremonies, ritual, trance, dance, etc., leaving none 'free' for the individual. Given this novel and somewhat tortuous theoretical excursion, the authors would still disagree that the individual lacks libido, 'free' or otherwise. The Balinese express aggressive and sexual energy in a variety of types of social interaction. The authors question whether libido theory is at all appropriate for application to the Balinese and have not chosen to utilize the theory for understanding Balinese character.

Negative Views of Bali

Somehow Bateson and Mead formed and presented a rather negative image of the Balinese. This is reflected, for example, by their interpretations about mothers and wives being witches, their characterizations of mothers as lacking thoughtfulness and not cherishing their children, and their representation of the people as generally having schizoid maladjusted personalities, to mention a few. Mead's statement that all the last-grade children and all the teachers in Bayung Gede were massacred in the political uprising in 1965 (Mead, 1972) is another example of careless reporting of data and negative implications. The statement is a gross error of fact: no schoolchildren were killed, and only three of the seven teachers died.[15]

1. Barnouw (1985: 123) came to similar conclusions: 'This tendency may have been expected by Bateson and Mead in the first place since before they went to Bali they had been fascinated by Jane Belo's preliminary reports on Balinese and trance.' Mead herself noted (in Belo, 1960: v): 'It seemed the ideal culture within which to plan a project on the cultural aspects of schizophrenia.'
2. Freeman's views of this issue are questionable (Rappaport, 1986). Barnouw (1985: 100) cited evidence that Boas was not 'the doctrinaire cultural determinist that Freeman made him out to be'.
3. Bateson was one of the theorists who were keen on the concept that parents or families were the cause of schizophrenia. They were called schizophrenogenic mothers, or parents. This theory has been largely discredited and discarded as a prominent factor in the etiology of schizophrenia and has been criticized for its destructive effects in therapy (Terkelsen, 1983).
4. However, environmental factors, particularly stress, are currently considered

to be contributing or precipitating factors in acute decompensation and the schizophrenic state.

5. After two months in Bali, Bateson wrote that he was impressed with the Balinese 'impenetrable dullness' (Lipset, 1980). His subsequent writings did not indicate a different attitude.

6. The following statement by Mead reflects a negativity towards the villagers and is possibly an ethnocentric intellectual snobbery. She wrote home about the 'most intelligent man in the village, the calendrical expert and the one who really thinks about ritual'. When he got sick, she treated him with 'salts and rhubarb and soda and a hot water bottle made out of a clay Dutch gin bottle'. She added, 'If he should die the village would be an intellectual wilderness.' (Howard, 1984.) One could argue that this was simply an example of Mead's tendency to exaggerate and of her colourful style of writing.

7. For example, they attributed the mental and physical slowness to a high prevalence of goitre (see Chapter 3 for more detail). To explain the cause of 'emotional withdrawal', they invoked the child-rearing pattern of a mother turning away from her child (see Chapter 5).

8. Neither Bateson nor Mead commented on the villagers' reaction to Bateson who must also have been a fearful stimulus because of his size (over six feet tall), white skin, and cameras. Some of their published photographs show evidence of discomfort of the subjects but most do not.

9. Mead used it one more time in her reanalysis of the Bali data (Mead and MacGregor, 1951).

10. This word is the name of a character in a play who eats in a greedy, quick, noisy, and repulsive way.

11. He said he learned English from the Dutch in Singaraja, Bali.

12. For example, Mead interpreted a child's behaviour as follows: 'Occasionally a very small boy, a five- or six-year-old whose musical virtuosity has brought him into the front rows of the metallophone players, will bitterly resent this temporary theft of his tool. He is too much absorbed in musical virtuosity to accept the notion that the hammer is also another toy detachable from his body.' Rather than interpreting the child's protest as being based on autocosmic play, the authors view his displeasure as a typical reaction of a small child—in any Western culture—in a similar situation.

13. Mead acknowledged her indebtedness to Erikson's influence (p. 27).

14. Bateson (1972: 118) noted that 'many Balinese actions are articulately accounted for in sociological terms rather than in terms of individual goals or values'.

15. The authors' information was from more than one reliable source, including a village headman of Bayung Gede.

Chapter 5
Misconceptions about Schizoid Balinese

BATESON and Mead made a broad generalization about the emotions and personality of the Balinese: 'It is a culture in which the ordinary adjustment of the individual approximates in form the sort of maladjustment which, in our cultural setting, we call schizoid' (p. xvi). They believed that this was relevant to the psychotic disorder, schizophrenia, and implied a cause and effect relationship. Mead wrote, 'In the most exciting scenes, rioting over a corpse, or at the climax of a cockfight, there are always some who stand aside, curved in upon themselves in the postures typical of schizophrenic dreaming' (p. 27). They subscribed to the idea that 'the bases of childhood experience' predispose to schizophrenia (dementia praecox) (p. xvi).

The Question of Schizoid Character

This likening of personality of all Balinese to a schizoid type and the association made with schizophrenia has the potential of grossly misleading the laity and perhaps some of the medical profession as well.[1] It has puzzled and antagonized the Balinese. The term 'schizophrenia' carries with it severe stigma in Bali. It is regarded as a chronic form of insanity (buduh), believed to be due to inherited factors and incurable. Most other psychotic disorders in the Balinese are not stigmatized because they are believed to be caused by supernatural forces outside the control of the individual and because recovery is complete.

In view of these considerations, it is important to clarify the term and concept of 'schizoid'. In so doing, related conclusions by Bateson and Mead about the emotions of the Balinese were found to be insupportable, erroneous, and misleading. Bateson and Mead did not define the term 'schizoid' nor did they specifically elaborate on the characteristics of schizoid maladjustment. In those days, psychiatric terms were not defined as specifically as they are today, but the general meaning of the term 'schizoid', as applied to personality, has not changed over the years (Allport, 1937; DSM-III-R, 1987). Firstly, it is regarded as abnormal. Secondly, the essential feature of schizoid personality is a pervasive pattern of indifference to social relationships and a restricted range of emotional expression beginning in early childhood (DSM-III-R, 1987). Schizoid personality is further described by American psychiatry: people with this type of personality prefer to be 'loners'; do not have close friends or only one other than the immediate family; choose solitary activities; appear cold and aloof; rarely express strong emotions such as anger or joy; may seem self-absorbed; and are often unable to express aggressiveness or hostility. A prominent psychiatry textbook of the 1920s (Brill and Bleuler, 1924) described schizoid characters as 'people who are shut-in, suspicious, incapable of discussion, people who are comfortably dull and at the same time sensitive, people who in a narrow manner pursue vague purposes, improvers of the universe'. At that time there was a related concept of latent schizophrenia which was considered 'a morbid psychopathic state' in which 'schizoid peculiarities' are not yet of psychotic proportions.

The question is: did Bateson and Mead find, and did the authors find, that the Balinese people in general fit these descriptions of behaviour and this type of maladjustment? And, if not, why were these terms used to characterize Balinese personality?

The authors' examination of Bateson and Mead's general conclusions about Balinese character indicate that they believed that the Balinese fit the term 'schizoid'. Mead stated in her conclusions: 'It is a character curiously cut off from interpersonal relationships, existing in a state of dreamy-relaxed dissociation, with intervals of non-personal concentration in trance, in gambling and in the practice of the arts' (p. 47); '. . . he is driven to fill the hours, so empty of interpersonal relations, with a rhythmic unattended industriousness' (p. 48). She also noted: 'Between the death which is symbolized by the Witch's claws and the graveyard orgies, and the death which is sleep into which he retires when frightened, life is a rhythmic patterned unreality of pleasant significant movement centered in one's own body to which all emotion long ago withdrew' (p. 48). Children steer clear of teasing adults and 'draw back (from adults) into themselves and then turn back on their own bodies for gratification'. 'The withdrawal, however, which marks the end of early childhood for a Balinese, and which comes anywhere between ages three and six, is a withdrawal of all responsiveness' (p. 33).

From the authors' knowledge and observations of the Balinese, both in the plains villages and at Bayung Gede, and in medical and psychiatric clinics in Bali, they can say with assurance that very few individuals have schizoid characteristics or schizoid personality disorder. On the contrary, they have been impressed with a readiness of expression of emotions in most aspects of everyday social inter-action. (This is discussed further in Chapter 8.)

Whereas it is rare to see a case of schizoid personality in the clinics in Bali, Suryani has found that inexperienced doctors undergoing training often diagnose schizoid characteristics in patients if they are not knowledgeable about *lek*, the feeling of embarrassment or 'stage fright' (C. Geertz, 1966) experienced when faced with a person of higher status. C. Geertz (1966) described *lek* as 'a diffuse, usually mild, though in certain situations, virtually paralyzing, nervousness before the prospect (and the fact) of social interaction, a chronic, mostly low grade worry that one will not be able to bring it off with the required finesse'. Young doctors have to be educated to recognize this normal behaviour of the Balinese and to distinguish it from schizoid traits or symptoms.

Bateson and Mead did not state that the Balinese or their behavi-our was schizoid; rather that their 'ordinary adjustment' approximated what in America would be termed schizoid. One interpretation of this is that this ordinary adjustment was not abnormal in the Balinese culture.[2] In other words, normal Balinese behaviour was like certain behaviour considered 'abnormal' in Westerners. This is supported by their statements about behaviours (e.g., withdrawn, little social interaction) that fit the definition of schizoid.

Mead's use of the term 'schizophrenic dreaming'(p. 27) was not defined; it is not a term used by the psychiatric profession and therefore has no meaning. Possibly Mead was referring to behaviour associated with hypnosis or dissociation: the separation of feelings or thoughts from usual consciousness. Neither Bateson nor Mead had any prior professional training or experience in psychiatry or with schizophrenic patients. However, it is important to note that she was likening the behaviour of normal Balinese people to Western schizophrenics. In the authors' observations of many cock-fights and videotapes of cock-fights, they have not observed schizophrenic-like or even dissociative behaviour in the audience. Mead's statement carries with it, for many readers, the implication that schizophrenia is relatively common in Bali. Since this is a serious misconception, available data will be presented to counteract it.

There are no accurate epidemiological data available at this time, but the best indication of the incidence of schizophrenia comes from Suryani's study of 113 consecutive first hospitalizations of psychotic patients admitted to the mental hospitals of Bali during the one-year period, 1984–5. Using standard criteria for diagnosis (DSM-III-R, 1987), only 4 per cent were schizophrenic. It is estimated that if an additional 100 cases of schizophrenia developed that same year but did not come to the attention of the psychiatric services, it would mean an incidence rate in Bali of less than one case per 100,000 over 16 years of age. This is quite a low figure compared with many other countries where it ranges between 7 and 14 per 100,000 (WHO, 1979) in the age group over 16 years of age.

Mead's concept of withdrawal of emotions into the body (p. 48) is amateur psychologizing: it does not fit any psychological theory. In Mead's use of this concept, the authors wondered if she was describing a real phenomenon. Perhaps she was thinking in terms of emotions (feelings of love, anger, jealousy) towards others some-how turned inward and later expressed in actions of ceremonies, dances, offerings, or somatic symptoms which are common in mental and emotional disorders of the Balinese. This could be regarded as similar to the way an artist or dancer might act out feelings in their activities. Even considering such theorizing, the authors observed spontaneous and direct expression of feelings, non-verbally and verbally, especially in eye contact. Anger in public is avoided or suppressed, although it is more likely to be expressed overtly in the privacy of one's home, because it is not polite to express anger, and if one does express it directly, one may as a consequence suffer the same or worse fate from some person (*hukum karma*).

Westerners may misinterpret some Balinese customs as evidence of little emotion or a lack of expressiveness. For example, when a Balinese is given a gift or when a Western guest at a dinner party comments to the hosts on the niceties of the arrangements or the food, the Balinese does not respond verbally. Rather, the response is non-verbal and takes the form of a subsequent return of good deeds or a gift. Another custom that explains minimal verbal response in some situations is that one should speak little if one knows little. A Balinese who ignores this custom is considered like the empty drum that makes a lot of noise when struck.

Interpersonal Relationships

The essential feature of schizoid personality is an indifference to interpersonal relationships (DSM-III-R, 1987). Far from being indifferent, the Balinese are highly attentive and attuned to interpersonal relationships. They place high value on maintaining them. The Balinese trait of suppression of anger is one mechanism that serves this purpose. The society's emphasis on co-operation is antithetical to schizoid personalities. The Balinese place such great importance on good personal relations that they will sacrifice job responsibilities for ceremonies in order to preserve good relationships.

Mead presented Balinese life as being 'empty of interpersonal relations' and associated this with a prevailing fear of 'some undefined unknown'. Again, in this area there are more inaccuracies and contradictions. The majority of the 756 photographs in *Balinese Character* deal with rituals, ceremonies, mother–child interaction, and child development. Most portray either individual activities or group activities in which there is no clearly evident social interaction. However, at least 100 photos and their captions (excluding those of mother–child interaction in nursing, bathing, etc.) show social interaction of many types, including mothers with children, children playing, women delousing, rowdyism, group synchronized behaviour at cremations and dances, sibling rivalry, father–child relationships, and painting faces of children.

Communities vary in the amount of opportunities available for social interaction. The cities and Bayung Gede are two extremes. In the cities there are numerous opportunities. In Bayung Gede there are much fewer, particularly for women because the husband is often out of the home working in the fields and the wife is either working (e.g., carrying water or in the fields) or home alone, usually with her small children, and she is busy. At the *banjar* men meet socially and a great deal of open discussion among equals takes place there. Because women are home and/or alone much of the day does not mean that they are schizoid. All of the persons interviewed at Bayung Gede were normal in their expression of emotion and in rapport, with the exception of the one elderly woman living in the banished area on the edge of the village, who appeared to be demented. Emotional expressiveness is discussed in Chapter 8.

Clubs (*seka*) are a prominent part of daily life, a rich source of interpersonal interaction, and were mentioned by Mead (p. 4). *Seka* are numerous and each individual generally belongs to several. Each focuses on one activity. *Seka* cover a broad range of activities of daily life, such as planting and harvest and creative activities such as dance, orchestra, and painting. In one village studied in which the houses are far apart, the men met daily in social drinking groups to talk, exchange information, and drink palm wine. Women meet and talk at the market and during bathing and clothes-washing. They also talk when harvesting rice and when labouring in groups.

The authors' observations and Suryani's personal experience growing up and living as an adult in several plains villages, and raising a family of her own, attest to the prominence of interpersonal relationships. For example, clubs or groups of young people often remain cohesive and active for decades and even lifetimes. As years pass by and some members move to different localities, the groups meet less frequently but still hang together. Social interaction is strikingly evident at gatherings of extended families which occur, for example, at the death of a member, travel to the mother temple at Besakih, marriage, birthdays, and other rites of passage. Together, much time is spent in relaxed chatting, playing with children, joking, and laughing. In repartee, joyful emotions are often powerfully expressed. The Balinese always try to make good relationships with their extended family and their community. Suryani (1988) found that persons will take a day off from work if their community or extended family is involved in ceremonies. They give more attention and place greater importance on such family and community social activities and on their own self interests than on their jobs.

These data contradict Mead's statements about lack of interpersonal relationships; there is no question about their presence and strength. It is curious that she concluded to the contrary.

1 Suryani interviewing a young woman surrounded by curious villagers.

2 Morning mist shrouding Mt. Agung, the holy mountain to most Balinese Hindus and site of the mother temple, Pura Besakih. It is one of the major points of directional orientation: *kaja*, towards the mountain.

3 The outrigger canoes of fishermen at Gumicik village. This photograph shows the other major direction of orientation: *kelod*, towards the sea.

4 A government building incorporating the traditional architectural style of Bali in the capital city of Denpasar.

5   A small snack bar (*warung*) where villagers buy food and a few household items. They also snack, sit, talk, and pass the time.

6   A village market in the mountains.

7 Farms and terraced rice paddies near the tourist city of Ubud.

8 A farmer tilling a rice paddy in the plains with the help of his water-buffalo.

9 Men and women working together to set rice plants.

10 Women harvesting and processing rice by threshing the dry plants against boards.

11 A woman and a young girl raking coffee beans drying in the sun.

12 The public bathing place, which is part of a temple, at Ketewel village in the plains.

13 A housewife from the plains washing clothes in a stream at Ketewel.

14 A Balinese Hindu temple in the mountainous area of Bedugul.

15 A gate to the sacred part of a Balinese Hindu temple.

16 The shrines of gods and ancestors at households in the plains are distinctly different from those at Bayung Gede. Each shrine is constructed of wood, brick, and a thatched roof.

17 A placenta is buried in the ground beneath this shrine at a household in a plains village. The placenta is the physical manifestation of one of the four 'sibling spirits' of the newborn (see Plate 40).

18 A clan praying together at a yearly family ceremony.

19 Two young women praying and being blessed at the temple belonging to their clan (*dadia*). The priest is sprinkling holy water from a bamboo utensil.

20 Offerings for the gods being borne by women in their finest clothes at a yearly ceremony in the village of Timbrah.

1 Food offerings, brought by women for a village ceremony in the plains, are placed on a platform in a temple pavilion (*bale*).

22 Young girls who will sing at the trance ceremony awaiting the procession through the village of Timbrah.

23 All dressed up awaiting a
village ceremonial parade
at Butabulan.

24 A *topeng* dancer with a
gamelan orchestra in the
background in the city of
Ubud. The mask and
elaborate costume are
traditional for this dance.

25 Several priests, in trance, dancing at the yearly ceremony of a clan in Denpasar.

26 A high priest conducting ceremonies for a family at Klungkung.

27 Priests in trance at a clan
    ceremony.

28 The puppet master
    (*dalang*) of the shadow
    play (*wayang kulit*) sitting
    (on the left) behind the
    flame which backlights the
    screen. A four-man
    orchestra is on the right.
    The village children gather
    in the rear area to watch
    and listen. Most villagers
    sit in front of the screen to
    watch the shadows of the
    puppets and listen to the
    lengthy, animated,
    humorous monologue of
    the puppet master.

29 Mt. Batur, the sacred mountain to the villagers of Bayung Gede. It is an active volcano.

30 A view of Bayung Gede. It appears much the same as in the photograph by Bateson 50 years ago.

31 The main intersection of roads at Bayung Gede.

32 A side-street in Bayung Gede with walls surrounding household compounds. This photograph is identical with one taken by Bateson 50 years ago.

3　The kitchen and parents' sleeping quarters in a household compound in Bayung Gede. The architectural style is the same as that shown in Bateson's photographs 50 years ago.

34　Household shrines of the gods in Bayung Gede. These are made of woven bamboo placed on tree branches stuck in the ground which grow and produce leaves. Contrast these with those in the plains (see Plate 16).

35 A teenager sitting in the
    children's building in a
    household at Bayung
    Gede. The picture of a
    traditional Balinese
    woman is placed side by
    side with a modern 'pin-up
    girl'.

36 A child 'nurse' and baby at
    Bayung Gede. The
    Balinese child is carried
    for most of the first three
    years of life.

37 A young father of Bayung
Gede holds his ailing
infant.

38 A woman with goitre,
common in this geographic
area of Bayung Gede.

39 Karba's 80-year-old uncle at Bayung Gede. Although stooped, he still works actively.

40 Two placentas placed in coconut shells hang in a tree at Bayung Gede. This custom is peculiar to this village and is different from the custom in the plains (see Plate 17). However, the spiritual meaning attached to the placenta is uniform throughout Bali.

41 Offerings at the village temple in Bayung Gede.

42 A warrior dance *(baris)* at a village ceremony in Bayung Gede. The costumes are identical to those photographed by Bateson in 1938.

43 Karba, who was Margaret Mead's favourite subject in Bayung Gede, posing with the authors 52 years later. He became a village priest in 1987.

44 The emotions displayed here contradict Bateson and Mead's statements that the Balinese are emotionally withdrawn.

5 A husband and his wife in Bayung Gede posing uncomfortably for the authors. They display *lek*, which is embarrassment in the face of high-status persons.

16 A young woman placing an offering containing food and flowers for the evil spirits which dwell near the ground. The wall of the family compound is in the background. The offerings (*mebanten*) in the tray balanced on her left hand will be placed at numerous locations known to be frequented by spirits.

47 The trunk of one banyan tree (a holy tree held in awe) near a small temple at Saba. The tourist standing near the centre indicates the size of the tree.

48 Rangda, the witch, in trance, being assisted by a man on each side during a ceremony at Kesiman.

49 A mischievous and playful *barong*, surrounded by accompanying villagers, moving through the village during the ceremonial days of Galungan. The villagers collect donations of money to be used in support of the local town administrative unit (*banjar*).

50 A *barong* mask.

51 A man in the plains grooming his fighting cock. The Balinese are seldom alone and generally spend time together in small groups such as this.

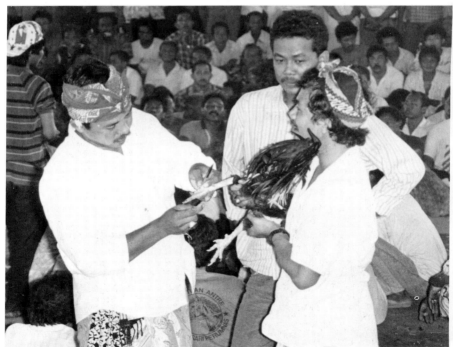

52 Men wrapping a razor-sharp blade around the leg of a cock in preparation for a cock-fight. This cock-fight preceded the village mass trance ceremony at Kesiman and is a symbolic spilling of blood to appease the evil spirits. Cock-fights are also occasions for betting and sport.

53 A *gamelan* orchestra playing at a clan ceremony.

54 A man self-stabbing himself with a kris at Kesiman during the annual ceremony of
Kuningan. The surrounding men monitor him and will remove the kris from his hands
when they deem it appropriate, usually after 20–30 seconds of self-stabbing. This represents
a climactic event in dances involving Rangda, and in some ceremonies.

55 Emotional expressiveness shown by children in Bayung Gede. They do not exhibit the schizoid behaviour Bateson and Mead stated were characteristic of the Balinese.

56 Women preparing rice cakes for a family ceremony in Gumicik.

7 Men attentively observing a temple ceremony. Rice placed on the forehead and temple shows that they have prayed.

8 A traditional healer (*balian*) discussing his methods of treatment with the authors. He is intently engaged in this social interaction.

59 An industrious middle-aged woman demonstrating a typical Balinese skill of balancing a load of coconuts on her head while walking.

60 A *balian* in Denpasar, in trance and possessed alternately by gods and by spirits of clients' ancestors. She not only treats illnesses and problems but also advises clients.

1 A *balian* standing at the carved, gold-encrusted entrance to his treatment pavilion in Bangli. The carving of a spirit over doorways is common in Bali and serves to ward off evil spirits.

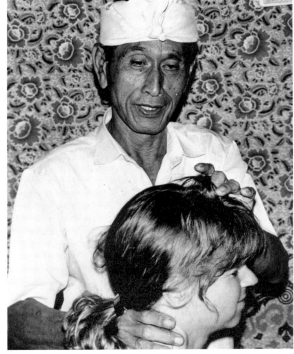

52 A *balian* in trance examining a Western client at Bangli. He is visualizing inside her head in order to make a diagnosis.

63 Pupils at the school where the outbreak of mass trance disorder (*kasurupan*) occurred in 1984.

64 The rock in the school grounds which a schoolgirl in trance said was inhabited by a spirit. It was made into a monument at the time of the outbreak of mass trance disorder in 1984.

Two of the authors' in-depth studies in Bali were centred on mountain villages: one of elderly persons who were interviewed extensively in their homes (Suryani et al., 1988) and the other of children in which villagers from various walks of life were interviewed (Suryani and Jensen, 1991; see also Appendix 2). It was the authors' impression that mountain villagers were less verbal, spoke less with each other than plains villagers, and showed less expressiveness in the face. Belo (1960) noted similar differences between the people of plains villages and the people of more remote mountain villages; she concluded that the former were friendly, gay, inclined to be talkative, more outgoing, and at ease with Westerners: 'They did not suffer from the "tongue-tiedness" and the strain which we found in the remote districts where the people were unaccustomed to such contacts.' Possibly Mead's general conclusions about lack of interpersonal relationships stemmed from her impressions of the mountain villagers of Bayung Gede. However, this would not fully explain it since she and Bateson also made observations in plains villages.

Mead (p. 12) stated that thoughtfulness[3] is '. . . extraordinarily out of key with Balinese character. Placating another, teasing another, flirting with another, fending off the approach from another—these are all habitual enough. But cherishing and thoughtfulness are absent even in the mother–child relationship to an astonishing degree, being replaced by titillation and emotional exploitation.' She stated an exception to this, an anomaly of this 'out-of-key behaviour', was in the thoughtfulness that older siblings pay to the younger: the parent admonishes the older child to 'take care of your younger sibling' (p. 12).

Mead's general assessment of lack of thoughtfulness is misleading. She correctly stated the older sibling's attention and the father's reassuring care of his child. However, she was wrong about parents and other adults. According to Mead, mothers give more attention to newborn and young infants and address them with polished (high) language (p. 7). This is because they think the baby is their husband's ancestor reborn. This fact contradicts Mead's statement of lack of thoughtfulness. The people of Bayung Gede whom the authors met casually offered to do anything they could to help them, often spending hours in helping with no expectation of pay. Karba and the village headman invited the authors back repeatedly with offers of help. When the authors attended ceremonies there and at other villages, as total strangers, they were sometimes spontaneously offered a seat and served with tea and snacks, with no expectation of reward. When the authors appeared uncertain of their way, people generally volunteered to help and went out of their way to do so. In crowded *bemos* (public transport) people often offered the authors a seat, as they also made room for each other. Possibly, Bateson and Mead met a cooler reception and got a different impression because the Balinese regarded them as fearful Dutch who can kill.

The Balinese are also thoughtful to each other as, for example, in sending gifts to former teachers and others to whom they feel grateful. When a person has a problem, such as sickness or mental illness, the neighbours will volunteer to help bring the patient to a *balian* or hospital in their own car or truck. As many as 20–50 neighbours and family members may bring the patient. Considering the minimal data presented by Bateson and Mead and the authors' own anecdotal observations, it would be inappropriate to generalize that lack of thoughtfulness is a trait of Balinese character. The data indicate the opposite: thoughtfulness is a highly developed behaviour in the service of maintaining good inter-personal relationships.

Mead's statement about mothers not cherishing their children is patently absurd. She apparently drew this generalization from her perception of the mother as teasing and emotionally frustrating by 'borrowing babies' (see below). In the authors' experience, both personal and observational, mothers are tender and loving, and they care for their children with a view towards the future: hope that their children will treat them the same way when they are elderly.

With reference to personality characteristics, it is worthwhile noting vignettes of two persons well known to Mead and Bateson who are stark contradictions to her presentations. One is Made Kaler, the 'incredible', energetic, attentive, skilled secretary, who had command of five foreign languages and who, in Mead's words, was 'just about the nearest thing to perfection that God ever made' (Howard, 1984). It is evident from Mead's own descriptions and from the authors' interviews that he was in no way schizoid, maladjusted, unintelligent, withdrawn, or lacking in thoughtfulness. He is a native of Bali and as Balinese in character as any. The other person is Karba, Mead's favourite subject personally, the subject of the film 'Karba's First Years' and one of eight children Bateson and Mead studied intensively

(Mead and Macgregor, 1951). She described him as the gayest, liveliest, and most responsive of the children she observed. His parents were not atypical for people of Bayung Gede but she noted that his aunt was a high-spirited person. Today, 50 years later, he lives with his fourth wife and one of his three grown sons in a traditional household about 40 metres from the main road intersection. His first three wives did not bear children so they parted, as is customary, childlessness being a serious problem. His wife tends a small store located in front of their house and he was recently made a local priest. The authors can say after a number of visits and interviews with him, from observing him and interacting with him at village temple ceremonies, and at a village wedding, that he is poised, thoughtful, ingratiating, curious, intelligent, sociable, calm, composed, successful, respected, and exudes an air of confidence and assuredness. He does not suggest in any way Mead's typical Balinese personality of resembling schizoid maladjustment. The personalities of these two individuals perhaps are sufficient to explode Bateson and Mead's conclusions but there were a number of others in Bayung Gede and in other villages that are equally illustrative and not atypical. What was in Bateson and Mead's mind when they described the 'Balinese Character' as schizoid and lacking in interpersonal relationships?

Borrowed Babies

Bateson and Mead used the term 'borrowed babies' for a sequence of mother–child interaction they called a game of mother tantalizing and teasing her child. Mead attributed the lifelong character trait of emotional unresponsiveness of the Balinese to a specific child-rearing pattern: the mother's (and other female caretaker's) teasing and tantalizing the 6-month to 3-year-old child by borrowing a baby in the child's presence, thereby provoking emotions of jealousy and anger, love or desire, and then turning away from the child and failing to make an emotional response to the child. Mead stated that once the child's pattern of withdrawal and unresponsiveness becomes established, it lasts a lifetime. Bateson and Mead illustrated this behavioural sequence in the films 'Karba's First Years' and 'Sibling Rivalry in Bali and New Guinea', and with still photos of two situations (plate 49, p. 152) although three photographs on this plate do not appear to be relevant (photographs 3, 4, 5).

The authors have observed the borrowing babies pattern but have an entirely different interpretation; a Balinese interpretation. They regard it as an educational or training experience which stimulates emotional maturity and self-confidence. Through the experience the child learns to control emotions of jealousy, unrestrained anger, and hostility stemming from frustrated desire. He learns this by solving the problem himself, rather than relying on his mother or other family member. This is illustrated in the film on Karba by the teased child attending positively to the baby in the mother's lap (i.e., offering water) and carrying the baby and by his leaving the stimulus that provoked his anger. A temper tantrum is the result of failure to solve the problem; he will have another opportunity at another time. The mother does not punish the child for failure, i.e., a temper tantrum. It is a fact that Balinese mothers very seldom punish a child. The problem-solving achievement of control of negative emotions is positively reinforced by the mother's affectionate contact, a sequence nicely shown in Bateson and Mead's sibling rivalry film.

Mead interpreted this game as a cause of the child developing emotional withdrawal and lifelong unresponsiveness. In this connection, she implied that the Balinese mother is rather cruel or unaffectionate, especially when compared with the New Guinea mother. Her tone is further revealed in the placement, in this plate of photos, of a picture of a statue of Rangda, the witch, holding on to a child who appears to be struggling to get away. Mead asserted that the child equates the mother with a witch. This is a misinterpretation: for the Balinese, Rangda is a symbol and portrayal of evil, not of mother (Bandem and deBoer, 1981; see also Chapter 4).

Mother Turning Away before Climax

Bateson and Mead described a sequence of mother–child interaction in which the mother or mother surrogate 'stimulates her child, but when he responds, she is unresponsive and never allows the flirtation to end in any sort of climax' (p. 148). Supposedly she breaks the sequence before the climax is reached. While the investigators never explicitly defined climax, they referred to a failure to consummate the child's rising emotion, in this case, with the mother's withdrawal of affectionate contact. Mead asserted that this is the cause of a cardinal characteristic of Balinese culture: lack of climax. She also implied that this pattern of the mother's behaviour is a determinant of the character trait of emotional unresponsiveness in the Balinese. The issue of climax is dealt with in Chapter 7. Here the authors will critique Bateson and Mead's data on the mother turning away and present their observations relevant to the hypothesis that mothers show this behaviour.

Bateson and Mead's Plate 47 (p. 148) shows nine photos, taken in the course of two minutes, of one mother with her child on her lap. They described the child fretting, then responding with affection, followed by the mother suddenly turning her head away, diverting attention, and showing a blank face. These photos are interpreted from a Balinese point of view as follows: in photo 3 the mother's attention is temporarily diverted by a peripheral stimulus while she allows her child to play with her nipples; in photo 4 it can be surmised from the mother's facial expression and body posture that the child had just painfully bit her nipple with his teeth; as the child continues to nurse and play with the nipple, the mother responded affectionately by patting and caressing; finally, the mother appears uneasy and the child appears sad. In summary, the photos do not illustrate the mother turning away syndrome but something else.

In the film 'Karba's First Years', Mead's narration focuses on the mother's turning away behaviour. However, the continuity of the film sequence is broken so that it is not possible to verify the true sequence. Mead stated that this pattern occurs in many contexts of mother–child interaction, including nursing, bathing, and teasing. She presented it as a common practice among the Balinese.

In attempts to replicate the above data, the authors observed countless episodes of structured and naturalistic mother–child interaction, specifically looking for the behaviour in question. They conducted observations in homes at Bayung Gede, in the plains villages, and at a large gathering of mothers and babies in Bayung Gede. Twelve mother–child couples were videotaped, all with infants and small children who were at the *banjar* attending a health education meeting. The camera was placed unobtrusively. It was clear from the recorded behaviour that it did not affect the subjects' behaviour.

In none of the above sessions did the authors observe the behaviour in question. Suryani could not recall it from her personal experience. The authors considered several interpretations of the above data and their negative results: (1) Bateson and Mead's observations were peculiar to a few mothers; (2) the pattern occurred infrequently; (3) it was peculiar to the mothers of Bayung Gede; and (4) the pattern dropped out of the culture. The first two seem distinct possibilities. If the third possibility were the case, one could not generalize to Balinese character. The last possibility is unlikely because mother–child patterns of significance are very slow to change. For example, the mother teasing game has persisted. Since the authors were unable to replicate Bateson and Mead's observations, serious doubt is cast on the assertion that the pattern of child withdrawal and lack of climax plays a significant role as a determinant of an emotionally unresponsive personality or culture without climax.

Bateson and Mead cited data on the infant, Karba, and his mother as a primary example of the mother interrupting climax, a behaviour which they believed produced a personality with schizoid characteristics. The authors' follow-up evaluation of Karba at 52 years of age provided evidence against the validity of their theory: Karba did not grow up to develop a schizoid personality, or personality characteristics resembling a schizoid personality.

More than a decade after the Balinese studies, when Bateson developed the double-bind theory of the etiology and basic process involved in schizophrenia, he referred to the photographs of a Balinese mother breaking climax as an example of double-bind behaviour (Lipset, 1980). In brief, the double-bind theory holds that a pathologic and/or pathogenic pattern of communication occurs in schizophrenic families in which one person signals a desire for a kind of behavioural response from another and then counter-responds to the evoked behaviour by rejecting it. It is as if one were to say to another 'I want this' and when the person responds accordingly, to counter-respond by saying 'I didn't want that and you were wrong', in effect, creating a situation in which the respondent cannot win. It appears that many years after the Balinese study, Bateson still believed in schizophrenogenic characteristics of Balinese mothers. In the 1960s the double-bind theory of schizophrenia was quite popular among American psychiatrists but today there are few adherents. Studies failed to support it as a cause of schizophrenia. Today it is regarded as archaic and potentially counterproductive in therapy with families (Terkelson, 1983).

Awayness

Bateson and Mead described a behaviour pattern they called 'awayness' in which there is a 'withdrawal into vacancy ... letting themselves suddenly slip into a state of mind where they are for the moment, no longer subject to the impact of interpersonal relations', a withdrawal that they said occurs in various contexts, but especially in parent–child and teacher–pupil relationships (p. 68).

The authors' procedure for evaluating the concept of awayness consisted of reanalysing the photos and by looking specifically for the behaviour at Bayung Gede, and other mountain villages and in plains villages. The concept was also discussed with several scholars of Balinese culture and Suryani reached into her own personal lifetime experience.

Bateson and Mead's substantiation of awayness is weak. They illustrated it with six photos, only two of which are possibly convincing instances. One, showing a woodcarver, illustrated awayness of very brief duration followed by a quick switch to animated, gay behaviour. The other is of a woman sitting at a food stall, her child near by, who appears to be tired or sad. The duration of these episodes was not noted. One photo is of a psychotic man, whose abnormal behaviour, probably schizophrenia, may have been confused with awayness. Made Kaler confirmed to us that this man was the only psychotic person in the village. The two photos of a woman and her child visiting them at their house in Bayung Gede appear to us to illustrate *lek* rather than awayness. *Lek* would be appropriate in this situation. The woman's hand over her mouth is consistent with *lek*. The two photos of a small boy at a birthday party were interpreted by Mead as seeking emotional contact but not obtaining it. However, this photo shows physical contact by the hand and body, both of which represent significant non-verbal interaction and are emotionally soothing to the Balinese. Mead's text does not provide enough description to distinguish the child's appearance from a moment of casual inattention, expectable of a child of any culture in such a situation. Finally, the photo of the leader of a dance club appears on inspection to show respite of a tired person or possibly exasperation, but not awayness.

The authors have observed awayness on several occasions and this behaviour is well known to Suryani. They provide a somewhat different description of it and a totally different interpretation from Mead's.

The Balinese recognize a pattern of behaviour called *ngeramang sawa*, which literally means 'absent thinking or emotion'. It is characterized by absence of thoughts, a staring or vacant-like facial expression, and inactivity, usually brief but lasting up to perhaps 1–5 minutes. It is usually brought on by a problem, such as a recent disagreement or by frustration, disappointment or simply fatigue. It is not seen very frequently. It often evokes the attention and interpersonal supportive behaviour of a friend or family member. The episode terminates rather abruptly. It is the authors' impression that such awayness behaviour is a dissociative state similar to meditation or a shallow level of self-hypnosis.

In their presentation of awayness, Bateson and Mead appear to have combined several different unrelated conditions, including a case of schizophrenia. However, they appear to have identified a true pattern of infrequent occurrence, known to the Balinese, but which does not resemble schizoid maladjustment. Rather, it appears to resemble disassociation[4] or a self-hypnotic state. In terms of function, it can be interpreted as episodic withdrawal and an alternative to experiencing feelings which would make one uncomfortable or expression of feelings which might threaten the harmony of interpersonal relations. Rather than disrupting or impinging negatively on personal relationships, its consequence may be interpersonal support.

Sulking

Sulking is a way of handling anger. Mead cited its occurrence in 2- to 4-year-old children, often as a response to mothers teasing and as an alternative to temper tantrums (pp. 30, 34). She stated that normally children outgrow this response after about the age of 6, a time during which girls take up the role as nurse-mothers and boys begin herding oxen or water-buffalo. When sulking persisted in older children, Mead attributed it to a combination of deviant temperament and a host of other social factors such as family problems, delayed weaning, adoption, and being the child of a mother who was regarded to be tainted with witchcraft by heredity. Mead did not mention it as an adult behaviour.

In the authors' experience, the Balinese recognize two similar types of sulking behaviour. In *ngerumuk* the person disregards the person with whom he is angry and looks down, muttering to himself. In *ngambul*, also an alternative to temper tantrums, the person goes off to be alone and is quiet. For example, a wife who has experienced disappointment or feels angry with her husband may go to her parents' house and *ngambul*. By the time her husband comes to get her, she has recovered. The Balinese interviewed associated disappointment and anger with *ngambul*. Alternative expressions of anger or modified type of temper tantrum in adolescents and adults is slamming furniture and going to bed and sleep. The Balinese see sulking as a way of avoiding a situation in which they are angry or disagree with someone. They do not debate or disagree openly. The Balinese consider *ngambul* normal behaviour, though not common in children and adults. No evidence was found that the causal social factors mentioned above by Mead are relevant.

Many of the above behaviour patterns observed or confirmed by the authors can be interpreted as serving to preserve the harmony of interpersonal relations and to avoid their disruption because of their paramount importance to the Balinese.

In summary, Bateson and Mead erroneously characterized the Balinese personality as schizoid, as cut off from interpersonal relationships and emotionally withdrawn. Bateson and Mead's data and the authors contradict this. Evidence of strong interpersonal relationships was cited. Mead was incorrect in characterizing the Balinese as lacking in thoughtfulness and in describing mothers as not cherishing their children. Mead identified a behaviour which she called awayness associated with withdrawal, but which the authors interpret as dissociation or a self-hypnotic state. Bateson and Mead described a pattern of the mother teasing her child by borrowing another baby and concluded that this leads to a sulking phase in development and to lifelong emotional withdrawal. The authors gave a Balinese interpretation to the practice of borrowing babies: it is positive training in learning to control emotions. Mead placed great significance on a pattern of mother-turning-away-from-her-child as a determinant of lack of climax in the culture, but the authors were unable to replicate observations of this behaviour. Therefore doubt is cast on the validity of Mead's conclusion that the consequence of the mother's turning away from her child is a life and culture without climax.

1. Wallace (1961: 224) stated: 'Such characterization of whole societies or cultures as mentally ill is rarely, if ever, defensible on scientific grounds; a society of psychotics is a contradiction of terms, and the use of a diagnostic label in national character evaluation exposes merely the author's hostility towards the subjects of his description. . . . The use of diagnostic labels such as paranoid, psychotic, and schizophrenic or words implying such labels, is never justified when referring to an entire society.'

2. Mead's works on Samoa (1928), Manu'a (1930b), and Arapesh (1940) indicate that she had a model of a culture setting up strong directives as to how a well-functioning personality should be, which made life very difficult for people who cannot fit into the demands of such a culture. She did not assume that those Balinese who fit their model of Balinese character were abnormal. Quite the contrary. She felt that those people would be the contented ones, but that there would be others—whom she would call 'deviant'—who did not fit, and who might have personalities more similar to those present in other cultures.

3. Definition: 'mindful of others'; implies concern for the feelings of others (Webster's Seventh New Collegiate Dictionary, 1965).

4. Dissociation is a psychological 'defence' or mechanism operating unconsciously, which involves a separation or splitting off of emotions or behaviours from an idea, situation, or another person. It is also defined as 'a lack of normal integration of thoughts, feelings, and experiences into the stream of consciousness and memory' (Bernstein and Putnam, 1986).

Chapter 6
Fear, Worry, and Trust

MEAD concluded that Balinese character is based on fear which, 'because it is learned in the mother's arms, is a value as well as a threat' (p. 47). She claimed that 'fear of many sorts becomes a pleasant emotion, since in childhood shared fear brought mother and child together' (p. 47). Some scholars might reject the concept of fear as the basis of Balinese culture on the general grounds that the concept of national character is controversial or has little merit (Favazza and Oman, 1980). Others may dismiss further consideration of the concept on the basis of oversimplicity, overgeneralization, or inadequate substantiation. The authors examined Mead's fear concepts, including the data and impressions presented to support them, because they felt the need for a more accurate portrayal of Balinese culture and they have found the issue of fear important in understanding not only normal behaviour of the Balinese but also the symptomatology and optimal treatment of mental disorders afflicting them.

Mead's use of the term 'fear' corresponds with the current definition given in a recent psychiatry text: 'an unpleasant emotional state consisting of psychological and physiological changes in response to a realistic threat of danger' (Kaplan, Freedman, and Saddock, 1980). For the Balinese, demons and other supernatural forces are realistic and potential threats, although they do not necessarily evoke fear (see Chapter 2 and the supernatural below).

Anxiety is distinguished from fear as follows:

... an unpleasurable emotional state associated with psychophysiological changes in response to an intrapsychic conflict. In contrast to fear, the danger or threat in anxiety is unreal. Physiological changes consist of increased heart rate, disturbed breathing, trembling, sweating, and vasomotor changes. Psychological changes consist of an uncomfortable feeling of impending danger. (Kaplan, Freedman, and Saddock, 1980.)

Mead described fear reactions in a number of situations. She described in some detail a fear that is instilled by the mother and deters the adult from 'ever venturing on an untrodden path' (p. 48). She asserted that the Balinese develop fear and anxiety if they lose their bearings (orientation). She concluded that they are always a 'little frightened of some unidentifiable unknown' (p. 48). She theorized that the parent instils fear into the child's personality. She wrote about the young man's fear that he will fail to get a charming wife and beget many children (p. 37). She interpreted two dances as personifying fear in the above situations. These and other kinds of fear associated with supernatural beliefs of the Balinese are discussed in greater detail in this chapter.

Orientation: Anxiety and Fear

Mead stressed that lack of orientation in terms of direction (north, south, etc.), day, and caste is the basic cause of fear, 'extreme anxiety and absolute confusion'; and that the existence of orientation is 'felt as a protection rather than as a straight jacket' (pp. 11, 48). In addition she stated that if a person loses his bearings, he may suffer from hours of illness and a tendency to deep sleep.

Because Mead used the terms 'fear' and 'anxiety' interchangeably, it is difficult to be certain which she meant. One assumption is that she meant fear because she used this term more than anxiety with reference to orientation. Possibly she meant both. Her reference to a disoriented state (*paling*) means confusion to the Balinese.

The authors' observations and knowledge of the Balinese do not support Mead's idea that anxiety and fear result from disorientation. Rather, it was found that loss of direction results in tension (*tegang*) and a state of confusion (*bingung*) in which it is difficult to pursue one's thoughts and speech clearly. This is comparable to a state of mild anxiety but clearly is not the 'extreme anxiety' indicated by Mead. *Tegang* has none of the physiological signs associated with anxiety. The tension and confusion clears as soon as orientation is clarified.

It was possible that Mead got her information about orientation distress from McPhee (1946), the composer and ethnomusicologist, because he described a single incident in the 1930s of a young Balinese man who appeared 'pathetic, lifeless and almost sick' when he felt lost and uncertain about his directions in a strange place, but suddenly perked up when he got reoriented. The case, however, appeared to be atypical to the authors.

The authors disagree with the assertion that lack of knowledge of the caste of the person one is addressing or of the day (e.g., with regard to scheduled ceremonies) causes fear or confusion. The first thing a Balinese does when addressing strangers is to ask where they are from, where they live, what their caste is, what their marriage status is, and whether they have children. All of these are used in rules of conversation. The Balinese always specify orientation in terms of the direction—e.g., east, west, *kaja* (towards the mountain), or *kelod* (towards the sea). They must know the person's caste in order to choose the proper level of language to use. If they are unable to speak a higher level of language when necessary, as is often the case in mountain villages, they feel embarrassed and apologize. If a Balinese does not know the day, for example when in a strange village, he immediately asks rather than suffer disorientation. The authors have never encountered illness or a tendency to deep sleep due to loss of bearing. Orientation is important for practical reasons and equanimity but it does not present a problem.

Fear Arising from Parents

Bateson and Mead theorized that the mother instilled fear in her child and then reassured him/her with a 'theatrical embrace'; a pattern that '. . . lays the groundwork for an ambivalent attitude towards fear', by which they meant both a penchant for theatrical performances and a fearful personality. In support of this conception, they wrote of the mother's 'fear laden cry' of *aroh* followed by 'scare words' such as 'snake', and subsequent 'theatrical' reassurance in the mother's arms (pp. 31, 147).

The authors have never observed this pattern although they specifically looked for it in natural and clinical situations. Scholars of Balinese culture have not recognized it. Furthermore, they disagree that *aroh* conveys fear. It is merely an expletive equivalent to 'oh my God', or 'aah!' Hence, Mead's psychological interpretation of a Balinese penchant for theatricals is far-fetched, at best, as is her portrayal of the mother 'laying the groundwork for the continuation of fear as a major sanction and stimulus in Balinese life' (p. 31).

Sometimes there are problems in translating from Balinese to English. For example, there are three words for worry and fear: *nyeh*, *takut*[1] and *jerih*. These words are used when speaking to persons of low, middle, and high castes or status respectively, although they are not exactly synonymous. Mead believed that the mother tells her child not to act afraid or to be afraid (*da takut* and *da jerih*, respectively) but does not follow through with enough reassurance to dispel the fear (p. 31). This translation of the words *takut* and *jerih* is incorrect, and the error may have led to her misconceptions about the role of fear in Balinese life. In Bayung Gede, as in the plains villages, *da takut* means 'do not worry', and is a comforting expression that would, for example, be said to someone before he goes into the forest. *Da jerih* also means 'do not worry', but this would usually be said *after* someone returned from the forest. Neither term means 'fear' or 'afraid' in this context nor in the context of mother–child interaction presented by Mead. It is easy to mistranslate *takut* from Balinese to English because there is no single English word that corresponds exactly with it. Balinese frequently use the word *takut* without meaning fear in ways similar to the Westerner's use of the English word fear. It often means worry or concern. In a recent study on the emotions of northern Balinese (Wikan, 1987), interpersonal fear was reported to be pervasive and 'ubiquitous' in the culture. The authors disagree with such reports or interpretations and attribute them to misconception of the words for fear and worry; both Westerner and Balinese can easily misunderstand each other on the concept of fear because of the incorrect or inaccurate translation.

Fear of strangers is a normal developmental stage in infancy (Bowlby, 1973). The authors have observed parent–child interactions that may have significant bearing on the child's fear of strangers. In Bayung Gede, a parent may respond to the authors' presence outside the household compound by directly picking up a small child playing alone. If the parent conveys fear by this action, it could reinforce a child's fear of strangers. On the other hand, some parents at Bayung Gede and in the plains allowed the child to play freely and independently in the authors' presence, without intervention. The authors have often observed a small child in his mother's arms react to their friendly approach, even just looking and smiling, by fretting and turning to the mother for reassurance or comfort. The mother then responded by cuddling the child and frequently by turning or moving away. The authors, in interpreting this situation, have attributed the child's behaviour sometimes to shyness and other times to fear of strangers. In contrast, most older children, youths, and adults were attracted to the authors and often gathered around them on the roads, in households of villages, and at ceremonies.

The Witch Plays: Fear and Parents' Roles

Bateson and Mead placed great emphasis on the witch play, 'Calonarang'.[2] They interpreted the witch and men who attack her as resembling the relationship between mother and child.

A traditional, widely and frequently performed play, 'Calonarang' features the classic witch deities, Rangda and Celuluk. In former times this play was performed in villages by their own players and by itinerant or visiting groups. Nowadays it is performed less but seen in television presentations, and a similar show, the *barong* and kris dance, is performed daily for tourists at Batubulan, near Denpasar, the capital city. Every Balinese child (and adult) is eminently familiar with Rangda and Celuluk. Every tourist sees the masks of Rangda, queen of the witches, displayed for sale in souvenir, woodcarving, and mask shops. It is truly a grisly mask with bulging eyes, long stringy white hair, tusk-like canine teeth jutting out from the mouth and a red and gold tongue, studded with small mirrors, about a half metre long that hangs out of an open mouth. The costume with 10-centimetre-long pointed fingernails and Rangda's devilish laugh add to the fearful stimuli (Covarrubias, 1937: 326; Belo, 1960). Mead described Rangda as terrifying and as a personification of fear itself (p. 35).

Rangda carries a magical white cloth on her arm which Mead stated is a mother's baby sling. Bateson and Mead stated that the word for the cloth (*anteng*) is the same as for a baby sling. The word *anteng* (or *slendang*) is actually a general one for a cloth that is used around the breasts, the waist, or the head as well. None of the scholarly studies of Rangda and her dances have given it Mead's interpretation. The *anteng* has been referred to as a white hip cloth of *ikat* weaving, formerly imported from India, with secret power symbols on it (Bandem and deBoer, 1981) which protect against krises or daggers (Ramseyer, 1986), as dramatized in the play.

Mead's psychological interpretation of Rangda was that of a 'reconstituted mother', one who displayed fear to the child and instilled fear in him: a 'teasing, powerful unsatisfying person who aroused one's emotions, only to throw one back on oneself' (p. 36) and likened the *barong*, the playful, reassuring dragon, who is pitted against Rangda in some dances and plays, to the Balinese father.

The authors are puzzled by Bateson and Mead's interpretation of Rangda as a mother figure. Rather, there is consensus that Rangda represents evil and symbolizes an exorcism of the powers of evil, witchcraft, and demons (Covarrubias, 1937; Belo, 1960; Bandem and deBoer, 1981; de Zoete and Spies, 1938). Rangda represents the power of Siwa, the god who can cause destruction[3] as well as well-being. Rangda is also reassuring: sacred masks of Rangda are often kept in the village temples and are believed to protect the village from harm, just as does the mask of the friendly *barong*; they can be benevolent forces in the life of the community (Bandem and deBoer, 1981). When good and evil representations are pitted against each other in dance, it is not important that one triumphs over the other or as is typical in the West, that the 'good guys' win. For the Balinese, good and evil forces are balanced.

Rangda is not feared but she is held in awe, like other things felt but not understood. Balinese are in awe of the banyan tree because it grows so big from such a small seed. It is a holy tree (*bingin*), one in which evil spirits dwell. The people make offerings to these spirits to honour them and to keep good relations so they will be benevolent and cause no harm. All things in the Balinese world, e.g., the sun, cars, palm wine, and food, have two sides (*rua bineda*): the good and the bad.[4] Which effect each has depends upon the individual's use of them.

The kris dance, which is part of the Rangda dance dramas, involves men, and sometimes women players, and occasionally Balinese members of the audience, who enter into a dramatic trance performance in which they fall to the ground at the wave of Rangda's cloth, press sharply pointed krises against their bodies, but suffer little or no ill effects upon being revived from trance. Mead interpreted the stabbing as a turning against oneself and a reaction to rejection after approach to the mother: 'Thus symbolically they complete the cycle of the childhood trauma' (p. 35).[5] The trauma referred to the sequence she described for mother teasing. This psychological interpretation appears to represent Mead's use of psychoanalytic concepts of the era.

Bateson and Mead's film titled 'Trance and Dance in Bali' portrays mostly the trances and the final parts of the Rangda and kris dance. In the beginning Rangda, the witch, threatens to spread plague and kills a mother's newborn baby. Mead's narration states that Rangda 'represents fear itself' and the friendly jovial *barong* (dragon) who comes on the scene represents life. Rangda and the dragon's male followers go into trance and the latter fall down at the wave of Rangda's white cloth and they perform the self-stabbing, which is harmless because they are in trance. Women in attendance sometimes go into trance and turn krises on themselves. 'Children with anxious faces watch.' A chicken is brought for offering to the dragon. All the people in trance are revived by sprinkling of holy water as the 'Balinese re-enact the struggle between fear and death and life-protecting ritual'.

The film is a dramatic portrayal of an authentic trance dance drama, something seen less often in Bali, although the dance is recreated for tourists without true trances occurring. The film shows graphically that one can press a sharp dagger against one's body without inflicting harm when in trance. The story is traditional and very familiar to all Balinese and it is no wonder they never tire of it because it is highly dramatic and may include members of the audience going into trance entering into the drama. In the film and in her writings, Mead equated Rangda with a murderous maternal figure.

The Balinese themselves offer an alternative interpretation of this drama. They feel that Mead incorrectly interpreted it as the struggle between fear and death and a 'life-protective ritual', and as symbolizing the mother figure. To them, the drama symbolizes the daily and lifelong conflict between good and evil[6] and the overcoming of the latter by balancing forces. For them, its theme is not death or fear, although the drama ends with the witch no longer threatening to incite plague or killing babies. She is subdued in a trance and the kris dancers enact the strength of the gods that possess them by pressing the sharp krises against their bodies and by coming through unharmed.

A Western psychological interpretation of Rangda that resembles Bateson and Mead's might go like this. Rangda represents a grotesque female, a widow, who eats and kills babies. The closest parallel in modern Western society is the Halloween witch who may threaten or frighten children (Rangda's role is for the entertainment and benefit of people of all ages). It can be assumed that there is such a destructive figure in the unconscious of most persons. The question arises as to why such a figure took form in the unconscious since mothers in general, Balinese mothers included, are in fact loving, nurturing, and giving. Possibly it derived from the experiences of young children witnessing their siblings die when they were very young. Because infant mortality was quite high in Bali until recent years, most children would have had an opportunity to witness one or more mysterious deaths of infants. The young child might interpret the death as being caused by the mother. In Freudian theory, an infant has impulses to devour its mother or eat her and the infant or child could project those impulses on to the mother, attributing to her powers to devour and destroy an infant. Rangda's mask has a good side as well and this could be a representation of the child's or adult's image of the good side of the mother. In the drama, Rangda, the mother, is not killed by the men with daggers because to overwhelm or kill her would be intolerable to the feelings of the observers.

The kris performance could be an example of the exorcism of evil which possesses the individuals in trance as a confirmation of the witch-like female figure in the unconscious of adults and children. In support of the latter, it was noted that the schoolchildren who experienced hysterical dissociation (trance) attacks (Appendix 2) reported frightening hallucinations of being taken into a forest by a tall woman with long hair and big eyes (characteristics of Rangda). The foregoing interpretations are consistent with Bateson and Mead's interpretation that Rangda represents the potentially fearful aspects of a mother figure.[7]

Rangda represents a woman but it is noteworthy that she is always played by a man. No authors have interpreted this aspect of the custom; possibly the practice represents the dual sex nature of evil. In their beliefs, the Balinese do not distinguish between the sexes with regard to good or bad. Male and female and the forces of weak and strong, good and evil are united in one god, Siwa (Covarrubias, 1937: 307).

The authors favour the interpretation of the Rangda and kris trance dance largely as the personification of evil and demons and the exorcism of evil from the self and the community (Covarrubias, 1937; Bandem and deBoer, 1981; deZote and Spies, 1938). Bandem and deBoer (1981) stated that the self-stabbing tests and demonstrates the strength and invulnerability of the god who possesses the dancer. It is therefore understandable that one kris dancer described his experience of self-stabbing as a show of devotion (*ngayah*) and not hostility turned on the self. The author's observations and Belo's (1960) report that a kris dancer felt anger prior to going into trance is consistent with exorcism.

Mead extended her theme of the bad Balinese mother (fearful witch) to an assertion that the young man fears he will fail to succeed in getting a loving wife but will instead find that he has married a witch: 'Generation after generation, men continue to dream of the princess and find themselves married to the witch' (p. 37).[8] She supported this theme from an incorrect reading of the theatre plot in which she described the prince who attempts to abduct a beautiful girl but instead gets her ugly sister, the 'Beast' princess who was dressed in the costume of the mother or mother-in-law. Mead was apparently referring to an *arja* dance drama but she misinterpreted it in several critical respects: in the real story, the king had two wives, one beautiful and the other unattractive and strong-willed, and there is no reference to the clothes of the latter as those of a mother or mother-in-law (Bandem and deBoer, 1981).

The authors looked at this question of the witch-wife in their study of marriage-related problems for which 54 men sought help at a psychiatry clinic in Denpasar, Bali. Neither in the patients' symptoms and complaints nor in the clinical assessment did the authors encounter any hint of men regarding their wives as resembling witches. Made Kaler, Mead's secretary, said he never perceived such an idea or attitude in the people of Bayung Gede; he regarded the idea as 'fanciful'.

Mead augmented her theory of the mother as witch with her views of the Balinese father as gentle, unconditionally loving and reassuring, like the *barong* (pp. 38, 187) which is considered the antagonist of Rangda (Belo, 1949). McPhee's (1946: 101–2) description of the *barong* is the most appealing:

At festive afternoon performances these creatures were high-spirited and full of whims, dancing a strange ballet, coquettish and playful at one moment, rolling on the ground like a puppy, and suddenly and unaccountably ferocious the next, snapping and stamping in the fine fury as the two dancers within the body synchronized their steps and movements with beautiful coordination.

But when, late at night, towards the end of some play, the *barong* made a dramatic entry, looming out of the darkness to the sound of agitated drums, it was no longer the friendly agreeable creature. It advanced slowly, with strange menace, its gold and mirrors shining dimly in the lamplight. Now it had become the mystic and supernatural form of king or saint about to engage in battle against the forces of evil, a conflict in which the last ounce of magic strength would be needed to put to flight the witch or demon foe. This was a dark moment in the drama, a moment of hovering on the borderline between reality and the unseen, for more often than not the dancers, carried away, identifying themselves perhaps with the beast whose body now enveloped them, fell into trance. Here a new drama might begin, for the *barong* often left the stage, to run quite wild into the night.[9]

The authors concur that Balinese fathers are strikingly tender, affectionate, and tolerant in interaction with their children. However, this fact does not justify equating the father with the playful *barong* in the classical dances. For the Balinese, the *barong* does not represent life as interpreted by Mead but it is a good, reassuring, protective, helpful, and entertaining figure. The *barong* is also spiritually powerful and he is held in great awe.

Children regard their parents with respect and devotion, not fear, in everyday life and in special events such as marriage and death of a parent. They are taught to accord honour and consideration to four types of teachers: parents (Guru Rupaka); teacher (Guru Wisesa); government (Guru Pengajian); and God (Guru Swadiaya).

In summary, the authors found untenable Mead's psychological interpretations of the mother and wife as a witch and the father as a kind and loving *barong*. Mead's interpretation of the witch

Rangda as a personification of fear is erroneous; instead, Rangda represents evil and is held in awe by the Balinese but her mask is benevolent as well. Such attempts exemplify the hazards of trying to interpret Balinese culture by using Western-based psychological concepts and theory. In order to develop more accurate interpretations of the roles of fear and worry in Balinese culture, there is a need for more data from rigorously designed studies, as well as the appropriate use of psychological theory and consideration of the beliefs held by Balinese.

Sleep and Fear

Bateson and Mead made the generalization that Balinese fall into deep sleep when frightened or in fearful situations. They interpreted this sleep as psychological regression and illustrated it with two examples in photographs (p. 191). Here, two men fell asleep while sitting in a group of villagers discussing their thievery. That they felt frightened was an inference by Bateson and Mead, possibly based on how they would feel in a similar situation. The authors and their Balinese informants have not encountered any Balinese falling asleep due to fear. However, Balinese will fall asleep when tired or, like other people, when feeling tired after experiencing a period of tension. When teachers see pupils acting sleepy in class, they suspect a problem at home and attempt to correct it.

The Supernatural: Worry, Fear, and Illness

To a Balinese, Bali is filled with gods. It is primarily the supernatural phenomena that are at the core of many activities of daily life, ceremonies, rituals, dances, plays, trance, physical and mental illnesses, and healing. These include demons, witchcraft, black magic, and *leak* or spirits. Evil spirits are often present. For example, one should not start a journey at midday or dusk because it is believed that evil spirits come out then and are more likely to disturb one at these times. These spirits are the focus of treatment by *balian*. Physicians and psychiatrists who practise Western techniques need to know about the supernatural and of the work of the *balian* in order to be effective in Bali.

Leak (pronounced, 'lay ack' and often spelled *leyak* or *lejak*) are witch-like spirits or creatures that are transformations of real people who live in the community.[10] Some persons in a village are generally regarded as *leak* and others are believed to be *leak* by individuals. Almost any disliked acquaintance presents a potential danger because of the possibility that he/she may be transformed into a *leak* at any time. *Leak* can practise black magic and thereby initiate illness of any sort, and they can even poison people, thus causing death. They generally come out in the night and are likely to frequent cemeteries. According to the beliefs of the people, Halloween-like activities occur: the goddess of death meets at midnight to dance and feast on the living blood of the dead brought back to life; entrails hang in trees, cauldrons catch dripping blood, and the roots of trees wind in and out of the skulls and bones (McPhee, 1946).

McPhee (1946: 227–8) described one of his experiences thus:

It was perhaps a week later that I awoke again, late in the night, with the same strange feeing that someone had called. It was an unusually warm night, and I went outside onto the veranda. I could not believe my eyes.

Across the valley, halfway down the hillside, a row of lights glowed with a soft pure brilliance. They seemed to move ever so slightly, floating up and down as though anchored. Suddenly they went out, as suddenly went on again, but now to shine in a perpendicular line, one above the other. They merged slowly, until only the central one remained, which now began to float slowly up the valley. All at once it vanished. But within a minute the lights were shining in a row once more, far to the north.

I went to rouse Durus and Sampih, who were sleeping in the next room. Look! I said. What lights can these possibly be? They are too pale for lamps, and besides, there are no paths where they are moving.

The *leaks*, said Durus, softly almost inaudibly. They must be from Bangkasa (the village across the valley) ... or from somewhere in the north, he added after a while.

We stood silently watching this magic display. The lights glowed and died, came close together, spread rapidly out in a long line. Slowly they floated back once more to where I had first seen them. One by one they went out, until only a single light remained. But all at once it was gone. They valley was in darkness.

All the next day I was haunted by the weird beauty of the scene I had witnessed the night before. It was as if the stars had descended. If it had not been for Durus and Sampih I should have been unable to believe it had not been part of a dream. But when I mentioned it to Cokorda Rai, and later to the perbekel in Pliatan, they were not surprised. Had I awoke out of an uneasy sleep? With a feeling of suffocation? There was only one explanation. Sorcery was in the air once more. It had only begun, and no one knew what was to follow.

Such experiences are reminiscent of Westerner's reports of UFOs. Another of McPhee's (1946: 141–2) experiences illustrates *leak* phenomena:

No one was surprised, then, when all at once things began to go wrong in the house. Misfortunes occurred, one after another, and as they accumulated everyone began to have a worried, hunted look. Rantun the cook slipped on the kitchen floor and broke her arm. Pugig stepped on a thumbtack and got an infected foot. The cat fell off the roof, actually fell, and for no reason at all, and was killed, while Kesyur and Sampih declared the garage was haunted. Night after night they would wake, they said, unaccountably rigid, jaws clenched, unable to make a sound. They heard the bicycle bells of Durus and Pugig ring out in the darkness, although there was no one else with them in the garage. Voices called their names from outside, but they opened the doors to find no one. And late one night, as Kesyur walked up the road alone to the garage, he saw, sitting silently among the bamboos, a great bird, large as a horse. . . .

In the morning, as Pugig brought up the coffee, he would point to drops of blood that ran in an unbroken line all around the outside floor of the sleeping-house. A fight between two tokes, the great lizards that now hid and croaked in the thatch, I suggested, but Pugig did not agree, for he would wash the spots away, only to find them again the following morning. One night I awoke to hear the loud ticking of a clock almost in my ear. It was rapid and metallic, like an alarm clock, and seemed to come from outside the wall. As I reached for my flashlight it began to travel quickly around the four walls of the room. I ran outside, but there was no trace of anything at all.

Everyone agreed, as I related the experience in the morning, that all this was the work of *leaks*.

These are excellent examples of how Westerners and Balinese see and interpret phenomena differently because of their different belief systems. The Westerner was startled and puzzled by what he saw. The Balinese accepted the events as commonplace because they were readily understandable to his mind.

Leak may present themselves in various forms—a monkey, a human figure, light, or wind—depending upon the degree of ability of the *leak*. It is believed that a small proportion of the people who can see, hear and speak with *leak* are more vulnerable to their harm. Seeing a *leak* can evoke fear. Individuals who are regarded as being 'warm' humans are deemed to have no power or natural ability to see *leak* and do not worry about them; people who are considered 'cold' humans have abilities to see and hear *leak*. Such visions and auditory phenomena are similar to hallucinations manifest as symptoms in psychotic persons in Western cultures. In Bali normal persons can experience hallucinations in their usual state of consciousness or in a state of meditation.[11] People are not concerned with *leak* most of the time; they take ordinary, semi-automatic precautions to be safe, comparable to the Western practice of washing hands before eating. As Bateson and Mead pointed out, the 'actual disruption of social life due to suspicion of witchcraft and black magic is very slight' (p. 261). Certain circumstances, such as being in the presence of a person who is a possible *leak*, is reason to be cautious. For example, a psychiatrist who works in a mental hospital, although feeling fine and healthy, might occasionally consult a *balian* for a 'check up' to be sure he/she has not somehow been affected by black magic or evil spirit since these may come from unidentified patients at the hospital.

Whereas supernatural forces represent a relatively frequent worry and, for some, occasional fear, the culture has many regular rituals and ceremonies to deal with them. Also the gods and good spirits are everpresent or stand guard to protect one and provide comfort and peace. They do not fear God but hold God in awe. Nyepi, a yearly celebration throughout Bali, focuses on propitiating evil spirits by offerings. One type of modern offering is strikingly apparent in the villages: the huge likenesses of evil spirits made of paper and wood. They take the form of the most grotesque monsters imaginable, sometimes doing horrible things such as eating babies, and invoke fascination and excitement but not particularly fear. Children are drawn to them and like to play around them.

Bateson and Mead presented data which show that from early infancy children are taught to pray. The Balinese often bring the hands together with a slight bow in daily greeting or departing. Not only are gods present in everyone's daily life and shape many activities, but temples to serve gods are in abundance. Every household has one temple, each with one or more shrines, and in addition, every family has one or more family temples for prayer and offerings.

A Sense of Trust

The authors concur with Bateson and Mead that most infants experience a great deal of human contact and closeness in the early years. The Balinese child is in physical contact with the mother or her surrogate (child nurse) for most of the day and night for the first three years of life. It is a custom that the child should not be left alone outside the home before he is 3 years old. He sleeps in his parent's bed until at least the age of 3. He is usually breastfed *ad libitum* for one to three years. For the first six months he is carried constantly and never placed on the ground or floor directly. After the six months' ceremony, the baby can sit on the ground and play by himself but he is always cared for carefully by a person and usually placed on the hip when moved or sometimes carried there as the mother works at home or in the fields. He spends much of his first few years of life being carried on the hip, often in a sling. In many respects he is treated like a god and he is never punished. He hardly ever hears a cross word. While it is not possible to provide substantiating data that all or most Balinese infants have these experiences, the authors' experience and observations indicate that they are common enough to be set forth as generalities.

This style of child rearing might appear to the Westerner as over-protective or undesirable. This could be an appropriate assessment if applied to a Western child. But in Bali this style is the norm and it cannot be considered deviant. The authors have encountered considerable difficulty in attempts to apply Western psychological theory to Balinese personality and culture. This was a problem with Bateson and Mead's work. However, some Western concepts and theories are applicable and Erikson's (1950) theory of human development is one of these; parts of it are useful at this point. Erikson characterized human development as going through eight stages, from infancy to old age, each stage denoted by terms that epitomize opposing or alternative enduring traits. The first stage is trust versus mistrust: a period when the child has the opportunity to develop a basic sense of trust in people and his environment which he will carry through life. This is also the period when basic mistrust in people and the environment can be developed. The relative development of each outcome for an enduring trait depends upon child rearing and environmental experiences. The first two years of life are the most important for the formation of these traits.

In formulating the theory, Erikson drew on a background of studies and knowledge of Western societies as well as non-Western cultures. Erikson's developmental theory has been durable since its inception 40 years ago and is an integral part of psychiatric thought today.

No attempt will be made here to develop a comprehensive or detailed application of Erikson's entire developmental theory to Balinese personality or character. Erikson's concept of trust is cited because it is worthy of consideration and is another way of looking at a possible character trait of the Balinese. If Erikson's theory is appropriate to Balinese child development, it nevertheless carries the risk of fallaciously assuming that one can infer adult character traits as effects of early infantile experience. Until a way is found to support such hypotheses, interpretations based on the theory might be considered statements of faith.

Viewing the Balinese infant from the perspective of Erikson's theory, the typical style of child rearing could be postulated to develop a personality with a strong basic sense of trust. The authors have been struck by the role trust plays in the fabric of Balinese life, in interpersonal relations and in relations with ancestors and the gods. To the Western observer, this may at times appear as blind trust or being naïve to a fault. When trust is broken there are feelings of disappointment but these are usually handled psychologically by invoking the concept of karma. The authors' perception is that basic patterns of Balinese child rearing produce a lifelong sense of trust. This contrasts with Bateson and Mead's emphasis on lifelong fear as the predominant outcome of child rearing.

It is not implied that a trait of trust is the only outcome of the rearing experience of the Balinese child; it is hypothesized that trust is one of many traits. Contact and security may favour trust but common experiences not focused on here could also shape other traits. For example, accusation or suspicion of witchcraft is common.

The deep belief in gods from the beginning of life until death and the strong sense of trust characteristic of the Balinese could be the chief underlying factors that account for the ability of Balinese to go into trance easily and quickly. In addition the *balian* learn to go into trance by observation and imitation as children. Trance and hypnotic states are identical in terms of psychic mechanism. As Orne (in Soskis, 1986) has pointed out, 'The skills of the hypnotist consist largely in creating a context where the patient can feel comfortable, trusting and willing to allow himself or herself to respond.' This is the same context in which the Balinese go into trance.

In summary, the authors take issue with Bateson and Mead's conclusion that Balinese culture is based on fear. Mead's reports of fear and anxiety in situations of loss of orientation and lack of knowledge of the caste of the person to whom they are speaking are unsubstantiated. There is little evidence of the mother transmitting fear to the child. Mistranslation of *takut*, the word for fear and worry, may have entered into Bateson and Mead 's misinterpretations. Mead's interpretation that mother-induced fear results in a Balinese penchant for theatricals and a fearful personality is questionable; the authors disagree with Bateson and Mead's psychological interpretation that the classical witch, Rangda, is a personification of mother and represents fear; rather, she represents the power of evil and is a reassuring symbol as well.[12] Observations about supernatural forces in Balinese life that can cause worry or fear and how they are dealt with by the culture are presented and Erikson's theory of human development is cited to support the hypothesis that the usual pattern of Balinese child rearing develops a personality with a strong basic sense of trust.

1. Mead's spelling of *takut* was *takoet*, according to the spelling conventions of the 1930s.

2. They used it in psychological interpretations of character: 'This drama throws more light on Balinese character structure than any other' (pp. 164–71).

3. Other gods balance: Brahma creates and Wisnu is for maintenance.

4. The Japanese also do not have a clear-cut dualism of good and bad, right and wrong. For them, goodness or badness is a relative matter, depending on the social situation (T.S. Lebra, 1976: 11).

5. Barnouw (1985: 125) critically reviewed Mead's writing on the Rangda plays and concluded that it is debatable if Rangda can be identified with a 'frustrating' mother. However, he accepted Mead's interpretation of Rangda's cloth as a baby cloth and Bateson and Mead's presentation of mothers as being frustrating to the child. He stated, 'Perhaps there is something to be said, then, for the hypothesis

that mother–child relations are re-enacted in the Calonarang drama.' This is another illustration of the influence of Mead and Bateson's writings on cultural anthropology.

6. For the Balinese, this includes forces or spirits that cause plague or death.

7. Elizabeth Collins suggested this interpretation.

8. This style of writing is typical of Mead and it is easy to imagine her saying it, as she does in the film 'Dance and Trance in Bali'.

9. Here, as is often the case, the *barong* (men) are in trance.

10. For detailed descriptions, see Covarrubias (1937: 322–5).

11. Psychotic Balinese also have auditory and visual hallucinations but these are not as brief and transient as those of *leak*, are associated with other signs and symptoms of psychosocial decompensation, and are not characteristic of or identified by the culture as *leak*.

12. The authors have often puzzled over what factors lay behind the formulation of their main conclusions and why they were at such variance with the findings in this book. While the many anecdotes heard from acquaintances or students of Mead, her biographers, and her own autobiography are intriguing and helpful for understanding the fascinating personality of Mead, a psychobiography along the lines of Erickson's analysis of world-famous figures such as Gandhi is avoided. However, the comments of one informant, who had a close personal and professional relationship with Mead in her later years, are notable. According to this informant who wishes to remain anonymous at this time, Bateson and Mead delayed in getting the Bali data written up because of the pressures of World War II activities and Bateson being in England at the time. Mead did her part of the writing with unusual haste. Bateson contributed the concepts of schizoid and psychological formulation regarding Rangda and the Balinese mothers' habit of turning awang. Bateson had separated from Mead at the time of writing the book and yet Mead was motivated to give as much credit as possible to Bateson's ideas in order to enhance his professional standing which lagged far behind hers.

Chapter 7
Climax in Bali

The 'No Climax' Concept

MEAD characterized Bali as a culture without climax (p. 48). Although Bateson and Mead did not explicitly define climax, they described sequences of mother–infant behaviour in which there is 'a series of broken sequences of unreached climaxes'. The mother stimulates the child to show emotion 'only to turn away and break the thread, as the child in rising passion, makes a demand for some emotional response on her part'. Mead reported that from about 18 months, the mother teases the child repeatedly and 'the stimulus to this never-realized climax becomes more patterned and more intense'; the mother and others 'tease and tantalize while the child responds with mounting emotion which is invariably undercut before the climax'.[1] Later, the child begins to withdraw and continues a lifelong pattern of withdrawal of responsiveness. Bateson (1987) wrote, 'It is possible that some sort of continuing [emotional] plateau of intensity is substituted for climax as the child more fully adjusted to Balinese life.' Bateson and Mead also stated that 'climax is absent from their sequences of love and hate' (p. 255).

Nearly a quarter century later, C. Geertz (1966) studied Balinese behaviour in depth and accepted Mead's conclusions about the absence of climax. In his writing on a related topic, the meaning of certain kinds of Balinese behaviour and the social nature of Balinese thought, he stated that 'social activities do not build, or are not permitted to build, to definitive consummations'; this was exemplified by patterns of quarrelling, artistic performances, temple celebrations, and dance. He also utilized this concept in his theory of Balinese culture patterns, in relation to concepts of time: 'Balinese time lacks motion because Balinese social life lacks climax. The two imply one another and both together imply and are implied by the Balinese contemporization of persons.' Bock (1988), Mrazek (1983), and Ketter (1983) repeated the climax concept and Bateson (1949) further developed it. McPhee (1948), studying Balinese dance, wrote that it is without climax. On the other hand, he also stated that 'trance [dance] frequently forms the climax of the ritual dances of the temple'. Also, Geertz and Geertz (1975) referred briefly to the climactic outcome of religious rituals, artistic performance, and title-group conflicts. In spite of these generalizations about absence of climax, Bateson and Mead mentioned climax in certain situations such as trance (pp. 156, 163, 167, 171) and the 'orgasmic climax' of men stabbing themselves during the kris dance (p. 168), and in the courtship dance (p. 172).

Bateson (1949) used the 'no climax' concept in his analysis of the 'steady state' of the Balinese cultural system. He employed two conclusions: (1) 'in general the contexts which recur in Balinese social life preclude cumulative interaction', and (2) 'childhood experience trains the child away from seeking climax in personal interaction'. (The latter was equivalent to avoiding 'cumulative interaction' in Bateson's terminology.) He hypothesized that these characteristics contribute to a characteristic steady state, or maximization of stability in the Balinese culture.

No writer has previously questioned the concept of a general lack of climax in Balinese culture. However, this concept can be questioned when the data are closely re-examined. Bateson (1949) and Bateson and Mead emphasized the mother's failure to complete what would, in other countries, be expected as usual emotional interactions between mother and child, thus resulting in an emotional plateau rather than climax for the child. Their anecdotal observations, supported by photos and a film, depicted three types of events: (1) nursing, (2) bathing the infant, and (3) the mother teasing the infant. However, the descriptions offered are limited in amount and detail and insufficient in themselves to support a broad generalization about limited climax. The illustrative film, 'Karba's First Years', showing behaviour of one mother with her small child shows broken sequences which do not fully support Mead's commentary. Furthermore, in Bateson and Mead's film, 'Childhood Rivalry in Bali and New Guinea', the same child (Karba) is immediately and climactically comforted following the sequence of teasing. As noted in Chapter 5, it was not possible to replicate data of mother turning away in an emotional interaction.

Climax in Events and the Arts

This chapter examines several behaviour patterns, ceremonies, and events mentioned by Mead and discusses additional data regarding Balinese events and patterns relevant to the concept of climax observed on multiple occasions.

The cremation ceremony in Bali is characterized by weeks of laborious and expensive preparation; on its final day it constitutes a festive occasion for surrounding villagers.[2] At this ceremony, which is at times carnival-like and at other times solemn in atmosphere, the corpse is raised into a tower, whose height and number of steps leading to the corpse platform signify the status of the deceased. Forty or more persons then carry the tower as far as several thousand metres to the cremation area. The corpse and offerings are placed inside a paper and wood coffin decorated to represent an animal such as a bull, selected to be appropriate to the caste of the individual. Finally, the tower and its contents are quickly set ablaze, producing a dramatic and climactic tower of flames. After the flames die down, most observers and participants leave for home. Rituals for dealing with the cremated individual's ashes take place at various intervals following cremation but do not detract from the culminating and climactic character of the cremation itself which is recognized by all Balinese as a landmark event.

This major traditional ceremony is one of the most striking examples of climax that Westerners are familiar with. It clearly builds to a definitive consummation point or climax, 'the point of highest dramatic tension or a major turning point in the action' (Webster's Seventh New Collegiate Dictionary, 1965). C. Geertz (1980) described the entire process as (1) 'a long crescendo of getting ready', (2) the ceremony of burning, and (3) 'finishing up'. Even Mead appeared to contradict her view of climax in describing cremation: 'the weeks of laborious preparation culminate in three days of ceremony'. At the cremation, the men carrying the tower 'shout, they leap, they lift their arms in threatening gestures, they whirl around and around in a mass of vigorously stamping, kicking and entangled limbs, falling down, trampling upon their fellows, hurling themselves into a pool of mud and splattering each other with howls of glee' (Belo, 1935).

A dramatic and climactic historical event occurred in 1908, when the most powerful and last ruling family in Bali, the Tjokordas of Klungkung, walked ceremoniously and suicidally into the annihilating gunfire of invading Dutch troops (C. Geertz, 1980). A similar event occurred in 1906, when the Badung ruling family, the king, his wives, his children, and his entourage, suicidally marched into a massacre by Dutch troops.

Boon (1977) regarded the place of death in Balinese traditions as an enduring, almost substantive, theme: 'If any complex of values could be said to cement the diverse strata, factions and times of Balinese culture, it is the premises around which death and cremation rites occur.' He predicted that if Bali's culture ever succumbs to political or tourist-induced upheaval, 'its death will take the form not of a quiet burial but of one last and total cremation'. These views underscore the principal significance of death and cremation in Bali and the climactic nature of cremation lends credence to climax as a basic aspect of ritual in Balinese culture.

Cock-fights, traditional in Bali for centuries, continue to be staged today. In many villages, one can see cocks restrained in little bamboo cages, or being gently stroked and cared for by their owners in preparation for fights. These fights, attended by males only, are characterized by shouting and gesticulating by the audience during the betting, followed by intense concentration as they watch the cocks fight, to a bloody, climactic death. Bateson and Mead also mentioned the 'climax' of a cock-fight.

The *barong* or witch dance is one of the most enduring and popular theatrical performances for all levels of Balinese society. From time to time, it takes place in many villages. To cater to tourists, it is also performed at several locations near the capital city of Bali throughout the year. Mead (1939) and Bateson and Mead (1942) described this performance in detail (see Chapter 6). Basically, it depicts conflict between good and evil spirits, the dragon and Rangda respectively; it includes comedy and exaggerated expressions of theatrical emotion. As Mead (1939) stated, it 'usually ends in a series of violent trances' and 'climax'.[4] The *barong* impersonators, in 'climactic posture' (Holt and Bateson, 1970), bend backward and press their krises (daggers) into the flesh of their chests, sometimes piercing the skin but usually not drawing blood, and finally fall to the ground rigid or limp, followed by revival through the sprinkling of holy water. In C. Geertz's view (1966), the 'fearful witch and foolish dragon' end combat without climax 'leaving everything precisely as it was' and the observer 'with the feeling that something decisive was on the verge of happening but never quite did'. In contrast, the authors' observations are similar to Mead's: that both Balinese and foreigners cannot help but sense climax at the conclusion. Similarly, the enduring and popular 'Calonarang' play ends in climax with the minister of the king attacking and fighting Rangda who appears dramatically from an elevated platform.

Bateson (1949) stated that 'in general the lack of climax is characteristic for Balinese music, drama, and other art forms'. He further observed that 'it does not have the sort of rising intensity and climax structures characteristic of modern occidental music, but rather a formal progression'. McPhee (1970) also stated that Balinese dance and music lack climax. In the case of temple dances, this appears to be accurate in the sense that these dances may go on for hours with no obvious finale or single culminating point. However, within the overall structure there are multiple episodes of mounting tension with release in joke or comedy.[5] Ethnologists (McPhee, 1948; Holt and Bateson, 1970) stated that trance dances can be seen as climaxes within temple dances.

The traditional music of Bali is played by the *gamelan* orchestra; it has a distinctive, easily recognized sound and rhythm because of the five-tone scale and the characteristic percussion instruments that are not used in Western music. According to McPhee (1970: 296):

The swift, aerial music of the Balinese orchestra, or *gamelan*, fills the open air with chiming resonance. Innumerable little gongs, large and small xylophone-like instruments with ringing bronze keys blend in an intricate polyphony that floats above the throbbing drums and periodic accents of deep and vibrant gongs. The air is shattered with a continuous shower of bright, percussive sound as the difficult music is performed by thirty or forty carefully rehearsed musicians.

The melody is repetitious. It does not reach climaxes resembling those of some Western classical romantic music. As McPhee

(1970: 311) put it: 'In this continually recurrent music, with no con-
clusive ending, no true beginning, the Oriental conception of time-
less, endless melody is revealed, revolving in smaller or larger cycles
but never advancing to a climax.' It is perhaps this quality that led
Bateson (1949) to conclude that Balinese music, as an art form, lacks
climax. However, some Balinese describe the beginning, middle, and
end parts of *gamelan* music. The 'drums throb continuously in agitated
crescendos and diminuendos that forever urge the dancers onward or
hold them back' (McPhee, 1948). Balinese *gamelan* music may be
comparable to some music of Bach and much modern popular
Western music (including rock) in terms of thematic repetition and
the lack of a single climactic emphasis.

A description of *gamelan* music does indeed fit the definition of
climax (McPhee, 1946: 37):

At first, I listened from the house, the music was simply a delicious confusion, a strangely sensuous and quite unfathomable art, mysteriously aerial,
aeolian, filled with joy and radiance. Each night as the music started up I
experienced the same sensation of freedom and indescribable freshness.
There was none of the perfume and sultriness of so much music in the East,
for there is nothing purer than the bright clean sound of metal, cool and
ringing and dissolving in the air. Nor was it personal and romantic, in the
manner of our effusive music, but rather, sound broken up into beautiful
patterns.

It was, however, more than this, as I was to find out. Already I began to
have a feeling of form and elaborate architecture. Gradually the music
revealed itself as being composed, as it were, of different strata of sound.
Over a slow and chant-like bass that hummed with curious penetration the
melody moved in the middle register, fluid, free, appearing and vanishing
in the incessant shimmering arabesques that rang high in the treble as
though beaten out on a thousand little anvils. Gongs of different sizes
punctuated this stream of sound, divided and subdivided it into sections
and inner sections, giving it meter and meaning. Through all this came the
rapid and ever-changing beat of the drums, throbbing softly, or suddenly
ringing out with sharp accents. They beat in perpetual cross-rhythm,
engaging the regular flow of the music, disturbing the balance, adding a
tension and excitement which came to rest only with the cadence that
marked the end of a section in the music.

Traditional literature of Bali includes a number of examples of
climax. For example, a famous love story in Bali is the Jayaprana
legend (Boon, 1977). It has become a 'classic pan-Bali cultural identity',

and is taught in public schools. It is the story of the difficulties of romantic love in a society which is highly stratified, particularly in matters of marriage. It is characterized by murder, suicide, and finally the re-uniting of the lovers in heaven. According to Boon (1977), 'The chaotic climax is achieved as the palace society runs amok and the raja finally kills himself.' Another classical story in literature involving marriage is the *arja* story of Pakang Raras (Boon, 1977). In this romantic love story, there is death and revival, culminating in the king recognizing the young man and giving his consent to marriage which is then 'celebrated amid universal rejoicing' (de Zoete and Spies, 1939).

One of the most typical and frequent ceremonies of Bali is the food offering at temples by household women. Tourist brochures commonly picture colourfully dressed women carrying even more colourful aesthetically arranged stacks of food, up to one metre high, balanced on their heads as they walk on paths through rice paddies and down the streets to the temple. They bring the offerings to the temple, place them on the altar, and then wait as a group near by, where they either talk with friends or sit on the ground or road in a way that is comparable to the way that Christians sit in pews waiting for church services to begin. Finally, they pray together, led by the priest, who purifies the offerings with holy water and blesses the women. They then file into the temple to retrieve their stacks of food and carry them home where they are consumed by family members. Since this ceremony is rather quiet, one might wonder if there is a climax. Following the definition of climax as 'a major turning point in the action', the turning-point appears to be the holy water blessing, followed by the women abruptly becoming active as they claim their offering. At this culmination, the women involved experience feelings of inner peace (see Chapter 8).

Each year in March, the Balinese celebrate a period of several days referred to as the New Year celebration, which culminates in Nyepi, a day of silence. Nyepi is a day when people stay in their homes, cars are not allowed on the streets, no electric lights are used, and there is very little noise except for roosters crowing in the morning and frogs croaking at night.[6] However, in the afternoon of this day, the children gather on the deserted main streets and play, as if to exercise the rare privilege of being free to go where ordinarily cars, trucks, motor bikes, and buses are busily travelling. On the day or two preceding Nyepi, adolescent boys in the city set off fire-crackers and sometimes home-made bamboo canons which make enormous booms at unpredictable intervals to chase away evil spirits. Women will start cooking for Nyepi on the day before because no cooking can be done on Nyepi.

For the past three years, on the day before Nyepi, a parade has been staged at night in Denpasar, replete with 'floats', each carried by 20 to 30 men and women who have descended upon the city centre from all directions far and wide. The floats are in the form of large imaginary monsters and evil spirits. It is traditional to carry them around the village to excite everyone to shouting and merriment. Three days preceding Nyepi, there is a similar converging upon beaches. Processions of men and women from all corners of the city of Denpasar, and beyond, carry effigies of the gods and offerings to a rendezvous located at Kuta or Sanur Beach, where the offerings are finally blessed. One can sense the build-up of emotion preceding Nyepi, but the climax is not loud nor dramatic as is often seen in Western culture (e.g., American's Fourth of July celebrations). Instead it is an impressive day of relative quiet and almost complete silence, except for the children playing in the evening. It is, however, both a major turning-point in action and a culmination point. The festivities of the days and night before lead up to it dramatically. Peaceful feelings and a release of tension accompany the day of silence, somewhat similar to the feelings of women after having their food offerings blessed at the temple.

Amok is a culture-related (sometimes called culture-bound) mental disorder which occurs widely in Malaysia and sporadically in Bali (Belo, 1935; Arbolego-Florez, 1985). In essence, a person suddenly, without provocation, behaves erratically, commits violent acts, some severe or lethal, and generally exhibits lack of control. The individual must be physically subdued; after some hours he reverts spontaneously to his previous calm personality and is generally amnesic about the episode. An individual may believe that he is possessed by an evil spirit who causes him to act unnaturally. *Amok* is an aberrant trance-like state. However, the Indonesian government does not regard the violence as excusable and homicide during *amok* is punishable by a jail sentence. Psychodynamically, *amok* is best understood as an outgrowth of repressed anger and aggression, typical of the Balinese, which suddenly explodes in an altered state or trance, similar to hysteria or dissociation. It can also be regarded as a climactic expression of pent-up anger, aggression, frustration, or rage. In this respect, it suggests a climactic type of mental disorder.

Milestones in the life cycle such as birthdays and the tooth-filing ceremony marking puberty are regarded by the Balinese as cardinal and climactic events.

Climax in Mother–Child Interaction

An example of climax may be found in a mother–child interaction described by Mead: the mother's intense 'theatrical exclamation', *aroh*. Mead stated that this practice laid the groundwork for the continuation of fear as a major controlling factor in Balinese life. As the child grows old enough to leave the mother and get into mischief, she calls to him with 'a histrionic fear-laden cry, *aroh*', followed by mention of any one of several other scare words, such as fire or snake, to which the child responds by running back to his mother, into her embrace, gaining attention and reassurance (p. 31). As described in Chapter 6, Mead mistranslated *aroh* and this expression does not necessarily mean fear. Nevertheless, one aspect of this interaction would be its climactic nature, raising tension to a peak, followed by release and comfort in the mother's arms. The authors were not able to observe this interaction but Mead's description of it seems to provide another example of climax in the culture.

Bateson and Mead's formulations about climax and character in Bali can be summarized as follows: the frustration of an infant and toddler's expression of a consummated emotion causes an emotional plateau, a state without climax, and this results in a later childhood and lifetime withdrawal of emotion and the absence of climax in individual interaction, events and the entire culture. Bateson and Mead, possibly influenced by the psychoanalytic thinking of the time, assumed that mother–child rearing practices, such as feeding and bathing the infant, generate the basic structure of character. Erikson (1950) used this approach in his combined psychoanalytic and anthropologic studies of two American Indian tribes.

The concept of a national character or temperament as an outcome exclusively of child-rearing patterns has not proven supportable either in psychiatry or psychologic anthropology, and it is not supported by developmental psychology. Increased knowledge has brought awareness of greater complexity and diversity, as well as the multiplicity of factors that determine character. For example, genetic factors are now acknowledged as determinants of some behaviours: variations in children's basic temperaments (e.g., irritability or calmness) are more likely to be determined by inborn biological factors (Thomas and Chess, 1977). Although early childhood environmental factors may have some influence on adult character, they have never been shown to be exclusive determinants. The biopsychosocial model of human behaviour includes biological, social, and psychological factors, which all interact throughout the life of individuals, as determinants of behaviour (and illness) (Engel, 1977; Fink, 1988). The climate and ecology (e.g., plains, forests inhabited by dangerous wild animals, or animals of prey) also shape behaviour patterns. Studies of ethology and animal behaviour draw attention to evolution as an influence on human behaviour patterns (Hinde, 1974; Jensen, 1980).

A Reconsideration of Climax

It may seem curious why the Balinese themselves have not cited, critiqued, or protested the issue of climax as elaborated by Bateson, Mead, C. Geertz, and others. Two explanations were offered by Balinese anthropologists: (1) the traditional politeness of the Balinese; and (2) difficulties in understanding English writing, particularly the styles of certain authors. The latter seems more likely.

It is curious that lack or presence of climax, in the sense described by Bateson and Mead, has not been reported as characteristic of other cultures. The question arises as to whether it has been seriously considered by other ethnographers. Since all humans are highly emotional creatures, it would be reasonable to assume that people of all cultures experience and even need climaxes, which relieve tension. The biology of sexuality offers a compelling argument for the implausibility of an absence of climax in any culture. The human orgasm is unquestionably a psychophysiologic climax (Masters and Johnson, 1966). One could hypothesize that this ultimate point in the progression of the sexual response cycle, 'generally believed to develop from a drive of biologicbehavioural origin clearly integrated into the condition of human existence' (Masters and

Johnson, 1966: 127) would likely be expressed in other human behavioural patterns in a manner parallel to maternal care and affection or sibling rivalry. The resolution period immediately following female orgasm is often described subjectively by American women as one of well-being, of feeling beautiful, energetic, friendly, and generous, and of profound and prolonged sensuous pleasure (Hite, 1976). Data on Balinese sexuality are not yet available but are needed for comparison.

The examples presented of climactic events or behaviour in Balinese society do not imply that most behaviour and social interaction of Balinese are of this type. Several scholars have commented on the relaxed, reserved, detached, steady, rhythmic flow of motion characteristic of daily life (Belo, 1935; Holt and Bateson, 1970) and on the social control and politeness that is so pervasive and strong in modulating the expression of some emotions (Wikan, 1987). For example in arguments, the Balinese are perhaps the opposite of the expressive Mediterraneans. Perhaps the apparent evenness of emotion in daily life is a manifestation of what Mead referred to as the withdrawal of responsiveness and emotion. In contrast, observations of ceremonies and dances presented here are graphic examples of overt and fervent emotional expression, as well as climaxes in certain classic and common situations. It is theorized that the Balinese avoid climaxes of anger in everyday interaction because they would disrupt the harmony of good interpersonal relations that they strive for and which are so important in their culture.

From their observations, the authors hypothesize that there are two types of 'climax' for the Balinese. One is the building up to a major turning-point in the action, and the height of dramatic tension, as illustrated by the cremation ceremony and the *barong* dance. The other is a major turning-point, culminating in feelings of inner peace and well-being, as, for example, experienced in the offering ceremonies and Nyepi. Analogies can be made with the psychobiology of the human sexual response. The first type is analogous to orgasmic phase of the sexual response cycle. The second type is analogous to the resolution phase immediately following orgasmic response. In this instance, it is as if the orgasmic response were muted or suppressed.

Thus, from observations of Balinese behaviour and events with reference to climax and from a review of the literature, it may be concluded that it is incorrect to state, and misleading to accept Bateson and Mead's view that Balinese life or culture lacks climax. Rather, climax is present in many cardinal aspects of the culture and must be considered in the psychologic anthropology of Bali. Climaxes in the forms of anger or disagreement are avoided because they would be too threatening to the harmony and balance that the Balinese strive for in interpersonal relations. Balinese climaxes take different forms from those in Western culture and are more likely to be expressed in periodic rituals, ceremony, drama, trance, and probably in some mental disorders, rather than in daily social interaction.

1. Bateson (1987) cited this pattern as a primary support for his conclusion that the Balinese culture lacks schismogenesis, his theory of spiralling or intensity-building interaction.

2. The ceremonies are well discussed and illustrated by Bateson and Mead (pp. 232–55) and by Covarrubias (1937: 359–77).

3. They were outlawed by the government (except at ceremonies) but, even though illegal, continue to be held regularly.

4. Covarrubias (1937: 331) also described the climax.

5. The induction of trance in ceremonies is accompanied by climaxes of *gamelan* music and the excited tempo continues until the people have fallen in trance at which point the music slows and becomes softer.

6. Mead was very impressed with this celebration because they arrived for the first time in Bali on Nyepi, by chance, and were able to get special dispensation to travel by car.

Chapter 8
Emotional Expressiveness

THE issue of emotional expression figured strongly in Bateson and Mead's conclusions about Balinese character. This is illustrated by the conclusions that Balinese character is based on fear, that the Balinese fall asleep when beset by fear, become anxious when they are disoriented as to direction or do not know the day or caste of the person they are addressing, are emotionally withdrawn, and withhold anger. Mead concluded that such patterns of emotional expression are the product of certain Balinese child-rearing patterns. Several of these issues have been discussed in other chapters (see Chapters 5, 6, and 9).

The field of mental health and disorders is directly concerned with human emotions, both their normal expression and their manifestations in psychopathology. It is generally believed that repressed anger which has no outlet causes psychiatric symptoms, particularly of a somatic type (Averill, 1982). In Bali, anger is suppressed; fights and arguments in public are rare. However, traditional trance dances are a dramatic vehicle for expression of aggression, anger, and other emotions not otherwise acceptable in everyday life. Abnormal states of trance with possession in Bali such as *bebainan*, a culture-related syndrome, may similarly be an outlet for socially unacceptable feelings (Suryani, 1984). As patterns of emotional expression are closely related to, if not highly shaped by, culture and as they also affect the kinds of symptoms of mental disturbances, it is important for mental health professionals to know as much as possible about characteristic patterns of emotional expression in cultures represented by his/her patients. This chapter describes ways in which the Balinese experience and express emotions, and discusses aspects of emotional expression in childhood, as well as Mead's conclusions about emotions in the Balinese, and the roles of emotions in some Balinese mental disorders.

The concept of emotional expressiveness as used here is distinguished from the term 'expressed emotion' or 'EE,' which has recently been introduced into Western psychiatry as characteristic reactions of family members to the patient's unacceptable behaviour. Instead, the authors are concerned with the ways in which emotions are expressed, displayed, felt, perceived, and responded to by the Balinese.

Two traditional cultural events each involving emotional expression characteristic of Balinese are cock-fights for men and temple offerings by women. They illustrate ways in which Balinese manifest and express emotions (in these behaviours). In both types of events, emotions are expressed both overtly in characteristic behaviours and internally without outward expression. At the climax of the event, emotional responses appear to be internally expressed.

Cock-fights

There are several descriptions of cock-fights in Bali (Bateson and Mead, 1942; C. Geertz, 1966, 1973; and Covarrubias, 1937). The authors' focus is on the feelings evoked in Balinese male participants in the event, their sequential progression, and their patterns of expression.

The authors attended and studied cock-fights in 1988–90 on the outskirts of Denpasar and in villages in the township of Gianyar. One of the Gianyar cock-fights was held in an unobtrusive open area among village houses, reached by a maze-like path. About 100 men of all ages, but primarily younger adults, gathered in a packed circle around a central area (*kalangan*) about 4 metres in diameter, with a few schoolboys perched on a wall. In keeping with tradition, no women were present except those selling snacks and drinks on the periphery. During an anticipatory period before the fights, the men squatted in the *kalangan* testing the cocks' reactions to each other. Suddenly, the *kalangan* was cleared and a man quietly solicited money from persons who were supporters of the cock owners. Two men finished binding each cock's leg spur with a four-inch long, narrow, polished, razor-sharp, dagger-shaped knife. Two owners brought their cocks into the *kalangan* and suddenly the audience began a torrent of loud shouting and gesticulation to attract partners with whom to make bets. They resembled the frantic behaviours of traders on a stock market or commodity exchange floor. After several minutes, the excitement subsided, and the cocks were positioned opposite each other and released. Immediately they began fighting, displaying erect neck feathers, and jumping on each other. In less than 90 seconds, one had plunged his knife into the other; the cock fell dead, bleeding on the spot.

During the fight, the audience leaned quietly forward, shoulder pressed tightly against shoulder, eyes intently fixed on the fighting cocks. The mounting tension they experienced was expressed through various facial expressions and in a chorus of groans emitted according to approval or disapproval of the action of a cock. The dead cock and victor were unceremoniously picked up and carried out of the *kalangan* by the owners. At this point, the audience quietly and without noticeable facial expression paid off or collected bets. In several minutes, they reassembled in the circle, resumed talking, and waited for the next fight to follow in 5 to 10 minutes. Other cock-fights observed in Denpasar were similar to that described above. Videotapes of these fights were studied to verify direct observations.

The mounting tension of the men anticipating the beginning of the fight sequence was obvious to the authors. The overt expression of emotion during betting was spontaneous, intense, and dramatic. However, the climax of death, clearly appreciated by all, elicited little or no apparent emotional response. Neither did the subsequent settling of bets.

It was only by questioning betters that the authors discovered their inner feelings during the kill and afterwards. The kill evoked feelings of satisfaction followed by feelings of good fortune by the winning betters and bad fortune, remorse, regret, or a sense of loss by the losing gamblers. The absence of outward signs of emotion at the kill[1] contrasted with the dramatic expressions during betting.

The covert inner feelings could be perceived only by the betters and the owners (who also showed no outward emotion). The Balinese consider it inappropriate to show feelings in such situations.

Westerners might gesticulate emotionally, cheer, smile, or talk at a comparable point in a sporting event. At this point, the Balinese participants invoked the philosophy of karma or suppressed overt emotional expression. There was a feeling of satisfaction that one's karma was being fulfilled either for good or for bad; whether in this life or the next. They tried to avoid expression of emotion to prevent others from feeling disappointed, upset, or angry. They also believed that if they were to express it, they would receive it in the same situation from another person (*hukum karma*).

The participants' feelings of happiness at winning or sadness at losing money might resurface hours later at home, out of the view of outsiders. There, overt expression is acceptable.

In summary, the cock-fight is an emotionally intense event with a building up of tension to a point of climax. At the preliminary stages of the cock-fight, emotion is expressed overtly. Climactic emotional responses are not evident to the observer but are felt internally by the participants. Various emotions associated with winning and losing tend to be suppressed or dealt with by utilization of the concept of karma, as it is understood by the individual.

Temple Offerings

Every 6 to 12 months, according to the Balinese calendar, the women members of each temple participate in these unique Balinese ceremonies. Any one woman belongs to at least four or five temples that have six-month ceremonies of this sort. So a woman goes through this activity at least 10 times in any one year, if not more often. The activity is widely recognized since colourful pictures of it appear in travel books and magazines. On the appointed day, one woman from each household (the women may rotate the responsibility) buys the best fruit and flowers they can afford, bakes rice cakes, and then arranges them in a colourful, cylindrical, and aesthetically pleasing design stacked up to one metre high, sometimes topped with a roast chicken and palm leaf crown ornament. With skill and practice, this can be completed in an hour or two. She then carries the offering on her head to the local *banjar*, returns home to bathe, dresses in her finest traditional Balinese costume and returns to the *banjar*. There she joins a group of village women who proceed to walk single file to the temple with stacks of food (offering to the gods) on their heads. She places the offering on the table of the pavilion (*bale*) in the temple and then joins her friends or family near by, talking and joking, with clear emotional expressions of happiness. The women wait near the temple to watch the priest bless the offerings with holy water. Then they pray in a group, and experience a 'serious' feeling (*hening*). The priest then blesses the women by sprinkling them with holy water, which evokes in them an inner feeling of peace, described as a calm, happy, good feeling. This is not shown in visible outward expressions. The women then rise, take their offerings, and walk home; on the way they talk cheerfully and joke with their friends. At home, the family happily consumes the food. The women's feelings of peace and fulfilment may last hours or throughout the rest of the day.

The Western observer would not be likely to see the climax of this ceremony because the women show little observable emotional expression at its completion. However, for the Balinese woman participant, the point of climax is the blessing when she experiences a consequent inner unmistakable feeling of calm and peace for which there is no outward or obvious expression. This ceremony illustrates, as does a cock-fight, direct expression before and after, but concealed emotional manifestation during, the climax.

Cultural Patterns of Emotional Suppression and Repression

Bateson and Mead focused on the ways children were reared and emotions handled, and related them to patterns of culture and Bateson (1949) connected patterns of child rearing with the Balinese 'national character'. Mead concluded that the Balinese show little emotional expression: 'a character curiously cut off from interpersonal relationships' (p. 47) and a life 'centered in one's own body to which all emotion long ago withdrew' (p. 48), having its origin in childhood between the ages of three and six. Bateson and Mead emphasized the repression and the control of feelings of aggression. These general conclusions have been accepted and repeated by other ethnologists (Ketter, 1983; C. Geertz, 1966), and have been discussed in Chapter 5.

These theses of Bateson and Mead can be evaluated by a consideration of the patterns of relevant emotional behaviour observed in the authors' studies of the Balinese. The Balinese express some types of emotions strongly, overtly, and spontaneously in many social situations but avoid expression of some emotions in certain situations. Examples of the former are: (1) joking, smiling, and laughing in everyday interaction among family and friends; (2) raucous laughter by the audience at theatre dramas in which exaggerated emotions of all kinds are portrayed; (3) gaiety and exuberance at certain ceremonies such as cremation and cock-fights (Covarrubias, 1937); and (4) friendly greeting of strangers along the road. In this latter situation most persons, especially children and youths, are often spontaneous and cheerfully assertive. They make sustained eye contact, smile, say hello, and comment or call out a question (e.g., where are you going, why are you walking, or why are you going alone?). If they do not initiate the greeting, they generally respond immediately to that of the stranger.

The Balinese suppress or avoid outward expression of emotions in many situations. There is a muting or absence of expressed anger in everyday Balinese social interaction (Belo, 1935) and argument in public situations is unusual, although disagreements are more openly expressed in the home. Arguments between males seldom end in fighting, being usually resolved before this through meditation by a village leader (Bateson, 1949). One seldom sees a fight or hears cross words in Bali.

The Balinese suppress humour and joking exchanges in more formal situations, such as at a meeting with the authorities, or when dealing with persons of higher status. For example, the interns as a group at the hospital joke, laugh, and tease while waiting around the ward but when they hear a superior approaching, they make a 'shhh' sound and become quiet immediately. Suppression of emotions was mentioned above, during cock-fights and temple offerings. Youths at a rock concert are strangely quiet by Western standards (relatively little shouting, jumping up and down, crowding around rock stars, or enthusiastic applause). The Balinese express some feelings non-verbally though seldom verbally. They seldom say, 'I love you' to anyone.

One way of looking at these types of behaviour is that they simply represent public conventions as to how, when, and where emotions may be expressed overtly or concealed. However, this book argues that the pattern of suppression of emotion is a function involving more than just custom: it is partly a function of the personality that controls emotional responses. Each Balinese learns and develops these psychological responses, which become automatic; they become durable parts of the personality. Psychologically speaking, the behavioural response pattern becomes internalized. This distinguishes the pattern from purely conventional behaviour or customs (which are also learned). Following this rationale, 'suppression of emotion' has been identified as a character trait (see Chapter 9).

The Balinese have several techniques to control anger and other emotions. They may avoid direct contact with the other person by leaving the house if the person is in the house, or concentrating on hard work if on the job. Anger can also be handled by invoking the concept of karma. Anger and anxiety and sadness may be handled by delayed expression or other processes. The small child allays anxiety or sadness by closeness to the mother or caretaker; the adult prays to God to help him handle the situation, or if needed, he goes to a *balian* for relief through a purification ceremony or advice.

The Balinese may suppress anger and sadness and substitute other behaviours and emotions in their place, such as laughter. It is clear that they in no way inhibit or suppress laughter when among peers. An example of this was observed at a family ceremony involving embalming a deceased member of Suryani's family. The authors spent several hours together with extended family members during which there was quiet conversation, punctuated with cheerful comments but no evidence of sadness. However, when driving home, the five family members in the car laughed and joked in the heartiest way for about 20 minutes as if in a situation of utmost hilarity. This reaction can be viewed as a healthy discharge of emotional tension.

The origin of the character trait called 'suppression of emotion' probably owes something to the child-rearing practices of Balinese parents. It is common for Balinese parents to instigate their children to be quiet at home and polite in public. Western observers frequently comment how well behaved Balinese children are in public places.[2] Much of this behaviour entails suppression of their emotional response (see Chapter 9). Children also learn to be quiet and polite by imitation, identification, and reinforcement. The whole community encourages the children to learn the culturally approved ways of handling anger, arguments, and fights; anger is to be suppressed.

Wikan (1988, 1989b) presented another view on the management or control of emotions along with detailed observations of grief reaction (bereavement) in a Balinese Muslim of north Bali which she believed was similar to the pattern of the Balinese Hindus. The Balinese women, especially young women, controlled the emotions of sadness by substituting a 'shiny face' and a sparkling and gracious façade. They used conscious, wilful effort to 'restructure the experience', even saw good in tragedy, and sought out situations of laughter and merriment. Wikan stated that they 'work on feelings to shape expression'. She viewed this psychological process of thinking/feeling or feeling/mind (*ngabe keneh*) as a combined process, a merging of feeling and thought. She also regarded this notion of managing feelings, especially anger, by conscious thought, to be motivated by a 'fear of sorcery' linked to notions of morality and health (i.e., if one prays and observes rules of etiquette and propriety one will be protected from dangers of black magic which could produce illness).

Some emotions are expressed directly, intensely, and exuberantly in dance and by the accompanying *gamelan* musicians (Belo, 1970; McPhee, 1946). Belo's (1935) early observations and analyses of 'Balinese temper' provide vivid descriptions of emotional expressiveness. At plays, when clowns cavort and when a joke is made, 'the entire audience rocks with mirth' (Belo, 1935: 131). She also noted the 'strong tendency to hold onto and caress each other in all relations where no sexual connotation is implied'. She observed then, as is common today, adolescent girls and boys in like-sex pairs strolling along a road, holding hands or with their arms about each other in a genuinely affectionate or warm manner. She wrote, 'Such gestures should not be misconstrued as evidence of homosexuality for they are no more than the habitual expressions of demonstratively affectionate people.' Travelling in Bali, Jensen has had many similar experiences: riding on a *bemo* (public bus), a young man, a total stranger, might rest his hand on Jensen's thigh as he conversed in a friendly manner.

Supernatural beliefs include awe of the gods as well as a belief in their benevolence. These beliefs, instilled in every Balinese from infancy, are part of the mechanisms controlling anger and aggression: interpersonal arguments and shows of anger do not reach crisis point or climax partly because of a desire to restore harmony (or balance) in the environment, between one's self, the outside world, and the gods.

In certain situations, such as when receiving an award or graduating from school, children and youth learn to withhold overt expression of happiness, although they feel it 'in their heart'; i.e., to do so would reflect conceit. At a later time, the happiness may be overtly expressed among friends or family. This pattern could be termed delayed emotional expression.

Some emotional reactions are dealt with by specific religious ceremonies. For example, anxiety and shyness of a couple over an illegitimate pregnancy, among members of the royal families in Klungkung, are relieved by a special ceremony (*madewa saksi*), witnessed by all men from the future husband's family and by the gods. The ceremony signifies acceptance of the foetus and anticipated child into the family. It has great consequence for the life of the child as well: without the ceremony he/she would have lifelong low status with all its implications of restricted emotional and behavioural interactions and privileges.

The Roles of Emotions in Culture-bound Mental Disorders, *Bebainan* and *Kasurupan*

Suryani (1984) described a mental disturbance of 27 women living in the compound of the premier royal family of Bali in Klungkung, a trance disorder which she called *bebainan* (see Appendix 1). Symptoms began suddenly and lasted about 15 minutes to an hour. The women who were studied described hallucinations and spirits speaking through them. The spirits usually told the traditional healer the purpose for coming, i.e., that they came to harm or kill the person whose body they had entered. The cause of the disorder could be understood in terms of an accumulation of stress, a restricted lifestyle of adolescent girls about which they felt resentful, and pressures on lower-status women to defer to higher-status families in precisely prescribed manners and language as they gracefully accepted affronts from the upper classes. Prospects of marriage or pressure of a newly married status were also sources of concern. These behaviours and stressful aspects of the roles were expected or required to be performed without overt expression of emotion. However, the women experienced associated inward emotions of anger, anxiety, and worry. Suryani hypothesized that trance behaviours (*bebainan*) provided sufferers with an opportunity to release feelings of frustration and anger without risk of widespread disapproval or stigmatization.

The authors studied participants in an epidemic-like outbreak of a trance disorder, which they identified as possession and named *kasurupan* (see Appendix 2). In 1984 in a relatively isolated village in the mountains of central Bali, 45 schoolchildren were suddenly afflicted with a trance disorder with hundreds of attacks in the group. The attacks were characterized by prodromal symptoms, trance, and recovery phases lasting from half an hour to five hours. After recovery, the children could recall and describe frightening and anxiety-laden hallucinations and dissociative phenomena during the trance phase. In these cases, the afflicted children's anxiety over having had an attack and the spectre of recurrence were considered to be the primary precipitating stressors. As a result of the epidemic, the entire village experienced intense concern and guilt over mistakes in their relationships with the gods and the supernatural.

Trance states are very common in Balinese culture, but are generally culture syntonic and occur in expected and socially accepted situations such as in theatre drama and ceremonies. In one village in Bali, with which the authors are familiar, about 25 per cent of the community inhabitants go into trance states at a twice-yearly ceremony.[3] Ritual dance, trance disorders, and therapeutic trance all have in common the process of emotional catharsis; relief of distress by expression of emotions not otherwise acceptable.

In theory, trance disorders and other dissociative disorders (DSM-III-R, 1987) are characterized by the use of the psychological defence mechanisms of dissociation and denial. These defences effect a replacement of unpleasant feelings with more pleasant ones, and allow the expression of feelings unacceptable to the individual or not permitted in everyday life in the culture (e.g., *bebainan* and multiple personality disorder), thereby preventing emotional distress. In the disorder of *kasurupan*, anxiety appears to have been the primary emotion causing the disorder. A mass trance disorder in Malaysia, similar to that of the Balinese schoolchildren, appeared to be a means for the children to express distressing feelings and erotic conflicts regarding the schoolmaster which they could not express directly (Teok and Tan, 1976).

The Emotions in Minor Mental Disorders

Suryani surveyed symptoms, problems, and the relative prevalences of various minor psychiatric disorders in 162 consecutive patients at the outpatient psychiatry clinic of Wangaya Hospital in Denpasar. Patients checked their perceived symptoms on a list developed by collaborators in a multicultural study of minor psychiatric disorders in Asia. Diagnoses according to DSM-III-R (1987) were made on the basis of psychiatric interviews. Demographics were: males, 62 per cent; female, 38 per cent; ages between 15 and 40 years, 88 per cent; married, 51 per cent; single, 45 per cent; education through secondary school or better, 74 per cent. Seventy-seven per cent had anxiety symptoms, and 62 per cent had symptoms of depressed mood or sadness. Symptoms such as sleep disturbance, difficulty concentrating, decreased appetite, and physical complaints could have been secondary to depression. The most common clinical diagnoses were generalized anxiety disorders (56 per cent), depressive disorders (29 per cent), and somatization disorders or multiple physical symptoms of various types with no identifiable organic cause (12 per cent).

These data indicate that disorders related to the emotions of anxiety and depressed mood (sadness) comprised the majority of minor psychiatric disorders presented at a psychiatric clinic in Bali. The third largest diagnostic category, somatization disorder (DSM-III-R, 1987), is also causally related to disturbances in emotions (e.g., anxiety and depression).

It is striking that no cases of phobia were noted (intense anxiety attached to specific stimuli) in these 162 patients. In the past year, Suryani has identified cases of phobia in Balinese. Phobias ranked first in prevalence of mental disorders in communities studied in the United States (Myers, Weissman, and Tischler, et al., 1984) Possibly Balinese with phobias such as fear of cockroaches or the dark do not come to psychiatric attention, or they are treated by *balian*. The authors have yet to hear of agoraphobia (fear of open spaces or of leaving the house) in a Balinese, the most common phobia in the West. A study of phobias in Bali might yield new insight into these disorders in Western culture.

In their epidemiological study to determine the status of physical and mental health and the prevalence of disorders in the elderly of one Balinese village in the mountain area of Kintamani, the authors found that a relatively high proportion of the elderly had symptoms of anxiety (18 per cent) and depressed mood (14 per cent) (Suryani et al., 1984). It was difficult to compare these data with Western reports. These subjects did not qualify for a diagnosis of depression and anxiety disorder. Prevalence of depressive disorders in the general population of the United States is 1–2 per cent (Myers, Weissman, and Tischler, et al., 1984). However, the authors' data suggested that elderly Balinese in this one village have significant problems related to these two manifestations of emotions.[4]

In summary, the authors' studies of emotional expressiveness in Balinese indicated that emotions are expressed overtly to a high degree in interpersonal relationships and in many public events typical in the society. At times, emotion is also experienced as inner feelings ('in the heart') but not expressed overtly, either verbally or by touching. Cock-fights and temple offering ceremonies illustrated the latter. Patterns of emotional expression of Balinese help one understand aspects of the culture and of individuals in health and illness. Emotional expression in children was briefly examined. Bateson and Mead's conclusions that the Balinese are emotionally withdrawn and cut off from interpersonal relationships were refuted. Two examples of culture-related mental disorders in Bali illustrated the relationship between symptoms, culture, and patterns or ways of handling emotion. Data were presented on frequencies of symptoms noted by patients with minor psychiatric disorders (e.g., anxiety and depression) which indicate the major roles of emotions.

1. Some cock-fights do not end with a kill but terminate in a drawn-out fight.

2. In their own villages, the children can be boisterous, lively, and emotionally aggressive in peer play (e.g., in soccer and tag).

3. Galungan, every six months (210 days), based on the Balinese calendar.

4. The elderly subjects gave a number of reasons for their symptoms, including physical illness, low finances, decreased memory, loneliness without family, decreased physical abilities, and feelings of loss of respect.

Chapter 9
Balinese Character: A Synthesis

THE preceding chapters focused on what Balinese character and culture are not and presented additional data from which alternative views to those of Bateson and Mead were derived. In this chapter, the question, 'If Balinese are not like that, what are they like?' is addressed.

The sketch of Balinese character presented here represents abstractions based on the authors' studies, observations, and intimate knowledge of the Balinese and their culture.[1] Some of the conclusions are definite while others may be regarded as hypotheses. While the elements of character singled out are considered to be characteristic of the Balinese, they are not necessarily exclusive to the culture; some are seen in other cultures, particularly in other parts of Indonesia and the Orient.

First, a background and definition of the term 'character'[2] is in order. The term 'character' has been used broadly in cultural anthropology to denote personality characteristics. It is little used by anthropologists today, but it was entirely acceptable in the era of Bateson and Mead's studies.[3] Psychiatry has long used and continues to use the term 'character', defined as the 'constellation of relatively fixed personalty traits and attributes that govern a person's habitual modes of response' (Kaplan, Freedman, and Saddock, 1980: 3315). Psychiatry makes no clear differentiation between personality traits and character traits. (Note that the term so used refers to an individual.) Bateson and Mead used the concept of character similarly. They abstracted it further to apply to that 'constellation of relatively fixed personality traits' that is either characteristic of most members of a society and/or that 'fits' best with the customary behaviour expected in a society.

Ruth Benedict, cultural anthropologist, and a close personal friend and contemporary associate of Mead, espoused the concept that culture is 'personality writ large'.[4] This was the thinking at the time of the Bateson and Mead studies. Since then, attempts to use the terms 'personality' and 'character' in connection with culture have been beset with controversy. Mead (1955) and Bateson (1987) argued for the concept of national character, meaning, in brief, the character or personality traits that could be considered typical for most members of an entire specific culture.[5] Many anthropologists rejected this concept on the basis that it was too simplistic or reductionistic and potentially misleading.[6] Some arguments against the concept of national character focused on findings from psychological testing, particularly Rorschach and other projective tests that showed wide variations within national groups. However, the fact that there are wide variations in personalities within a culture does not mean that there are no common elements. There may also be similar traits within the group. Bateson and Mead mentioned the issue of variation when they wrote about the 'great contrast in content with virtually no alteration in form' (p. xv). Using a thematic apperception-type psychological test on the Japanese, Caudill (1962: 131) found that there were commonalities, some emotional themes, and 'variation in emotional patterning that nevertheless has its major and minor themes'. In the same vein, the authors argue the concept of national character and assert the hypothesis that the Balinese culture produces and is characterized by some character traits that the people have in common. (This is not a substantiated conclusion based on research.)

Some cultural anthropologists in America consider Bateson and Mead's *Balinese Character* as basically wrong in its assumption that there is a common character to most (or even many) Balinese and that this is systematically related to the Balinese culture. Some might also consider this an unprovable notion and hold that similarities of 'character traits' are illusions, based on external impressions. They might regard character traits as conventional ways of behaving which would come under the category of 'culture'. They disagree that people make cultural directives part of their personal character. Rather, they believe that people conform to cultural directives. This same viewpoint would hold that the differences between Bali and America represent cultural differences, not matters of character, and would invalidate Bateson and Mead's conclusions and the conclusions in this chapter as well.

Nevertheless, the concept of national character is viable and expounded by some contemporary cultural anthropologists and sociologists.[7] Wallace (1961) presented the theoretical viewpoint of anthropologists who subscribe to the concept of national character or what he called 'basic personality'. He viewed patterns of a national character as 'the articulation of a large number of components into a structure or pattern'. He defined this pattern as 'a set of intricate, dynamic interrelationships among different aspects of a personality or character' (Wallace, 1961: 149). The term 'basic personality' or 'national character' applied to any culturally bounded group and 'tended to connote a more thorough-going use of the psychoanalytic theory of personality' (Wallace, 1961: 149). However, he disavowed partiality to any particular theoretical schema. The term, as he recognized it, did not imply a particular type of social organization nor a particular theory of personality; 'it merely refers to a structure of articulated personality characteristics and processes attributable non-statistically to almost all members of some culturally bounded population'. According to Wallace (1961: 150):

In method, the approach to national personality, character, or basic personality rests on the cultural deductive principle ... that is, the analyst first prepares an ethnographic description and then infers from the ethnographic data the intrapsychic structures of the members of the society.... Generally the maintenance system of the culture—the essential economic institutions of the kinship, political, education structures dependent thereon—is considered to be responsible for determining the nature of the basic personality structure.

[The] basic motivational structure is assumed to be learned, usually in infancy and early childhood; later experience, however, and especially stressful experience, may lead to the development, or use, of various institutionalized mechanisms such as religious belief and ritual.

The authors concur with these viewpoints: that individual Balinese learn character traits from example and teaching, growing up in the family and the community, and by participation in the community. As such, many of the character traits of an individual are shaped primarily by learning.[8] People growing up in Bali have the character traits that they have because of the cultural environment (i.e., parents, family, and community) in which they grow up. This is consistent with the concept of 'cultural determinism' as set forth by Mead, but it does not disavow the possibility that some character traits, such as shyness and aggression, are partially determined by genetic and even biologic components. There is evidence, for example, that shyness has a genetic basis and that, since teenage males become more aggressive after puberty, they may be responding to developmental biologic (e.g., hormonal) factors.

Cultures are unquestionably characterized by behaviours and practices, or customs, many of which give each culture its distinctive quality.[9] For example, suppose it is stated that in Bali most individuals and groups go into trance easily and that hypnotizability is a characteristic of the Balinese (a hypothesis as yet unproven). It would not be objectionable to use the term character trait to denote hypnotizability as it is manifest in Balinese individuals or in the culture as a whole. Trance phenomena are functions of personality factors and traits, as well as of cultural beliefs and attitudes (e.g., expectations and rules). Since there is clinical value in thinking in general terms of the ways most people in a culture typically behave and the psychosocial reasons why they do so,[10] the term 'character' is favoured with regard to culture.

Culture and character or personality may be easily confused and differentiation is important. Culture, or behaviour which is customarily done by the people (e.g., ceremonies, prayer, cremation, traditional healing, dance, cock-fights, offerings, rice planting, and clubs) is not assumed to be imbedded in personalities. Rather, personality or character traits are psychological or emotional mechanisms which perform such customary behaviours. The people express personality traits in all customs of the culture.

Character traits are not considered as the same as behaviour conforming to cultural expectations or what the people in the society regard as proper behaviour. For example, if a Balinese were to leave his culture and live in a foreign culture, he would not leave his Balinese character behind nor could he shed his personality traits and assume traits entirely like the people in the foreign culture no matter how much he might wish to or try to live by the cultural norms of that culture. The psychological explanation is that some aspects of the Balinese culture with its attendant behaviour patterns, rules, and values become internalized as part of an individual's personality, presumably as a result of child-rearing and lifelong experiences and manifest themselves as character traits.

Balinese character, as defined in this book, is a collection or constellation of character traits that are manifested by a majority of the people of Bali.[11] This meaning and use of the term 'character' in this chapter is close to that of Bateson and Mead (see Chapter 1). Balinese scholars use the term *karakter*, (a derivative of the Western word) with a meaning similar to the one adopted in this book. It is important not to reify the terms 'character' or 'culture'. They are not entities but abstractions. In this book, culture is viewed in context as it is the specific context in which an event (e.g., a ceremony) or a behaviour takes place that gives it much of its intended and perceived meaning (Bateson, 1987; Hobart, 1985).

The concept of probability is relevant to the use of the term 'character'. It is not necessary for every village or every individual to show each trait or all the traits; it need only involve most. Technically, quantitative data, statistically treated, would seem desirable but is not usually feasible to obtain;[12] judgement must be used and estimates of probability must be relied upon.

In the use of the concept of character traits, one has to guard against the mistakes of earlier anthropologists and psychiatrists who oversimplified the trait profile of a culture or misrepresented the distribution of traits in a culture. In addition, the authors recognize the hazards of attempting to attribute the development of national character as a whole to certain styles of childhood rearing behaviour patterns such as those associated with toilet training, swaddling, or weaning, as was sometimes done a number of years ago.[13]

The character traits proposed in this book are descriptive behaviour patterns which have been identified or observed (e.g., co-operation-devotion and conformity) or abstractions related to psychological or psychiatric theories (e.g., trust-belief). The terms chosen for traits denote primarily the way in which most Balinese behave or feel (e.g., conformity and tranquility). The reasons why they so behave are included in so far as the data permitted.

Explanations of the reasons for character trait behaviour lie in cultural expectations (e.g., of parents, peers, family, *banjar*, and religion) or they may be manifestations of personality. However, they are usually a combination as well as an interaction of both factors. For example, the Balinese culture expects each family to have a son. In addition, personalities of prospective or aspiring parents have been shaped to desire one in order to lead a satisfying life: they feel the need for it from within themselves. Psychologically speaking, this value or directive of the culture has been internalized and become part of their personality. Thus both the culture and the personality of the individual act and interact to motivate a marital couple to behave in ways to achieve a son in the family. Similarly, in the case of trance, both cultural expectation and personality interact to induce the state of trance. In this respect, the authors' conceptualization of the relationship between culture and personality is consistent with what anthropologists term the 'two systems' view (LeVine, 1932: 58).[14] It seems likely that in the expression of every character trait, some aspect of cultural expectation or directive would be operative.

In their description of traits, the authors have included perspectives of the Balinese and of Western psychiatry, as applicable, bearing in mind that Western psychology and psychiatry can be inappropriate when applied to the Balinese. For example, the phenomenon of visual hallucinations can be normal in the Balinese but is generally abnormal in the Westerner. Only those English terms with similar meanings for the Balinese are used. To enhance clarity for the Balinese as well as readers from wider Indonesia, both the Balinese (B) and Indonesian (I) words for all concepts have been used, whenever possible.

The Question of Cultural Change, 1936–1989

The issue of change in Balinese culture over the last half century is relevant to the authors' revision of Bateson and Mead's work. How different might the Balinese have been in the 1930s compared with now? Cultural anthropologists concur that a few decades is a relatively short time for any significant change to occur in basic aspects of a culture such as child rearing, religion, kinship, marriage, and law.[15] Similarly, Inkles (1979: 415), a sociologist, pointed out that although American national character is dynamic; it has 'remained the same in many respects despite massive changes in size and composition of the population, its level of education, its patterns of residence, and its forms of work' over a period of many decades. In the case of Bali, Mead addressed the issue of possible change in the 40 or more years after Dutch occupation, including the advent of automobiles, more tourists, imported cloth, etc.: '... two characteristics of Balinese culture are the ready acceptance of those small details of custom and technology which can be absorbed without changing the basic premises of life, and the utter inability and unwillingness to contemplate any more drastic changes' (p. 262). According to Bateson and Mead, for centuries the Balinese have been both adapting to and resisting cultural details associated with 'the higher centers of the Hindu, the Chinese, and Dutch'.[16] They felt that the Balinese culture underwent superficial changes as a result of culture contact but the Balinese character remained unchanged, despite exploitation, violence, and modern technology (pp. 261–3). Belo (1960) stated that 'culture contact [from outside and tourist influences] in Bali did not necessarily lead to weakening of tradition, but more often to accommodation of new factors to the old ways', and her information indicated that ceremonial life, dance, ritual, and trance had remained essentially unchanged in the 30 years following her original studies in the 1930s. In 1972–3 Muller, anthropologist and long-term resident of Bali, traced all of the people and dances described by Belo in the mid-1930s and was impressed by how they had remained the same 38 years later (personal communication). Covarrubias (1937: 255) similarly observed that the Balinese assimilate new and foreign ideas into their traditional forms. 'This enables the islander to create new styles constantly, to inject new life steadily into their culture, which at the same time never loses its Balinese characteristics.' More recently, Ramseyer (1986: 239) stated that the Balinese absorbed material culture without a break in tradition and 'that the basic values shaped by religious and communal social interactions have remained remarkably intact'.

The authors concur with these scholars. In addition, they agree with the observations of Covarrubias (1937) regarding the basic components of the culture, including religious beliefs, relationships of people to the community, extended family, ancestors, most ceremonies, offerings, dramas, dances, architecture, farming, and trance.

Trance ceremonies in two villages in 1935 described by Belo—one of a *balian* (1960: 23) and the other of kris stabbing (1960: 104)—are nearly identical to those observed today.

Following the advent of taped music Suryani witnessed the temporary decline in village *gamelan* orchestras, but they made a vigorous comeback a decade later. Since the advent of television, there has been a coincident decline in the number of dance performances in the villages and a disappearance of the traditional itinerant dance groups that visited the villages, including Bayung Gede. In keeping with the tenacity of Balinese customs, the authors predict that there will be a resurgence of dance in the not too distant future. According to Bandem (1990), that renaissance is now in effect. The sacred dances continue to be performed in Bayung Gede, as in many villages. Five years ago the government decreed that only persons who pray be allowed to enter temples, and at the Galungan ceremonies at Kesiman only villagers are allowed to enter the sacred temple, an example of efforts to control tourist and outside intrusions on the culture. Balinese culture is a living system that is dynamic and not static. In spite of surface changes, especially as evidenced by technology, it is remarkably stable in its basic elements (Suryani, 1988). The reasons for the stability of the customs of Balinese culture are detailed below.

Bali has a consistent history of gradual and harmonious assimilation of the intrusive influences of other cultures. Rarely have threats to stability resulted in unusual mass action or violence. In 1939, the police interrogated foreigners about their private lives and homosexual practices and jailed some, including artist Walter Spies (Howard, 1984: 209) in a movement that affected other Pacific Rim countries. An episode of mass violence involving multitudes of Balinese citizens throughout the island, as well as other parts of Indonesia, occurred in response to threats of a communist takeover of the government of Indonesia in 1965.

Changes along with evidence of stability are evident at present. Increasingly, major economic strength is held by Chinese merchants, Javanese, and capital investors from outside Indonesia. However, locally the Balinese Hindu maintain political and administrative control as much as ever. Although materialism has increasingly affected the Balinese, especially the younger generation, and television programming has had its effects, these still happen within the context of the conservative forces of the culture. Balinese youth may wear Western jeans and aspire to a motorcycle or a car with stereo speakers, but they still wear the traditional sarong when they eagerly attend traditional drama and dances presented at traditional local sites, even in the popular tourist cities of Ubud and Kuta Beach.

The stability of the Balinese Hindu religion contrasts with events in Lombok, a neighbouring island close to Bali. This island, with similar terrain and weather to Bali, was colonized in the seventeenth century by a royal Balinese family and many of the Muslims of Lombok were converted to or influenced by the Hindu religion of the Balinese colonists. In the early 1900s the Dutch conquered Lombok, taking over the government, and the Balinese rulers lost their place. In 1990, the majority of the people are Muslim and fewer are Hindu. Interestingly, some temples in Lombok show a mixture of Hindu, Muslim, and animistic influences. The authors visited two that were Hindu in structure but had blue colourfully painted entrance doorways (Balinese temple structures are generally unpainted) and stone-lined ponds for sacred eels, as well as shelves for sacred stones (animism). The sacred stones, one foot long, were lined up, dressed in cloth, for purposes of promoting healing. The eels, according to the priest, promote the powers of healers: if the eels appear they are believed to exert such power. In order to attract the eels, the authors bought three hard-boiled eggs which the priest, an old woman, distributed in the flowing water while clapping her hand against the stone edge. After some moments of suspense, two eels, with one-inch diameter bodies poked their heads out of crevices and snapped at the eggs. The authors were considered to be lucky and imbued with augmented healing powers. The Hindu priests in Lombok expected payment for contacts, and even relatively brief conversations, a custom distinctly different from that of the Balinese.

The Balinese may be in a good position to cope with future shock and the 'third wave' of revolution and lifestyle that Toffler (1980) asserted is rocking the West. Because the Balinese are firmly rooted in immutable practices that originated in the dim and distant past, they have not experienced any of the major causes of this disruptive modern lifestyle revolution, especially family fragmentation or breakup. The computer store and fax machine operators put out offerings to the gods every day in the same traditional way. In spite of electronic innovations, they continue to lead familiar, stable, comfortable lives. They adapt to modern technology with flexible stability and accept it without losing the close-knit family structure and traditional practices that could give them the best of both worlds.

Recently, a group of 25 Balinese scholars convened to discuss the issue of preserving the character (*karakter*) and Balinese-ness (*kebalian*) of Bali. Suryani presented the authors' view of stability and its basis in religion, family, community, and ancestors as described below. One speaker cited the decline of the Balinese language in favour of Bahasa Indonesia as an eroding factor in identity. Immigrants from Java and other parts of Indonesia were cited as factors in changing identity. One suggested closing Denpasar to further influx of Indonesians from the other islands, as has been done in the Indonesian capital city of Jakarta. The effects of tourism—e.g., the transformation of the Balinese from being a generous and helpful society to being a materialistic one—were noted. Concern was also expressed about the relatively recent influx of prostitutes into tourist centres. The Balinese Hindu religion was cited as an indicator of identity. Bandem expressed the opinion that the power of Balinese art (*taksu*) derives from its religious base. A suggestion was made that the state Department of Religion encourage *banjar* to teach the concepts and meaning of religious customs. That this meeting was held is evidence of local awareness of the threats posed to desired distinctive features of Balinese culture—i.e., its character and identity—by current social forces and changes.

No major changes are envisioned in the backbone of Balinese culture, of which a basic characteristic is the maintenance of equilibrium of forces and other factors based on Balinese Hindu religion. However, adaptation to disturbances in cultural equilibrium will continue to take place and some mental disorders, which are forms of adaptation, will continue to be shaped in form and symptomatology by the pervasive determinants subsumed under the Balinese character.[17]

Bateson and Mead's Contributions

Mead stated that 'no appeal has ever been made to him [a Balinese] to achieve in order to validate his humanity, for that is taken as given' (p. 48). This conclusion about character was not elaborated upon nor supported by data. It merely states the absence of a quality in the Balinese that, by implication, is characteristic of Western cultures, i.e., the need to achieve. The authors wondered if this reference to achievement could have been generated out of one of Mead's own personal life themes: a striking lifestyle of achievement, or possibly her theoretical focus on what is known in anthropology as 'negative instance': a pattern, general to many cultures is absent in one culture. This was purportedly the chief strategy used by Mead in presenting the Samoans as lacking adolescent turmoil and crisis and thereby supporting the doctrine of cultural determinism (Freeman, 1983). The part of her statement regarding the 'given' aspect of 'humanity', may have been related to the honorific attitude towards and indulgent care of newborns and small children. It is true that Balinese children are provided with much care, attention, and physical contact in the early years of life. For the first 6 months, the infant is regarded as holy. Children are believed to be close to the gods and surrounded by them until 3 years of age. Since the souls of the baby are those of their ancestors, they have high status and one must address them in the appropriate high language and cannot punish them. The Balinese interpret a baby's smile as a response to the gods teaching or playing. A special area in the parents' sleeping room is reserved for the baby's shrine with a place for symbols such as the umbilical cord and for offerings to the god of the baby (Dewa Kumara) and the 'sibling' spirits. From birth, each Balinese already has a secure place among his closely knit family, community, ancestors, and the gods.

Mead's comment that 'If a man follows the prescribed forms, he may expect safety—and if that safety is still meager, there will be a different turn to come in another incarnation' (p. 48) touches on two concepts important to the Balinese. The first concerns the security and comfort one has by following the prescribed routines of offerings, rituals, ceremonies, traditional work patterns, etc., that fill much of everyday life. Doing right by the family, community and gods brings rewards according to the principle of karma and ensures a comfortable niche in one's environment and future lives. The second important concept is reincarnation. Mead provided a brief description of this cornerstone of Balinese Hindu life (pp. 44–5). Persons from cultures who do not live by a concept of reincarnation will find it hard to appreciate its significance and power for one's lifestyle. As described earlier, the soul is inevitably recycled through a series of bodies until it achieves final unity with God (Chapter 2). Every Balinese has another chance at life and hopes that it will be better the next time around.

Bateson and Mead identified 'continuity' as a characteristic of most aspects of Balinese life and they contrasted this with life in a Western culture which is marked by climax, 'commas and periods'. An example of this continuity is the soul of the great-grandparent in the great-grandchild (p. 255). The authors agree with the characterization of continuity but not with the concept of lack of climax (see Chapter 7).

Mead characterized the Balinese as 'vulnerable, but deft and gay, and usually content' (p. 48). This does not sound like a description of people manifesting schizoid maladjustment and indeed it is not. It is a refreshing statement from Mead about Balinese character. Examples of spontaneous emotional expressiveness can be found in Chapter 8. The Balinese are engagingly cheerful and friendly and contagiously so. As Suryani said to Jensen on his first visit to Bali, 'If you stay in Bali a little longer, you will smile more.'

In addition to their contributions of ethnographic data, Bateson and Mead preserved in notes and on film the customs and dances performed, such as the phenomenal little girl trance dance (pp. 74–5),[18] still enacted in certain villages. In this particular event a young girl, untrained in dance, performs like a virtuoso dancer while standing on the shoulders of a moving man; in addition, she sometimes dances on the ground over hot coals without appearing to feel the heat (Belo, 1960: 180). It seems likely that Bateson's extensive film footage would possess data useful in verifying a number of cultural patterns relevant to Balinese character.

Basis of Balinese Character

Mead concluded that fear, instilled through child-rearing practices, is the basis of the Balinese character (p. 47). However, as shown in Chapter 6, the authors disagree with this idea, as they do not regard any single emotion or combination of emotions as a valid basis of character. Furthermore, no child-rearing practices that might have a bearing on the basis of character have been identified. This, of course, does not preclude the possibility that child-rearing practices, and innate and biologically determined behavioural and emotional manifestations of child development, play roles in the transmission of culture (Trevarthen, 1983). Child rearing in Bali could be a fruitful area of cross-cultural study.

A conceptualization and generalization of the basis of a cultural or national character is seldom attempted by anthropologists. However, aspects of Balinese culture that are so elemental and pervasive that they can be regarded as fundamental forces shaping behaviour and character have been described in this book. These forces have their roots in two basic interrelated systems: (a) the Balinese Hindu religion (Hookyaas, 1973) and, (b) the extended family, community (*banjar*) and ancestor system.[19] They exert their effects in spite of the fact that most Balinese cannot explain the principles of the religion. Indeed, the majority of Balinese carry out the various rituals and ceremonies out of simple faith or as a matter of custom. Most ceremonies require community participation and this is willingly given because it is a means to acquire good social relationships.

As pointed out in Chapter 2, the basic elements of the Balinese Hindu religion are (a) the five principles of Hindu–Dharma belief, and (b) the concepts of the three factors of microcosmos, macrocosmos, and God, and the 'sibling' spirits. It was also noted that the family, ancestors, and community are tightly enmeshed and interdependent. No one, except a vagrant or schizophrenic, can function without being a part of all three. Every Balinese is imbued with this trilateral system from birth, and this early imprinting of an individual (to use an analogy from the field of ethology), coupled with regular and frequent reinforcement, lasts throughout this life and the lives thereafter. These two systems are regarded not only as the basic forces that shape Balinese character but also as the main factors accounting for its stability and durability. In interrelated functions, associated rituals, and ceremonies, the two systems account for much of the uniqueness of the culture, the distinctive characteristics that are clearly Balinese.

All foreigners who have visited Bali know that ceremonies are a striking aspect of the life of every Balinese. They are manifestations of the family community ancestor system and the religious system, which, in function, are inseparable.[21] Ceremonies (B and I: *upakara*), and offerings (B: *mebanten*; I: *mempersembahkan*) are part and parcel of the elaborate and colourful customs borne by the two systems. A number of examples showing how ceremonies and offerings generally go together have been presented. These do not refer to discrete behaviours or patterns but to complexes of behaviours, sometimes involving numerous individuals, that are oriented towards identified goals and performed with clear purpose.

Rituals and ceremonies range from the individual and the private to the masses and the public (Hookyaas, 1977). Individuals make offerings of freshly woven small palm leaf baskets (*banten*) filled with flower blossoms, incense, etc., at home shrines and gates, crossroads, at a stream crossing, near their business, and neighbourhood. Public buses may stop briefly along the way to make small offerings at shrines erected along the roads.

There are ceremonies for acquiring a car or motor cycle and several for building a house, both at the beginning and on completion. In order to commence building Jensen's house in Bali, the authors consulted the high priest of the area to decide on a propitious date and time. When they arrived at his home, he was sitting on the floor of his pavilion making a wood carving for a temple. He explained that he gets inspiration for the design of the carving while meditating; in this way each piece he makes is an original creation though it follows traditional forms. He consulted the Balinese calendar and the *lontar*, his old palm leaf books which contain information about religion. Then he said that the proposed site, which is by the sea, is close to an area well known to harbour powerful evil spirits, so it would be necessary to make proper offerings in order to establish good relationships with these spirits so that they will not harm the house or its occupants, but instead will provide protection. On the appointed day and time, the authors picked up the high priest at his house, along with his two assistants, many baskets of offerings, and a bamboo shrine that he had made.

Seven o'clock in the morning was the appointed time for the ceremony but it took an hour after that to assemble the people to help dig the hole in which offerings were to be placed and to erect the shrine. The priest conducted his ceremony with the appropriate prayers, bell ringing, and chants calling for the evil spirits, and placed hundreds of offerings into the shallow pit to be covered with dirt by Jensen and the contractor. The offerings included many kinds of rice cakes, different fruit, a full roasted chicken with head and legs intact, as well as special freshly made palm leaf decorations.[22] Finally the shrine for the gods was erected and offerings were made to them. By the time the ceremony was finished, the sun had risen further in the sky to make the day quite hot but the priest was very tolerant of the delays and time required. The authors experienced a feeling of peace following the ceremony. Each day during the construction of the house the workers would place an offering on the shrine to ensure continued good relations with the spirits and protection of the house.

Character Traits of the Balinese

In this book, the authors have conceptualized the following traits of the Balinese character: trust-belief, industrious creativity, hierarchical orientation, co-operation-devotion, conformism, son-generativity, and hypnotizability. Four aspects of emotions were also identified as character traits of the Balinese: tranquility, non-verbal expression of emotion, controlled emotionality, and, passive acceptance.[23]

The term 'trust' corresponds with Erikson's term for a stage of human development which theoretically became a basic attribute of the personality, expressed throughout life (Erikson, 1950). However, in no way is it implied that this term and concept which is the same or similar to Erikson's is exactly interchangeable with his, although they have some things in common. Due caution has been exercised in applying Western psychology to the Balinese because of the risk of misinterpretation. As Hobart (1985) pointed out, 'to import explanatory theories tend[s] to make nonsense of ethnography' and it makes more sense to characterize Bali in terms of their own cultural idioms.

There is in the Balinese a strong trait of trust-belief (B and I: *percaya*). This sense of trust was discussed at length in Chapter 6. *Percaya* means both trust and belief and these two attitudes go hand in hand. From birth to about three years, the child is in contact with a kind caretaker virtually all the time. Child abuse, especially of infant or toddler, is almost unheard of in Bali. From infancy through maturity, the Balinese develop and maintain an unfailing belief in the gods along with the other principles of the religion, which not only provide them with a sense of security but also play a governing role in their behaviour.

The Balinese grow up to trust their parents and elders because they have always been taught to respect them. They trust the priests, high priests, and *balian* who are needed by the gods for communicating their wishes and directives to the people. They trust the village headman and the *banjar* headman and believe the laws of the community are in their best interests. They place unflinching trust in their ancestors' traditional customs, believing that these will help them succeed and have a good life. This is why they honour God and their ancestors, and give them regular devotion and offerings. The sense of security experienced by the Balinese is enhanced by their feeling of closeness to their ancestors, community, and the spirits, both their own spirit companions (i.e., the 'sibling spirits') and others.

The power of trust-belief is illustrated by the following summary of treatment by a *balian*. A family once consulted a *balian*, who was a trance medium, because of concern over the death of a family member and family problems which they believed were caused by evil persons in their village. When the *balian* fell into a trance, he spoke first as God who informed the family that the woman's death was caused by two persons, a man and a woman, not relatives, but neighbours who put a spell in the deceased woman's household gate. This caused her to lose interest in things, to suffer from various ailments such as epigastric pain, vertigo, and irritability, and finally to die. Following this explanation, the *balian* was possessed by the soul of the deceased woman. She said, 'Yes, I died because someone wanted to hurt me. For this, I am still distressed. I want revenge, but don't you do it yourself. I will do it. This is my business. I'm sorry I died quickly. I only care about my children. After my cremation I hope you will have good relationships with others. Don't try to find out who killed me. You must try to make good relationships with everyone. Don't worry about my life. I still have a good chance to make a good life for myself. I will help you from my world.'

In an interview immediately following this visit to the *balian*, family members said that originally they had a great urge to avenge the woman's death and the death of several other family members and that they wanted to know who had been causing them problems, but after listening to the *balian*, they had changed their way of thinking even though they believed they knew the persons responsible for their troubles and their relative's death. The family had complete trust and belief in the *balian*, the god, and the ancestor's spirits. After the session with the *balian*, they felt satisfied and were no longer revengeful or even distressed. This remarkable (and rather rapid) change of mind and attitude, which in a comparable Western context might have taken several psychotherapy sessions to achieve, was brought about by just one visit to the *balian* possessed by the soul of the deceased woman and speaks to the psychological power of trust-belief.

Industrious creativity (B: *glitik* and *prataktik*; I: *rajin* and *kreatif*) refers to the self-initiated industrious trait of the Balinese personality and character. Mead stated that by 6 years of age many children would have taken responsibility for work roles (pp. 212–15). The student who does all his homework or the obedient, dutiful servant is referred to as *seleg* (B). The Balinese are conscientious and hard workers. Adults stay at tasks which Westerners would consider arduous, tedious, or boring. In so doing, they are relaxed and sociable but not generally lazy. Perhaps this characteristic is common to a number of Asian cultures.

Mead emphasized a rhythmic, 'unattended industriousness' (p. 46).[24] On the contrary, the authors have not been impressed with 'unattended' quality of most workers. The lone rice paddy cultivator skilfully attends to his work. Harvesting rice is routine work, but the harvesters are attentive to it and socialize intermittently. Even the human 'scarecrows' who drive the birds from the rice paddies are alert and attend to specific stimuli. Women spend hours making countless palm leaf woven baskets for offerings; they do it with deft and semi-automatic movements because they are so practised in the art and socialize at the same time. At Bayung Gede the authors observed the studied attention of men painting designs on dance costumes, hour after hour. Balinese musicians are attentively absorbed and focused: 'I remembered the dramatic-looking young man who drummed so feverishly, his eyes fixed on the dancers as they moved across the stage. His energy seemed to flow into every accent of the music, every motion of the dancers, through their bodies and out into the fragile hands that were forever forming new and beautiful designs.' (McPhee, 1946.)

Industry and creativity (I: *kreatif*) have been combined as a trait not only because they are denoted by the same word in Bahasa Indonesia, but because the latter is generally expressed in the process of performing the former. Most Balinese are industrious but it is difficult to gauge what proportion are creative. Creativity is expressed in daily life by innovations and variations in performing ceremonies and the arts, including painting, dance, wood-carving, and music. New 'deliciously exciting music' was 'taking the island by storm' in the 1930s and the style of *gamelan* music was always changing (McPhee, 1946: 26, 41). Furthermore, the arts are widely practised by the average person: the peasant farmer by day may be the musician or dancer at night.

According to Djelantik (personal communication) the painter (artist) seeks security in the regular traditional forms or copies of model works, 'but there is a fire that burns that seeks expression'. Although a painting may appear to be an imitation of another, originality is expressed in it in relatively obscure small changes. An example from the field of *gamelan* music is when a flute player, following a regular melody, suddenly changes the melody and perceives the change as a surprise, more lively and vibrant. Such a relatively small change in musical expression is analogous to the small change executed by the painter. Similarly, family ceremonies show variation and creativity. The food arrangements for offerings follow rules but are expressions of creativity in a manner analogous to Japanese flower arrangements. The arts reflect an unconscious integration of nature (the environment), religion, and community.

Some changes in ceremonies represent a creative adaptation of technology. For example, the cremation fire was formerly made of wood but these fires were expensive, undependable, lengthy, and laborious. The Balinese now use a torching kerosene burner. If they should carry this technological adaptation further by switching to a Western-style cremation oven, the family would still carry the corpse in the tower and the priest would carry out the same ceremony but he would push the button to start the oven. Some ceremonies become simplified for economic reasons but the underlying meaning remains the same.

The authors also observed the creative narrations of the men at the evening parties in the village selected for their palm wine study (Suryani and Jensen, 1990). Made Kaler composed a nine-verse poem (Mead, 1977) in honour of Bateson's mother on the occasion of her visit to Bali in 1936, one verse which went:

Njonjah[25] we all love you
But we don't know how we can show that to you
Only God knows and he will probably tell you
If not by day then in a dream of you

This touching verse illustrates not only creativity but also thoughtfulness, sensitivity, expression of emotion, and the essential role of religion in everyday life.

Hierarchical orientation (B: *linggih* for caste and *sor singgih* for speaking; I: *jenjang*) refers primarily to caste and status which are ever-present in social interaction and play roles in personality and emotional comfort. The authors' experiences with members of the royal family of Klungkung, of the Ksatria caste, is an example: the *puri* (palace) has received only five foreign visitors to the household in the past 20 years, because of the possibility of embarrassment to either visitor or royal family if etiquette were to be breached. However, even the lowest caste household has rules of etiquette. The first question asked by Balinese who meet for the first time is, 'Can you tell me your caste, please?' (*Titiang nunas antuk linggih?*). In addition to its social and emotional ramifications, caste lends a person identity and stability. A Balinese can rise in status by virtue of wealth and a woman can rise in caste by marriage, but most Balinese retain a sense of his/her given caste in which he/she is most comfortable.

The Balinese are preoccupied with etiquette and a critical part of this relates to rank and hierarchy basic to Hinduism (C. Geertz,

1980). Commenting on cremation, Geertz stated, 'The whole ceremony was a giant demonstration repeated in a thousand ways with a thousand images of indestructibility of hierarchy in the face of the most powerful leveling forces the world can muster—death, anarchy, passion and fire.' Cremations still go on, little changed, except that wives of deceased royalty no longer make a suicidal jump into the fire of the corpse.[26]

Mead illustrated the function of status and the importance of levels to every Balinese, even those of the lowest caste such as all the villagers of Bayung Gede, by citing their effects on various aspects of Balinese life, e.g., language use; amount of contribution to village ceremonials; share of chicken one receives at a feast; postures and gestures (pp. 7–16). Many aspects of levels are a function of custom and others become part of the personality.[27] Attention to the many details of status is quite automatic and without stress. Status is an aspect of social rank. Vying for status was evident in the competition in arts and warfare between the royal families (*raja*) of Bali in earlier times. Today, some Balinese with accumulated wealth occasionally attempt to augment personal status by flaunting material possessions such as a house or a car or by having unusually elaborate and costly ceremonies. However, the majority of the people do not strive for status through money because they have very little of it. In traditional marriage ceremonies, they may strive to show status by having their best spokesman represent the family in negotiations and by gathering as many of the extended family as possible for the ceremony.

The careful attention the Balinese give to how high a person sits or stands in relation to a person of different status, the significance of the highest point of the body (the top of the head), and its placement in relationship to the environment when one sleeps (e.g., towards the sacred mountain or *kaja*), the number of steps of the cremation tower, etc., are all aspects of custom and related to hierarchical orientation. Bateson and Mead referred to these under the concept of elevation and respect (pp. 75–83). Even the type of wood used in construction of shrines, houses, and service buildings is selected according to the Balinese belief in high, medium and lower woods (i.e., jackwood, teak, and all other types of wood respectively).

Co-operation-devotion (B: *ngayah/nguopin*; I: *gotong royong*) is a striking aspect of many activities and jobs but nowhere more evident than in the clubs (*seka*) (see Chapter 2), the irrigation systems (*subak*), ceremonials of the families, and at the *banjar*.[28] For example, a *dadia* (extended family or clan) may have periodic ceremonies, some of which involve dozens of the related extended families, numbering hundreds in all. Preparations which involve the construction of special temporary structures for preparing food and offerings, for presenting the offerings, and for eating and sleeping take weeks to complete. The ceremony itself can last several days. All the people are provided with food daily. In preparation each day, they work for hours, synchronized and sociable, doing their allotted jobs. It is a symphony of motion. Over a hundred guests may attend the ceremony. Such an undertaking is highly complex and requires utmost co-operation, with each person doing his/her part in keeping with tradition and custom. The schedule of events has been worked out carefully in advance but is somewhat flexible because it follows 'Balinese time': an hour or two, more or less, when it all comes together and happens.

As a personal illustration of typical co-operation, one day while motoring in the country the car came to a rolling halt with steam pouring out of the hood. A few minutes after opening the hood, the authors were surrounded by about five men assembling from a stopped truck, a little store, and a house near by, and several curious children who proceeded to work together quickly and efficiently to obtain water, fix the radiator, and get the car running again—with pleasant smiles and refusal of money.

Co-operation is associated with a sense of devotion or dedication to friends, family, and village. *Ngayah* means not only working for the *banjar* but also working for family and relatives. For example, a friend with whom you have developed a good relationship might offer you assistance with your ceremonial preparations or help you build a house as an expression of devotion and with no expectation of reward.

Conformism (B: *manut*; I: *taat*) is reflected in the traditional ways of doing things such as strictly following the rules of the *banjar*, attending traditional family ceremonies, and planting, growing, and harvesting rice.[29] There are often good reasons for such conformity. Government introduction of a new, higher-yield rice strain brought about a change in the ecology which eventually negated the expected benefits and caused disruption by making the farmers dependent on government loans, and the use of expensive petrochemical fertilizers (Poffenberger and Zurbachen, 1978). This caused the farmers to abandon their traditional rice storage customs, making them subject to market fluctuations and resulting in a loss of security. This experience led many farmers to switch back to the traditional methods. The centuries-old tradition and system of paddy irrigation that ingeniously moves water from the mountains through countless paddies until it flows into the sea has been eminently efficient and productive. It is controlled by the farmers' co-operative groups and, like all matters of rice growing, is presided over by a high priest and the goddess of rice. Government attempts to improve the system were not entirely productive (Crowley, 1987). A computer modelling of the traditional system proved its excellence.

Mead emphasized that Balinese follow routines of the calendar and prescribed forms of behaviour. Indeed they do: one can depend upon most of their rituals and ceremonies as much as an American can depend on the Fourth of July celebration, but there are many small variations within the general pattern. Possibly, conformity makes innovation appear to be a gradual process. The bulk of Balinese art and some handicrafts tend towards a 'static state' with imitation and copying (Djelantik, 1986). However, there was a period of outstanding innovation and creativity in dance in the 1920s and 1930s and dance has continued to evolve up to the 1980s (Bandem and deBoer, 1981: 81, 132).

The trait of conformism lends a quality of timelessness and stability to the culture and could be an element in the Balinese resistance to cultural change, for better and/or for worse. The Balinese are likely to be spared the 'future shock' of Western cultures: 'the shattering stress and disorientation we induce in individuals by subjecting them to too much change in too short a time ... so powerful today that it overturns institutions, shifts our values and shrivels our roots' (Toffler, 1971).

According to Erikson's theory (1950), generativity, meaning to raise and nurture offspring, is one of the eight stages of normal personality development, general to all cultures and strongly rooted in biology. To the Balinese, the main purpose of marriage is

BALINESE CHARACTER: A SYNTHESIS

to have children. In many cultures it is of paramount importance to have a male heir in the family and this is true of Bali, where a son is essential to perpetuate the family (*purusa*), to inherit the land and house, to support their livelihood, and to take responsibility for important ceremonies. Sons are also important to help the family at the *banjar* and to lead the way for the soul of their parents to go to heaven. This imperative of the culture and personality may be termed 'son-generativity' (*meled madue putra lanang*, literally, need to have a son). Pursuit of it can result in anxiety or depression for some couples, rejection of wives, divorce, the acquisition of multiple wives, and the possibility of a husband becoming a surrogate son who is required to move into the household of his wife's family, and be subjected to their pressures and demands.

Tranquility or peace (B: *rahayu*, I: *selamat, damai*) is an inner state of emotion that combines feelings of calmness and an absence of sickness, problems, and conflicts because all burdens have been given to the gods. It is a feeling that the Balinese experience in various contexts, e.g., when making offerings, receiving blessings, and on Nyepi, the day of silence. It is also achieved by meditation. The feeling is not experienced continually, but intermittently. When life is stressful or anxiety intervenes, peace is lost for a time but it always returns.

Non-verbal expression of emotion (B: *semita*, literally expression of emotion in the face; I: *mimik*) is a trait that often strikes and puzzles foreigners visiting Bali. Verbalization is not the way that the Balinese express emotions. It is not their custom to say 'thank you' or comment on the dinner being good or delicious. At traditional dance or music performances, they do not applaud at the end as is the Western custom nor do they applaud a speech or lecture. However, the Westerner need not be disappointed. When the Balinese receive a gift, gratuity, or positive verbal acknowledgement, either from his own countryman or a foreigner, he may acknowledge it with a slight nod of the head, bringing the hands together as in prayer, or by no obvious mannerisms at all. The foreigner may misinterpret this to mean that he does not like the gift or is ungrateful, and wonder why he does not say anything. However, the Balinese show appreciation by subsequent deeds, not words. They feel the positive emotion 'in the heart' but express little outwardly. This has a deeper meaning than words and reflects more 'psychic power'.

Emotion is conveyed primarily by the eyes and to a lesser extent by other facial expressions, as is evident by the Balinese habit of sustaining eye contact and looking directly at a person. A look is generally more powerful than words and eye expression is striking in dance and also evident in wood-carving, though not in painting (except of dancers). Parents seldom make a positive verbal response to a child for good work and they do not physically touch or give hugs to older children, choosing to express approval in other non-verbal ways. They are good at eye contact. They teach their children to look the other person in the eyes and the face and to listen when initiating a good relationship and they emphasize the importance of learning to read facial expressions. The foreigner is often unable to appreciate the meaning of Balinese emotional expression because of sharply different expectations, based on their own customs.

Observable behaviour does not always reveal internal feelings. For example, the Balinese may appear outwardly happy at a funeral but still harbour feelings of sadness within. Such inner feelings are generally not obvious to casual observers, especially Westerners.

The Balinese have words to acknowledge a gift, e.g., they say *titiang nunas* (meaning 'I take it', 'I accept it') when addressing a person of higher caste or status, and *tiang ngidih* when talking to one of similar caste or status. However, the feeling that goes with 'thank you' is expressed 'in the heart'. In recent years they have introduced words equivalent to the Western 'thank you': *titiang matur suksm*a, and *terima kasih*, in Balinese and Indonesian, respectively.

Colour is used for non-verbal emotional expression, as it is in many cultures, but the Balinese have their own characteristic way of using it. The Balinese liking for bright colours and contrasts in colour is evident in their food offerings, such as coloured rice concoctions and many kinds of tropical fruit, their dress, and their ceremonial decorations. The otherwise bland coloured temple structure is turned into a riot of coloured cloth, banners, umbrellas, and other decorations for ceremonies. Multiple colours are less obvious in Bayung Gede where the villagers tend to use single colours contrasted with black.

The trait of control of strong emotion or controlled emotionality (B: *nabdabang kayun*; I: *menahan perasaan*) is considered a virtue by Balinese. This pertains to anger as well as elation. The trait has some basis in religion and myth. An example is the story of 'The Temptation of Arjuna' from the Mahabharata myth, in which Arjuna sits in meditation, unmoved by the tempting lascivious maidens around him. Popular paintings show him 'asking strength from Siwa to overcome the demon Kala. On either side a smiling, teasing nymph (sent by the demon) attempted to distract him. Others danced seductively in transparent draperies, while below, old Tualen, the faithful attendant, made shameless, indecent love to still another nymph whose willingness was all too apparent' (McPhee, 1946: 188). The religious principle of harmony and balance of the emotions as well as all things in the universe are powerful influences. The Balinese control of anger and aggression was noted by Mead on several occasions. 'Interpersonal emotion is systematically discouraged'; 'there is an absence of display of aggression, and anger is expressed with greater smoothness of speech'. The authors concur in these observations of control of anger. Of course, the Balinese also experience feelings of anger but they learn early in life how to deal with these feelings by a number of psychological mechanisms in addition to suppression, including walking away, avoidance of conflictual persons or situation, sublimation, karma, delay of expression, and sometimes sulking.

Suppression of emotion (*negtegang bayu*) be it anger, aggression, or sadness in social life is, by Western definition, a conscious act of controlling and inhibiting an unacceptable impulse, emotion, or idea (Kaplan, Freedman, and Saddock, 1980). Possibly, the psychological defence mechanism of repression is involved at times: an unconscious process that serves the function of keeping unacceptable impulses or emotions out of one's consciousness. For the Balinese, walking away from a situation of disagreement is a non-verbal act of rejection, signifying that the other person's position means nothing. Avoidance of a person is another non-verbal show of rejection and also serves to protect the individual from a rekindling of feelings of anger through association with the person who could elicit the feelings. Engaging in hard work, talking with friends at one's *banjar*, or exercising are forms of sublimation. Other means for coping with anger utilize Hindu mechanisms: trust or faith that God will handle the problem; belief in reincarnation, leading to a resigned acceptance of mistakes, sins, or acts in one's own previous life; and karma, i.e., the offending person's acts will be reflected in a future life. In general the Balinese culture reinforces suppression of emotion: the better one can control emotion (*bayu sabda idep*), the better one is considered to be. Violence sometimes occurs but is atypical. The Balinese are also noted for their lack of overt sexual behaviour in public: they are never seen to kiss or hug and couples do not hold hands. To do so would be impolite and unacceptable.[30] Sexy and seductive behaviour is, however, seen in some dance and drama. However, affection between peers is common in public: males and females of all ages may hold hands with persons of the same sex as they walk. Warm affectionate hugs and embraces are lavished on little children. An observer can easily sense the interpersonal warmth, the opposite of schizoid behaviour, in a Balinese.

Passive acceptance (B: *nrima*, meaning receive; I: *menerima*) is a mechanism of adjustment to life situations that one regards as unchangeable or for which there are no perceived alternatives, i.e., 'nothing can be done about it'. If the Balinese must wait a long time for personal service or are stuck in a traffic jam, they may experience a brief period of negative feelings but then this is followed by a sense of resignation; they do not become resentful or attempt to avoid the delay. They are patient in the face of what many Westerners would regard as frustrating inconveniences. The Balinese do not think in terms of changing the system or implementing measures to prevent such inconveniences from occurring. This pertains to private and public issues, including increased taxation, a 30 per cent government hike in electricity rates, and frequent interruptions in public services such as electricity and water. There is little personal reaction and there are no public protests. Similarly, the university students do not dissent or demonstrate. While the absence of dissent may be considered a custom, the authors postulate that it owes something to personality.

Passive acceptance results in minimizing the degree of anger and frustration which could otherwise be experienced as stress. Westerners are markedly different in their reaction to inconvenience or perceived unfairness, and are quick to complain or express public outcry. It is the contention of the authors that passive acceptance is learned early in life by parents' admonitions to accept gracefully the words of the elders and the ways things are done, without expressing disagreement, argument, or protest. It is also possible that the custom of carrying the infant and small child in a sling or on the hip may have contributed to the formation of a passive acceptance trait.[31] The traits of control of emotion and passive acceptance combine to lend a dimension of tolerance to everyday life. Possibly this relates to Mead's statement that the people are 'usually content'. However, such a generalization, if valid, would need to be considered with regard to the various kinds of behaviours and facets of the culture.

Many foreigners visiting Bali are often struck by the friendliness and tolerance of its people. A number of traits and customs could contribute to this, including control of emotion, passive acceptance, eye contact and smiles, and a readiness and willingness to respond to requests for help, particularly from persons of higher status, a quality that accords additional respect. The Balinese tolerate with grace even the most raucous public behaviour of some heavy-drinking tourists.

The word 'hypnotizability' is used to denote the trait of trance in the Balinese which almost always includes the possession state.[32] Trance (kasurupan, meaning possession by evil spirits and kalinggihan, meaning possession by a god) is a discrete behavioural state which occurs in a variety of contexts including ceremonies, dance, and healing sessions. Trance states probably occur at various times in most of the populace. Trance continues to occur as a symptom of certain culture-related mental disorders (see Appendices 1 and 2) and some traditional healers go into a trance in order to treat physical and mental illness. Mead was correct in her conclusion that trance states are essentially hypnosis. In 1938, Belo (1960) recognized Balinese trance as a state of 'altered consciousness'. Somewhat later, Ludwig (1966) coined the term 'altered state of consciousness' for hypnosis and it has held favour ever since. Most trance states of the Balinese differ from hypnotic/trance states of Westerners with regard to the aspect of 'possession'. The Balinese nearly always experience possession but Westerners rarely do so. Mead described the little girl trance dance, the witch and kris dance ('Calonarang'), and 'seers' who are possessed by gods or ancestors (who speak through them), and she stated that in trance, strong emotions of grief and striving are expressed which are never otherwise appropriate except in drama (p. 5). In these respects, the authors agree with her reporting and interpretations. However, her following statement misconstrued the effects of trance on the society in general: 'These trance states are an essential part of Balinese social organization, for without them life would go on forever in a fixed and rigid form, foreordained but unguessed in advance' (p. 5). Trance states are an important aspect of the Balinese culture but the conclusion that without them life would go on forever in a fixed rigid form is questionable. There is no evidence that trance phenomena in Bali have such a general effect. Possibly, Mead meant to draw attention to the observation that trance behaviour may be highly unpredictable and is emotionally expressive.

Trance is a state in which the Balinese can overtly express intense emotion, such as anger, jealousy, and physical violence, without social disapproval. In trance, the individual is possessed by a spirit, so his behaviour is not within his control and he cannot be blamed for behaving the way he does; in possession, the individual is believed to be receiving or expressing feelings and information from a god or a spirit. Trance in dance and ceremonies allows for the expression of many kinds of emotions without threatening to disrupt the bonds and harmony of the community and it sometimes clears up dissatisfaction (Belo, 1935: 135).

A visitor to Bali can observe trance in several situations, e.g., he can seek out the traditional healers who use it. Trance is less commonly seen in ceremonies, although at the time of the Kuningan ceremonies at the village of Kesiman in Denpasar about 100 participants will go into trance. The trance of the fire dance is performed almost daily at Bona approximately 20 kilometres from Denpasar and at Butabulan 8 kilometres from Denpasar. The show at Bona begins with the *kecak* dance in which most of the 80 men of the chorus are in trance, then it continues with the little girl trance dance (Sang Hyang Dedari) and ends with a fire dance

(Sang Hyang Jaran) in which a man dances with a symbolic hobby horse for about 10 minutes on fiery hot coals from burning coconut husks, leaving little doubt that he is in a real trance. Before the *jaran* dancer begins, a chorus entices him, chanting in Balinese, to the effect, 'Go on, go to the fire. It's good; it's not hot. Go'.[33] His impassive facial expressions of staring and blankness during trance and while coming out of trance are typical. He suffers no burns because of the physiological changes in pain and tissue responses that occur in the trance state (Chapman, Goodell, and Wolff, 1959). The authors ascertained by interviews with the dancers about their experiences before entering, during, and after their performance that all of them were in trance.

In observations of trance dance and ceremonies in Bali, the authors have been impressed not only with the necessity of trust and belief but also with the role of singing, music, monotonous voices encouraging the persons, and a general expectation and positivity towards the trance state by the subjects and those in the audience. The attitudes and behaviour of the spectators towards the dramatic, exhilarating experience are important factors in inducing trance and in the behaviour of the trancers. Based on observations of trance in the Balinese, the authors believe that the majority of people in most cultures could enter trance if they had personalities with strong belief and trust, as well as a willingness to go into trance, and if they were subject to strong environmental support. It is estimated that approximately 95 per cent of Western populations are hypnotizable to some degree (Brown and Fromm, 1986).

The trance disorders studied by the authors, *bebainan* and *kasurupan*, afflicted 27 individuals from a group of 296 (12 per cent) and 45 persons from a group of 215 (21 per cent) respectively (see Appendices 1 and 2). Trance-possession occurred in an estimated 25 per cent of the participants and a variable number of the audience as well in ceremonies such as those involving self-stabbing by krises. In certain circumstances it has been reported that virtually an entire village population is capable of trance-possession (Belo, 1960). To test the hypothesis that most Balinese have the capacity for trance, one could administer standard hypnotizability instruments to representative samples of the population. This and other types of studies of trance in Bali could lead to a better understanding of hypnosis and dissociative disorders in Western cultures.

Trance states may enter into exercise and sports: the authors watched a group (club) of about 200 young adults gathered on the beach near Sanur engaged in synchronized exercises, resembling the movements of t'ai chi, which the men called 'meditation sport'. After these were over, the men sat in pairs in a long line awaiting a brief ritual in which the man sitting at the head of the line facing the pair brought his outstretched arms and open palms slowly up near their chests until they quivered and then placed his palms firmly, one against each man's chest. The two men, arms extended with hands positioned near their knees, were motionless and silent, with eyes staring; they appeared to be in deep concentration, in meditation, or in a shallow trance state during the 4–5 seconds of hand contact. Then the leader slowly dropped his arms and the two men arose quickly for the next pair to advance into position for the same procedure.

In attempts to explain why so many Balinese appear to possess the capacity to go into trance (hypnotizability)[34] and in efforts to gain a better understanding of hypnosis, Western scholars have uncritically accepted some of Mead's unsubstantiated statements and erroneous conclusions. For example, Gill and Brenman (1961: 7) believed that the personality characteristics of dissociated states in the daily lives of the Balinese could be traced to Mead's interpretation that the core of the Balinese personality derived from the mother's undercutting of the child's climax of emotional expression causing withdrawal and lifetime unresponsiveness. They regarded these kinds of withdrawal behaviour as 'aborted forms of trance, and since they are universally present among Balinese, they form an important line of evidence for our inference that almost all Balinese have the capacity to go into trance'.[35] These theorists further interpreted Mead's descriptions of child-feeding practices and aspects of digging up the corpse for the funeral ceremonies as, respectively, 'unconscious fantasies of oral incorporation' and 'the Balinese struggle against unconscious cannibalism', both of which they related to trance. Lewin (1945: 85) interpreted the little girl trance dance as 'an equivalent of infantile masturbation, and repetitive of the erotic sleep during the primal scene'. He concluded his explanation of Balinese trance thus: 'We seem to have a conversion symptom, neurotic sleep, which is a genital manifestation of the oedipus complex, a reminiscence of the primal scene.' These interpretations are highly speculative as well as unprovable. Whatever psychological or psychoanalytic interpretations Western scholars wish to make of Balinese trance, it is unfortunate when they base them upon erroneous concepts or upon snatches of Bateson and Mead's selected observations. The authors' observations of Balinese child-rearing practices indicate that theoretical generalizations, based only on Bateson and Mead's writings or observations without considering the meaning of the behaviour to the Balinese, will be of little merit in the study of Balinese customs.

Hypnosis may be far more common in Western society than generally believed. Tart (1986) made a case for a generalized phenomenon of hypnosis in much of daily life in Western society. In other cultures such as those in Asia, Africa, and certain parts of the Caribbean, trance is a common aspect of the culture and of culture-bound syndromes (Bourguignon, 1973; Simons and Hughes, 1985).

As Gill and Brenman (1961) described the relationship between hypnotist and subject: 'Not only does the subject become childlike and subservient, he also participates in the omnipotence of the hypnotist; and the hypnotist is not only omnipotent and directive, but he also participates in regression and subservience of the subject.' They emphasized a 'fluid interpenetration of hypnotist and subject' which they surmised is more clearly visible in the Balinese culture. The fact is that the Balinese are very rarely hypnotized by a hypnotist. In some ceremonies singers and music facilitate the trances. They enter into trance spontaneously at the pleasure and choice of the gods and when this happens they feel fortunate to be chosen. The subject and the god participate in a relationship in which the god is omnipotent.

In addition to the character structure of the Balinese discussed above, there are other traits, such as the tendency to accept the words and orders of some leaders, teachers, or authorities without question. As an example, Balinese students do not ask questions or disagree with the lecturer or professor (unless specifically invited), in sharp contrast with American students. Although this generalization may be valid, it should be considered within the broader aspects of the culture.

The presentation of character traits as well as the literature to date is notable for its relative lack of consideration of sexuality; a large part of life and significant behaviour. In Hobart's words (1985), 'it is an area over which the Balinese have drawn a polite veil'.[36] At present there do not seem to be any appropriate and acceptable ways to survey the sexual responses and behaviour of the Balinese. This may seem naïve, timid, or wrong to Westerners who are accustomed to reading about sex and to Western physicians who are taught to inquire about the sex life of their patients in order to diagnose and treat sexual and other relationship problems. On the contrary, this is a sharp illustration of cultural difference.

Parents always teach their children to be 'careful' in relationships with the opposite sex, because pregnancy before marriage would be an embarrassment for the family, and they would be less able to care for a child than the married couple. If a daughter becomes pregnant, the parents ask her to marry the man who made her pregnant, because it is important that a baby is born of a father through marriage in order to establish inheritance rights.

Sexuality is expressed in the arts in various ways, including drama, painting, carving, and dance. Paintings may show a man with a large penis or a woman with voluptuous breasts. Some sculptures of gods show them in erotic postures. In dances, such as the *joged*, the women dancers act seductively and erotically. In drama and puppet shows, sexual topics are presented in ways that stimulate laughter by the audience.

In social groups, people often make sexual jokes and sexual interpretations of comments because they are not referring to individuals. The authors have observed the custom of joking and expressing curiosity about the heterosexual relationships and courtship of youths. In serious discussions, it is difficult for youth to talk about sexuality, to explain how they feel, or to relate experiences.

Drama performances in villages present situations in which young people may see and choose a girlfriend or boyfriend. At these performances, all spectators stand very close together, but a young man may stand very close behind a girl of his choice and sometimes touch her. If the girl is interested in the man, she will not avoid or reject such advances but if she does not like him, she expresses rejection.

In the villages there is a custom called *nganggur,* at which three to five men go together to a woman's house in the daytime to talk and joke with her. If one of this group likes or loves the woman, he will visit her alone next time. This event seldom happens in the cities, because the parents there monitor their daughters more closely: young urban women are allowed to receive friends at home only in the evenings at which time the entire family is present.

Before menstruation, a girl is considered holy. The gods may choose such a girl to use her body (by possession) as may be observed in the little girl trance dance. God may also use a married person's or man's body but that person must first undergo a special ceremony to purify his or her body and mind. After this ceremony by the priest, he or she can no longer engage in sexual activity and must devote their lives to God or to humans. Parents are not unhappy if their daughter marries late or remains unmarried because an unmarried woman is highly valued. The Balinese call such a woman *nyukle brahma cari,* which means 'the holy woman, still a virgin, loved by God'.

Since marriages may be terminated verbally and no legal divorce is required, a man who 'divorces' and remarries has in effect more than one wife to whom he may provide material support. Occasionally but less often, the wife leaves her husband. Extramarital affairs generally take the form of secret liaisons. In cities, these may be carried on for years on a regular basis with the same partners even though both might be married. The authors have no idea of the prevalence of this, only that it does occur. It is not acceptable or even possible for unmarried couples to live together. If a couple were to do so, the *banjar* leaders would simply require an immediate marriage.

There is very little information on violence except with regard to *amok,* a culture-related syndrome (see Chapter 7). Types of violence typical in the West such as homocide, stabbing, and fights are relatively rare and gangs of youths do not exist but at this point, there is insufficient knowledge of violent behaviour in Bali to relate it to character.

Occasionally, the authors have been asked to identify negative aspects of character, with the implication that the aspects identified so far are all positive. However, the characteristics in this chapter have not been designated as positive or negative because to do so would mean making judgements relative to some other culture or ethnocentric ideal. As an example, Mead stated that everywhere there is a tendency to crowd too many offerings on the altar shelf, to pack too many flowers in a young girl's hair, or to carve too many scrolls and flowers on a stone gate' (p. 3). This is analogous to a Balinese stating that the buildings in New York are built too high and with too many windows.

Further research into the character of the Balinese could take several approaches. One involves the use of objectively scored psychological scales or tests. For example, the Stanford Hypnotic Clinical Scale (Morgan and Hilgard, 1978–9) and the Dissociative Experiences Scale (Bernstein and Putnam, 1986) measure the extent to which the population is highly hypnotizable and uses dissociation as a psychological mechanism, both of which would relate to the extensive use of trance and self-hypnosis in many aspects of Balinese life. Another method of research into character would be prospective in-depth studies of individuals similar to the authors' current studies of suicide in Bali. A third approach is illustrated by Inkles, Haufmann, and Beier's (1958) use of standardized questionnaires and psychological tests in studies of adjustment of the Soviets to their political system and the Dutch and Danes' attitudes towards life satisfaction, a sense of burden, and control of one's life (Inkles, 1989).

Adolescence

There are no published data or reports relevant to the social adjustment or mental health problems of adolescents in Bali. No psychiatrists or mental health professionals specialize in this age group. Recently, David Rosenthal and the authors undertook a study of juvenile delinquency in south Bali. Other information on this subject is based on Suryani's clinical work, talks she has given to adolescents and their teachers in high schools, and her experience as founder of a group of professionals and adolescents which works towards establishing preventive mental health programmes for adolescents in Denpasar.

Preliminary information is remarkable. The rate of juvenile delinquency is very low. Only sporadic cases are observed in Denpasar and in villages. In Bayung Gede villagers have not encountered juvenile delinquency for many years, do not recognize a general pattern of adolescent turmoil or crisis, and have not seen drug or alcohol use by adolescents even though alcoholic beverages are readily available. The Balinese in general do not expect adolescence to be a period of turmoil or crisis. When adolescent pregnancy occurs out of wedlock, it presents a problem but the family makes an effort to solve it by arranging a marriage before the baby is born. The child becomes accepted by family, community, and religion through marriage. Custom dictates that marriage, even if it is only short-lived, is essential for the child's benefit.

Bali has a juvenile justice system[37] but no juvenile detention facility. Government-employed counsellors meet with arrested adolescents to work out solutions to problems which might otherwise result in imprisonment. High school teachers and students told Suryani that they do not see the kind of adolescent adjustment problems that she related as typical of Western cultures and as described in the literature. They seldom see overt crises, children running away, street children, or drug use, abuse, or selling. Some adolescents brought to the psychiatric clinic for evaluation reveal disagreement with parents and instances of disobeying them. Teachers may note poor concentration and underachievement in these children. There are no data on adolescent rape, theft, indecent exposure, or violence; however, sporadic instances are reported in the newspapers.

The only information available about adolescent suicide is from Suryani's survey of cases at Wangaya Hospital: in 1968–78 most suicides occurred in the 20- to 25-year-old age group; in 1984, there was an increasing trend in the 15- to 20-year-old group. The Balinese Hindu religion is a strong deterrent to suicide because it considers suicide to be an offence against the gods, a reason for punishment, and a wrong way to die, a mis-death (*salah pati*). The Balinese believe that the soul of a suicide faces difficulty in going to heaven and requires a special ceremony by the family to correct the problem.

Present information indicates that adolescence in Bali is a period of life relatively free of overt turmoil, crisis, trouble, and delinquency. In 1927, Mead published her startling findings that the Samoans fitted this description (Mead, 1928; Freeman, 1983) but she failed to recognize it as a characteristic of the Balinese. The absence of adolescent problems in Bali is so striking that it is hard for the Western observer to miss. Mead must have noticed that Balinese adolescence is easy and trouble-free like the Samoans' but not sexually permissive. Mead may have ignored it because the theme of her book *Coming of Age in Samoa* was an easy sexually permissive, problem-free adolescence, a case of 'negative instance'[38] in anthropology. For Mead to have acknowledged such mentally healthy and positive traits in Balinese adolescents may have been incompatible with her and Bateson's theorizing about child-rearing patterns resulting in schizoid characteristics of the Balinese.

In summary, this final chapter presented the authors' conceptualization of the primary basis, as well as some traits, of contemporary Balinese character. The fundamental nature of Balinese customs has not changed significantly in the 50 years since Bateson and Mead's study. Balinese character is based on two systems: the Balinese Hindu religion and the family–community–ancestor system. A number of traits were identified: trust-belief; industrious creativity; hierarchical orientation; co-operation-devotion; conformism; passive acceptance; son-generativity; tranquility; non-verbal expression of emotion; suppression of emotion; controlled emotionality; and hypnotizability. It was noted that adolescence in Bali appears to be a stage of development relatively free of the turmoil, crises and problems, and juvenile delinquency characteristic of Western cultures.

In 1951, Mead wrote, 'Today I can look at pictures of young Karba and wonder, "What will you be when you grow up? How may you not affect the future of the world?"' The answers to those questions are now known. Karba, respected by his fellow villagers, as a father, priest, and village headman, admirably carries on the traditions of Bayung Gede. Some of his knowledge is incorporated into this book for people of many nationalities to read. Made Kaler is another Balinese whom Mead judged well. He acknowledged Mead's motivational impact on him and made his mark on Bali by establishing an innovative school which germinated into a university.

These two individuals, whose lives touched one another 50 years ago, but who subsequently lived quite different lives in many respects and at some distance apart, are pure Balinese—intelligent, creative, solid citizens, in a land of the gods. Mead would have been impressed with and proud of them both.

1. This was the method of Bateson and Mead (p. xvi) and is traditional in studies of culture and personality (see Wallace, 1961: 129).

2. In the 1930s, psychologists sometimes used the term 'character' as a synonym of personality but 'character' tended to be identified with the volitional, ethical, and moral aspects of behaviour (Allport, 1937). Most recently, the terms have been used interchangeably.

3. Mead and Ruth Benedict have been credited with the conceptualization of the relationship between personality and culture termed 'personality-is-culture'. They rejected the conceptual distinction between culture and personality. 'Both culture and personality refer to configurations of behaviour that are manifested and carried by individuals but are characteristic of a group.' (LeVine, 1932: 53.) Benedict and Mead were trying to prove that personality patterns not only varied across human populations but were integral parts of pervasive, culturally distinctive configurations that gave them meaning and apart from which they could not be adequately understood. Personality was, in other words, an aspect of culture, the aspect in which the emotional responses and cognitive capacities of the individual were programmed in accordance with the overall design or configuration of his culture (the 'cultural patterning of personality'); social relations, religion, politics, art, and recreation were programmed in accordance with the same design (LeVine, 1982: 53).

4. The term 'personality writ large' is often attributed to Benedict (1934). Possibly she meant that some culture patterns are like personalities.

5. Wallace (1961: 149) used the term 'basic personality' for the concept of national character.

6. For discussions of the controversy, see Favazza and Oman (1980) and Barnouw (1973: 213–36, 487). For a positive position and review by a sociologist and psychologist, see Inkles and Levinson (1969).

7. This is particularly true of anthropologists, sociologists, and psychiatrists working in the large Pacific Rim countries of Japan (Devos, 1962; Caudill, 1962; Doi, 1962; T. S. Lebra, 1976) and China (Weizhan, 1985; Li, Yang, and Yang, 1974; Song, 1985; Bond, 1986; Yang, 1986; Tseng et al., 1990), who utilized the concepts of orientations, traits, and behavioural patterns as characteristic of the cirucumscribed specific culture. Inkles, who has utilized the concept of 'national character' in his sociological analyses of Americans (1979), Russians (1958), Dutch (1988), and Danes (1988), stated, 'Modal personality may be extremely important in determining which new cultural elements are accepted in an acculturation situation,

which institutional forms persist in a society, and changes in the character of such institutions.' (Inkles and Levinson, 1969: 491.)

8. Inkles (1953: 588), a sociologist, held a similar view: 'Taken at a single point in time, any social system can be seen as a more or less integrated institutional structure in which the balance of cultural influences and institutional pressures tends on the whole, through its influence on significant parental figures, to produce a socialization process for the child, and to create a social–cultural milieu for the adolescent and adult, which yield personality constellations generally adaptive for life in the given society.'

9. Kroeber (1948: 587), anthropologist, believed in this concept when he wrote: 'There can be little doubt that some kind of personality corresponds to each kind of culture.'

10. The authors' studies of a trance disorder and of mass hysteria in schoolchildren are examples (see Appendices 1 and 2).

11. Similarly, Wallace (1961: 148) regarded national character as 'a structure of articulated personality characteristics and processes attributable, non-statistically, to almost all members of some cultural bounded population'.

12. Wallace (1961: 152) referred to such data treated statistically as modal personality.

13. Erikson tended towards this approach in his study of the Yurok Indians (1950: 153). For other examples, see Favazza and Oman (1980: 487–9). Gorer (1943) attributed predominate aspects of the national character of the Japanese to strict early toilet training. This has been criticized as too sweeping a generalization (Barnouw, 1973: 486).

14. As LeVine described it, 'This conception represents (modal) personality and socio-cultural institutions as two systems interacting with each other. Each system is comprised of interdependent parts and has requirements for its maintenance. Both sets of requirements make demands of individual behaviour, the personality system for satisfaction of psychological needs, the socio-cultural system for socially valued performance in the roles that are institutionalized in the social culture.'

15. Wallace (1961: 161) stated that 'changes in basic personality (or national character), furthermore, are usually granted to be very slow and become noticeable only after efforts to restrain or channel culture change have failed and after the basic personality has suffered gross and painful distortion under stress'.

16. Even after the Dutch conquest (finally complete in 1906), the Balinese kings (rajas) were reinstated in roles of government administrative authority under Dutch district officials (p. 262).

17. See Inkles's observation on modal personality in note 7.

18. Bateson's extensive film footage is filed in the National Library of Congress.

19. The two systems are aspects of what LeVine (1932) termed the 'socio-cultural institutions'. Wallace (1961: 150) referred to such essential institutions as the maintenance system of the culture and regarded them as 'responsible for the nature of basic personality structure'.

21. Covarrubias (1937: 405) concluded that 'their whole life, society, arts, ethics—in short, their entire culture—cannot, without disrupting the entire system, be separated from the set of rules which are called the Balinese religion'.

22. These offerings are placed on the ground because the evil spirits are believed to hover near the ground. Offerings for the gods are placed on the elevated platform of the shrine because the gods inhabit the high places.

23. In a similar vein, T. S. Lebra (1976: 39) identified empathy and dependency as primary character traits or behaviour patterns of the Japanese.

24. Mead did not clarify the meaning of this term. It appeared that she meant the Balinese worked almost automatically without being conscious of effort or movement.

25. *Nyonyah* (current spelling) means 'foreign woman'.

26. See Geertz and Geertz (1975) for a description of this old custom as practised in 1847.

27. The Japanese may have a similar behaviour pattern called 'occupying the proper place', which means one's awareness of the place assigned to one in a social group, institution, or society as a whole and one's willingness to fulfill the obligations attached to that place (T. S. Lebra, 1976: 39).

28. T. S. Lebra (1976: 22) used the term 'belongingness' to characterize a normative pattern of interaction of the Japanese. This included the need to establish an identity, as is done by asking where and for what company you work, when greeting a stranger for the first time. 'Collectivism' is expressed by 'an individual's identification with the collective goal of the group to which he belongs' and 'togetherness' denotes a feeling of being more alive in a group. The latter is similar to the Balinese tendency to crowd (*rame*) described by Mead (p. 3): '... temple courts overcrowded with offerings and where three orchestras are playing different pieces within easy earshot of each other and two dramatic performances are going on a few feet apart ... a theatrical performance about which the audience packs so tightly that the smallest child cannot worm its way from the front row (where the smaller children sit by well accepted custom). . . .'

29. T. S. Lebra (1976) used the term 'conformism' to describe the Japanese characteristics of going along with one's peers and pressure to conform with group norms. The Balinese express this characteristic at the *banjar* and ceremonial activities.

30. To express sexual feelings in public would be akin to behaving like animals, i.e., creatures of a lower order than humans.

31. According to Mead, many children are carried almost throughout the day until the age of three years, and the authors have observed this to be a common practice.

32. For the Balinese, possession means that the body is used by the gods. They perceive a 'power' or a god entering their body and acting and speaking through them.

33. Instrumental music and 'encouraging' songs commonly induce trance in many cultures (Rouget, 1985)

34. Recent studies have revealed that dissociative experiences occur in a high percentage of normal Westerners (Ross, John, and Currie, 1990). The psychological mechanism called dissociation is operative in trance states.

35. What Gill and Brenman called 'abortive forms of trance' could be dissociation, and if this psychological mechanism was used frequently by Balinese children, it could conceivably make for a high prevalence of hypnotizability.

Westerners manifesting multiple personalities, a condition involving the mechanisms of dissociation learned in childhood, are highly hypnotizable (Bliss, 1984).

36. Using a type of thematic apperception test (i.e., making up a story for a picture), Caudill (1962) identified a character structure of the Japanese: a general emotional pattern he called 'an emphasis on non-sexual satisfaction'. This meant that the typical close personal interrelationships has to be protected from disruption by the intrusion of sexual impulses or behaviours. Possibly the Balinese share this pattern.

37. This is known as *Bimbingan Kemasyarakatan Pengentasan Anak.*

38. The concept of negative instance held that the absence of a pattern of behaviour that is commonly seen in cultures is evidence of cultural determination of that behaviour.

Appendix 1
The Case of *Bebainan* in Bali: Culture and Mental Disorder*

THIS was an investigation of 27 cases of *bebainan*, a disorder which Balinese believe to be caused by sorcery (Suryani, 1984). The most common symptoms were sudden feelings of confusion, crying, screaming, and shouting, followed by an inability to control one's actions. The victims, mostly female, reported suddenly 'losing control of themselves'. Some cried out continually for no reason (82 per cent), some spoke, giving voice to the *bebai* (see below) that they felt possessed them (44 per cent), whilst others were silent (11 per cent), and a few ran *amok* (11 per cent). Only a small number of respondents could not say how they felt or acted during an attack (7 per cent). In the majority of cases, attacks were brief, lasting $\frac{1}{4}$ to 1 hour.

In an attempt to control troubled and uncertain feelings during the prodromal stage, sufferers usually went to a bedroom. After lying down, they suddenly found that they could not control themselves anymore. They cried out or sobbed or talked to themselves against all attempts to calm them down. Most (81 per cent) were lying down at the time of an attack, 15 per cent were standing or walking, and 4 per cent were running around aimlessly. If restrained, 89 per cent said that the more they were restrained, the greater was their capacity to resist. None could say how they gained the extraordinary strength. For example, a female sufferer who was restrained by six men was still able to struggle free.

Bebainan is an illness which the Balinese believe to be caused by the possession of the soul of the ill individual by a malignant spirit called the *bebai*. The term *bebai* (meaning evil spirit in old Balinese) refers to both the malignant spirit and its material representation. The latter is an embodiment of Balinese belief in the supernatural characteristics of the newborn. In Balinese religion, it is believed that at conception the 'soul' of the mother and that of the father intermingle to become the foetus (*rare ring*

*Reprinted in part by permission of Kluwer Academic Publishers.

jeroning garba) which assumes the quality of a supernatural human being (*manusia sakti*). This quality remains with the foetus until the newborn reaches the age of six Balinese months, i.e., about 210 days. Belief in the powers of the newborn has inspired some Balinese, who seek to practise sorcery or black magic (*ilmu pengiwa*), to capture those powers and transform them into those of a *bebai* (Weck, 1937).

Bebai may be made of different raw materials such as an aborted foetus, a baby which has died before or during delivery, a placenta, a bud of the banana tree, which is still very young and is commonly used in ceremonies (*pusuh*), an egg of a black hen, the water which has been used for bathing a corpse, or the brain of a murdered person. The type of material used determines the power of *bebai*. For instance, a *bebai* made from an aborted foetus of a female high priest (*pedanda istri*) would be much more powerful than another made from the foetus of an ordinary woman. A very powerful bebai is called 'king of *bebai*' (*raja bebai*).

Having found the material needed, the sorcerer then proceeds to treat the object as a baby. Like a real new baby, the *bebai* undergoes the normal series of ceremonies, performed for it immediately after 'birth', after one (Balinese) month and seven days, at the age of three months, and finally at the end of six months. Unlike a human baby, after the last ceremony the *bebai* is taken to the cemetery where a special ceremony is performed. At this ceremony, the sorcerer makes offerings to the gods, entreating them to bestow on the *bebai* the greatest powers possible. If the request is granted, the sorcerer then gives the *bebai* a name, usually simply 'human baby' or *bayi wong*. Afterward, back at home, the sorcerer prepares rice and other dishes specially for the *bebai*, which is now truly treated as a precious and precocious child. This next period lasts until it reaches the age when a normal child begins to talk. During this period, the *bebai* is not only fed regularly but is also given special offerings on Kajeng Kliwon (an important Balinese religious day which comes every 15 days). Finally, now that the *bebai* can 'talk' and 'understand', it is regularly consulted by the sorcerer to ascertain its 'maturity'. Only when it is fully mature is it ready to be used. At this stage, it is said to have acquired 30 powers or to have become 30 *bebai* in one. These powers can be used either by the sorcerer-owner, rented out, or sold.

Each of the 30 powers or manifestations of the *bebai* has a particular name and produces a particular symptom through the person it possesses. For example, *I Bebai Bongol* makes its victim unable or unwilling to talk. On the other hand, *I Bebai Sebarung* makes the person in its possession very talkative and rude. Another example is *I Rejek Gumi*, presumed to have 108 *buta* (evil spirits) under its command and therefore known as the king of *bebai*. This *bebai* attacks its victim violently in the pit of the

stomach, making the victim enraged before rendering him or her unconscious. The victim is likely to die unless help is quickly obtained.
Although each power or manifestation of the *bebai* has a distinct name and
a distinct mode of attack, the various manifestations are supposed to be
very co-operative, and to be ever ready to help one another to subdue victims.
Not every hated person can be attacked or possessed by *bebai*. The
impervious individuals are those who are free of sins, who are wise, or who
have mighty amulets. The vulnerable persons are those who are believed
to be weak either in mind or body and those who are sinful.

Most commonly, a person falling into the possession of the *bebai* is
reported to experience a sudden sense of blankness, loss of desire and
will, and confusion. These feelings are accompanied by a stomachache or
headache and ringing in the ears, followed by a loss of vision and a feeling
of cold starting from the feet upward to the pit of the stomach. Finally, the
victim loses all control and either cries uncontrollably, shouting and
screaming, or incessantly talks angrily to himself or herself. Sometimes,
the afflicted person becomes violent, exhibiting unusual strength.

Once in control, the *bebai* is believed to be capable of harming or even
killing the individual. Usually, however, its power can be mitigated and
overcome by a traditional healer (*balian*). Sometimes a spiritualist (*ahli
kebatinan*) or a Balinese Hindu high priest (*pedanda*) is consulted. But
since the illness is considered to be impure (that is, affliction by a lower
form of spirit), help can be obtained relatively easily only from the *balian*.
The high priest is usually reluctant to come into contact with this illness.

Puri Klungkung encompasses the residential quarters or compounds
of the family of the former King of Klungkung. It consists of Puri Agung
or the grand compound where the King and his principal wives (including
the queen) lived, Puri Agung Semara Negara where the younger royal
wives resided, Puri Agung Saraswati where the still younger wives of the
King had their quarters, and three other *puri* (i.e., Puri Anyar, Puri Kaleran,
and Puri Semarabhawa) where the brothers and sisters of the King and
their families have their residences. At the time of the fieldwork,
conducted in June and July 1980, the *puri* accommodated a total of 59
families or households with a total of 296 members.

In the past, a *puri* girl would at adolescence (following her first
menstruation) be taken out of school and confined to the *puri*. From then
on, she would be taught to weave, to prepare offerings, and behave properly
in accordance with the intricate etiquette of the *puri*. For her, the outside
world only appeared through the cracks and openings in the walls of the
puri. In the past decade, however, this tradition has undergone a slow
decay. A number of *puri* girls have continued their education as far as the
university, and some have outside employment in government bureaucracy

and in private enterprise. Nevertheless, almost all of the female members in the *puri* have been trained in the weaving of the Balinese traditional sarong (*kain songket*), the Balinese hat (*udeng*), and the shawl (*selendang*). And in general they are still unrebellious. They seem to be complacent and willing to accept the decisions of their parents and families.

In the *puri* as a whole, the older generation of men generally have more than one wife while most of the younger generation have monogamous marriages. All the wives in each polygamous marriage live together in the same compound, apparently quite harmoniously, each one putting the interest of the husband above her own. They appear to comply with the expectation that they should be completely obedient to their husband and, at the same time, be able, generally through weaving, dressmaking, or retailing, to support themselves and their children with minimum help from him. At any rate, none of the wives expressly expects to be completely supported by her husband. They accept support from him, of course, but without exception they recognize the need to be self-supporting. In effect, each wife with children is the head of her own household.

Suryani administered formal questionnaires and interviewed all of the members (296 persons) in the compound of the descendants of the former royal family of Klungkung. Twenty-seven individuals, mostly female from 16 families had experienced *bebainan* at least once. All these individuals, who were between 10 and 76 years of age, were included in the sample. The control group consisted of 215 individuals, *puri* residents who were between 10 and 75 years of age.

When the first signs of an attack occurred, all family members who happened to be in the immediate vicinity of the victim rushed to his or her side to render assistance. As mentioned above, relatives always tried to physically restrain the sufferer who might be shrieking, writing, crying, or running around aimlessly. At this stage, families had a lot of discussion about where to find a suitable healer to treat the victim. Close family members usually had no hesitation in making the diagnosis of *bebainan* as the symptoms were easily recognized and *bebainan* was regarded as a common illness. It was also considered a condition which must be treated by traditional healers (because of the sorcery involved) and which lay outside the power of modern doctors and paramedics to cure. In 93 per cent of cases recorded in the survey, the family immediately sought the help of a traditional healer. In 30 per cent of cases, the help of a Balinese Hindu high priest was sought in addition to, or as an alternative to, the healer's ministrations. In only 11 per cent of cases was the patient taken to a doctor or paramedic. In some of these cases, the close relative took the sufferer to a doctor (not accepting the diagnosis of *bebainan*) while other relatives sought the help of a healer as well. A mere 3.7 per cent of cases did not receive any treatment at all.

In most cases, the healer would be summoned to the house-yard of the victim. Several healers living close to the *puri* were the ones usually summoned to treat *bebainan* cases. On some occasions, close relatives would go to the house of a more distant healer for advice and medicines, but rarely was the victim taken outside the *puri* walls.

The healer usually arrived while an attack was in progress and typically the sufferer would cry out in fright at seeing the healer, and ask for mercy. In fact, it was the voice of the creature possessing the sufferer (the *bebai*) which was believed to be talking through its victim. The *bebai's* utterances varied little in content and tone from one victim to another. Sometimes the healer interrogated the *bebai* who had possessed the victim, asking, for example: 'Where do you come from?', 'Why are you here?', and so on. After such a session, the healer prepared to exorcise the *bebai*. Some healers used holy water, or certain ritual objects. Another common technique was to squeeze the thumb of the victim, so that the *bebai* was forced to cry out in pain (through the victim), asking for mercy and promising not to bother the person again. Often the *bebai* would only leave the body of the victim after its demands for certain foods or offerings were satisfied. When food was asked for, it was not necessarily food which the victim would normally have found appetizing. After the victim had returned to normal, the healer gave the family a supply of holy water or oil, which they were advised to administer regularly so that there should be no recurring attacks. During and after the attack, several close relatives of the victim were occupied with carrying out the healer's instruction, e.g., preparing food, making the small inexpensive offerings usually required.

In cases where the healer was delayed in coming, the distressed relatives of the victim might seek help from other *puri* households in treating the attack. Close relatives sought out other residents who had experience in handling cases of *bebainan* and who might have reserves of holy water and other medicines on hand. Thus *bebainan* attacks provide opportunities for informal co-operation between *puri* households, a temporary breakdown of otherwise rigid behavioural codes. Some time after the attack, on a pre-determined day, the afflicted person underwent a purification ceremony which was thought to have a calming effect on the sufferer. It was performed by a very high-ranking priest who had a special relationship with *puri* residents. The ceremony itself was small, brief and inexpensive, and was performed at the priest's house. This ceremony provides an occasion for the former victim to leave the *puri* briefly.

Basically, the same procedures were followed for first and recurring attacks. Apart from the purification ceremony mentioned above, no special attention was bestowed on the *bebainan* sufferer when not experiencing an attack.

Analysis of the psychological and social pressures acting on these women suggested that *bebainan* attacks provided sufferers with an opportunity to release feelings of frustration and anger about conflicts engendered by their social environment which they had no means to resolve. The victim benefited psychologically from the disorder because it was one of the few ways in which women in particular might give vent to negative feelings without risk of widespread disapprobation or stigmatization. However, *bebainan* was not instrumental in altering access to resources within the restricted environment of the royal compound, nor did it empower the victim within this environment in any but the most transitory ways.

From the psychiatric standpoint, the most compelling characteristics of *bebainan* are its sudden occurrence and the temporary character of its impact. During its attack, the victim suffers a severe impairment of consciousness and sense of identity and loss of control over motor functions. But these symptoms disappear completely at the cessation of the attack. There is no amnesia for events during the attack. *Bebainan* cannot be regarded as a form of psychosis, even of the reactive or atypical type; it is neither an organic mental disorder, nor a form of neurosis. Instead *bebainan* can be considered a form of dissociation, specifically trance with possession, which is understandable only in the context of local Balinese culture.

It is highly significant that within a year after Suryani's study of this long-standing disorder, it ceased to occur in the palace population. Because of this, some families regarded Suryani as having magic powers. The authors regard the disappearance of the disorder under the circumstances as consistent with it being a community-wide culture-related dissociative disorder with possession. It is hypothesized that the families' relaxation of restrictions on adolescents took the pressure off them and decreased their resentments. Possibly this, and related changes in the community which reduced the stress-producing customs and the education which Suryani provided about the nature of the disorder, removed some of the mystery of the illness, and were the primary factors responsible for its curious disappearance. It still occurs sporadically in the wider Balinese population.

Appendix 2
Mass Hysteria in Schoolchildren: *Kasurupan*

SURYANI made a clinical study of an outbreak of dissociative disorders (*kasurupan*) in 45 elementary schoolchildren (Suryani and Jensen, 1991). It illustrates a trance disorder and how Western trained psychiatrists need to develop an intimate and thorough knowledge of the Balinese culture as it affects behaviour, personality, and mental disorders, and clinical strategies.

In January 1984, a number of schoolchildren in a mountainous area of central Bali began to experience spells characterized by sudden onset, fainting, unconsciousness, crying, visual hallucinations, anxiety, and occasionally automatic dancing (lasting minutes to hours) with complete awareness of events of the spell after recovery. The number of children afflicted (45 of the 215 schoolchildren), the frequency of the attacks (65 per cent had 6–15 episodes; one had 30; some had several per day), and the apparently contagious nature of the disorder, interfered severely with the functions of the schools and caused fear in the children and community. It was apparent that this problem touched the entire community, as well as the children experiencing the mental disorder. Treatment efforts by traditional healers and psychopharmacotherapy advised by psychiatrists were ineffective. Education and government officials from the region became concerned and involved.

The village heads and associated government officials invited Suryani to investigate the problem. She visited the village on several occasions and interviewed teachers, school officials, community members and afflicted children, examined one child during an attack and surveyed 19 victims by structured interview.

The spells consisted of three phases: prodromal symptoms, trance, and recovery. The prodromal phase was characterized by weakness (90 per cent), a feeling of emptiness in the head, piloerection on the neck, closing of the eyes and difficulty opening them, and intense fear of impending events. This phase lasted from 2 to 10 minutes.

The trance phase was characterized by hallucinations and dissociative phenomena. The experiences varied in details but had common elements. Many victims lost their hearing and the ability to hear voices around them. Most (70 per cent) saw a woman or a man, usually a big, 'horrible' woman with yellow or red-coloured matted hair, a red or black face, hairy arms, and long hair hanging down or fixed behind the head (45 per cent), sometimes appearing like a giant or Rangda, the witch in classical Balinese drama well known to all Balinese. Some saw a woman with light-shaded beautiful skin. Some reported that this woman took them for a walk in the forest (in front of the school) and spoke to them, but they could not speak back. In the forest, they cried from fear, saw little men and snakes with big bright eyes, and then were led back to school by the woman or man. A few experienced being taken to the forest along with another child from school to whom they were unable to speak. On one occasion when 17 girls had attacks simultaneously, two sixth-grade children suddenly sat up and told of being 'possessed' by two women spirits who were sisters; the older one lived in a large stone, partially buried in the schoolyard, and the younger one lived in a stone hidden under a classroom of the school. The spirits asked for floral offerings to the supreme God and for a traditional Balinese *gamelan* orchestra so they could teach the children to dance. The teacher complied by turning on taped *gamelan* music. At the first note of the *gamelan*, all the children who were experiencing the attack suddenly arose and the two girls danced *legong*, a classical Balinese dance that most had probably seen performed in the village but had not before learned to do themselves. The other 15 children then performed *legong* spontaneously. When the music ended, all returned to sleep-like behaviour. The trance phase lasted about 40 minutes.

The recovery phase was characterized by sitting up, expressionless, confused and anxious with weakness of neck and body muscles (70 per cent). After a few minutes, most of the victims continued with their schoolwork as usual but a small number were fearful and went home.

A number of responses of the teachers and community were significant. Soon after the episode began, they recalled an episode two years before when two children suddenly lost consciousness (*pingsan*) at school, were taken home, and recovered after about six hours with several recurrences. They were treated by a traditional healer (*balian*), who said the cause was a buried small temple on the school grounds that offended the gods. At that time the community promised the *balian* they would build a new temple but had not done so because of a lack of funds. With the onset of this new outbreak of a similar disorder, the community quickly built the temple on the school grounds. This effort along with ceremonies and offerings to the gods was fruitless. The 'spirit' rock on school grounds was fenced off. Teachers became fearful and unable to teach effectively because of these interruptions. The school authorities transferred some victims to another school; however, this caused additional attacks in other children in that school and they were returned. The *balian* believed the attacks were caused by the gods who were angered by the villagers' mistakes. Non-afflicted children feared being attacked, and the news media expressed alarm.

Examination of a 13-year-old child during an attack revealed a pale face, flickering eyelids, and resistance to efforts to open her eyes. Pupillary reflexes and deep tendon reflexes were normal. Her extremities were cold, but her heart rate was normal. Fifteen minutes later, she was crying and breathing slowly (five respirations per minute). Eye movements resembling nystagmus were noted. Fifteen minutes later, she sat up, was unresponsive to questions, and had cold extremities. Fifteen minutes later, she spoke slowly with an expressionless face. Forty minutes later, she returned to her normal behaviour and could recall her experience well.

Interviews with victims included questions about their relationships with parents, peers, and siblings, and about their life out of school. There were no reported changes at home except fear that the 'big woman' would follow them home. They typically reported a home life, lacking communication with parents and with inadequate opportunities for play, because of the lack of immediate neighbours. Working or doing school homework were their chief activities. They did not report sleep problems but some felt fearful at night. At school, the pattern of play with peers went on as usual but fear of another attack persisted.

It was clear from these studies that the attacks represented a dissociation phenomenon or trance. The stressor for most victims in this study was anxiety among the children and teachers. A specific stressor for the children initially afflicted could not be identified. There was evidently a high degree of suggestibility involved as evidenced by the 'spread' of attacks to new contacts, including two adults.

Suryani observed that the temple built on the school ground was not properly oriented in its location according to the traditional Balinese Hindu religion. She became aware of the many visiting strangers (i.e., officials, news media, and curious outsiders) and their apparent disturbing influence on the village and its people who previously were relatively isolated from outsiders.

Various possible approaches to the problem were discussed. First, diagnosis was necessary. Arriving at a diagnostic term to be used in the management process with the community involved taking into account its suitability not only for individual 'patients' but for the community and even the country as a whole. It had to be acceptable within the culture if it was to be workable. For example, labelling the behaviour 'hysteria' would insult or anger the people and destroy rapport; using the term 'epidemic illness' would cause fear in the Balinese people; the diagnostic term 'dissociative disorder' would be incomprehensible and if used with the people would destroy confidence in the psychiatrists. This situation presented a dilemma to and generated conflict within the psychiatrists. The diagnostic term finally chosen was possession (*kasurupan*), a concept known to Balinese, understandable and acceptable to them. This term does not carry with it an implication of illness or stigma; rather, it is part of normal life in Bali.

Next, a treatment and intervention strategy had to be developed. There was no precedent for treatment of this kind of disorder in Bali. Pharmacotherapy was ruled out because prior experiences had shown it to be ineffective. Individual and group psychotherapy was considered but regarded as impractical in view of the urgency and extensiveness of the disorder. The epidemic nature of the problem suggested public health strategies. It was agreed that multiple aspects of the culture had to be taken into account and brought into harmony or balance with psychiatry. The final plan developed combined clinical and sociocultural elements.

The main components of the plan were outlined to the community leaders, and to health, education, and religious officials at a meeting held in August 1984, one month after initiation of the study. The characteristics of the disorder were explained, the diagnostic label of possession (*kasurupan*) was used, and specific measures were advised:

1. The high priest (*pedanda*) was recommended as the primary healer. This decision was based on his traditional role in treatment of mental disturbances, his high status in religious matters, and the prior ineffectiveness of local *balian*. The villagers would regard the high priest's intervention as appropriate since the community believed the cause of attacks were supernatural forces (anger of the gods) and the attacks did not represent disease.

2. A new temple should be built to correct the error in orientation of the existing newly built temple on the school grounds. This rationale adhered to the concept of 'balance' of forces traditionally believed to cause mental disorder. A proper temple is regarded as the source of all community power.

3. Teachers would allay fears of the children by reading and teaching traditional stories from the Hindu epics, *Mahabharata* and *Ramayana*, which feature positive and benevolent spirits. These stories are consonant with Balinese Hindu belief.

4. The village should be closed to all outsiders including the investigators. This was intended to reduce confusion, stress, and fear engendered by outsiders.

5. Individual psychotherapy was offered if needed.

These suggestions were accepted and all were carried out immediately. The high priest directed the temple change and the ceremonies of purification. Teachers had more confidence and a fresh direction of teaching; village life returned to its usual pattern. Within one month after the initiation of the plan, all attacks ceased. At yearly follow-up visits during 1985–90, no further attacks were reported.

Glossary

amok	a culture-related dissociative or trance disorder characterized by a sudden episode of uncontrolled violence and amnesia
anteng	a cloth tied around the head or waist, or a magical cloth used by the witch Rangda to fend off men in trance attacking her with krises
aroh	an exclamation meaning 'aah' or 'oh, my God'
atman	the eternal soul
balian	a traditional healer
balian matuun	a spiritual specialist
banjar	the governing and organizational unit of a village
banten	woven young palm leaf trays for offerings
baris	sacred warrior dances
barong	a lion, dragon or pig-like figure which features prominently in Balinese dramas and ceremonies, especially during Galungan
Bayung Gede	the mountain village originally studied by Gregory Bateson and Margaret Mead in 1936–9
bebainan	a culture-related dissociative disorder typical of Bali
Betara Sri	Hindu goddess of rice
Betara Surya	the Hindu sun god
Betara Wisnu	a Hindu god who takes care of the world
bingung	a state of confusion
Brahmana	the highest caste
brumbum	a 'middle' colour made by mixing all colours and a symbol of the god Siwa
buduh	a chronic psychosis
buta	demons or evil spirits who torment people
Calonarang	a classic drama featuring the witch Rangda

kasta	the stratification system, denoting status by birth (or for woman by marriage) from highest to lowest: Brahmana, Ksatria, Wesia, and Sudra or Jaba
dadia	the clan system
desa	a village
dewa	a manifestation of God, a god, or holy ancestor
dokar	a one-horse buggy taxi
dupa	incense smoke
Galungan	the ceremony held every 210 days, celebrating human victory of good deeds over bad
gamelan	traditional orchestra or music from Balinese xylophone-like instruments, drums, gongs, and flutes
Garuda	the eagle-like bird from Hindu mythology which is a symbol of Indonesia and frequently depicted in wood carvings
glitik	a trait denoting industriousness
gong orchestra	orchestra with gong instruments
hening	a peaceful feeling
Jaba	the lowest caste, formerly called Sudra
jaran	a hobby-horse used in a fire dance
jerih	'do not worry'; related to bravery in a struggle
joged	a sensual or seductive dance by women
kabupaten	a geographic district; one of eight in Bali
kaja	direction towards the sacred mountain
Kajeng Kliwon	the ceremony held every 15 days, according to the Balinese calendar
Kala	a sibling spirit that influences bad thinking and deeds (If a person has a good relationship with Kala, the spirit will help him.)
kalinggihan	a trance involving possession by a god
Kanda Mpat	the four 'sibling spirits' with which one is born
kangin	the direction 'east'
karma	the result of deeds, good and bad, accumulated throughout one's life or in previous lives
kasurupan	trance with possession and also a dissociative (trance) disorder
kecak	a chorus of men for a popular dance called 'monkey dance' performed for tourists
kelod	direction towards the sea, associated with the unclean and evil spirit activity

kris	a dagger or short sword
Ksatria	the second highest caste, which included the former king's families, and their descendants, who originally held positions in government
Kuningan	the ceremony held on the 10th day after Galungan
leak	a person whose spirit can disturb or harm people or cause mysterious events
legong	classic dance performed by women in colourful costumes
lek	feeling of embarrassment or shame, particularly when interacting with a person of higher status
lontar	Balinese sacred 'books' inscribed on palm leaf
madewa saksi	a special ceremony to relieve anxiety and shyness, e.g., in a case of illegitimate pregnancy
mantera	holy chanting to call the gods
manusa yadnya	the individual's life cycle ceremonies
mecaru	a ceremony with offerings and sacrifices to placate the demon deities and Kala
mecor	a sacred oath-taking ceremony of the *banjar*
mligia	the ceremony marking unification with God in the Hindu religion; same as *ngukur*
ngabe keneh	a psychological process of thinking/feeling
ngaben	the death ceremonies, including cremation
ngambul	sulking quietly or alone
ngeramang sawa	a state of non-thinking or no emotions
ngerumuk	grumbling or muttering to oneself while in a state of anger
ngukur	the ceremony marking unification with God in the Hindu religion; same as *mligia*
ngrupuk	a ceremony to placate evil spirits
nyeh	feelings of tension
Nyepi	a day of quiet and peace celebrating the new year
nyumbah	devotion to older or dead persons
otonan	a birthday celebration held every six months, according to the Balinese calendar
Panca Wali Krama	the ceremony held very 10 years at the mother temple involving all Balinese
pawintenan	a ceremony marking the attainment of the status of a holy person

pedanda	a high priest from the Brahmana caste
pemangku	a priest with less authority than a high priest
percaya	trust and belief
puik	punishment which involves not talking to the person being punished
punarbawa	reincarnation or rebirth
pura	a temple for the extended family
puri	a palace of former kings or a house of the second and third castes
Rangda	a classic witch in dramas and ceremonies, as well as a symbol of a goddess
sakti	strong spiritual power of a person, gods, or the supreme God
sanggah	a house shrine
Sang Hyang Widi Wasa	the Supreme God
Saraswati	the Hindu goddess of knowledge
seka	interest and working groups or clubs of the village
seleg	hardworking or industrious
subak	the irrigation system based on religion
Sudra	the lowest caste
takut	worry or fear depending on the context
tegang	feelings of tension
tirta	holy water
tri hita karana	concept of harmony and balance of the Balinese Hindu religion involving three factors: microcosmos, macrocosmos, and God
tuak	palm wine
Tumpek	every 35 days by the Balinese calendar; considered to be important for holding ceremonies for specific environmental elements (such as Tumpek Uduh for plants)
upakara	ceremonies
wadah	a tower for the corpse at the cremation ceremony
Wesia	the third caste, which originally functioned in business

Bibliography

Allport, G. W. (1937), *Personality, A Psychological Interpretation*, New York: Henry Holt & Co.

APA (American Psychiatric Association) (1984), *Psychiatric Glossary*, Washington, DC: American Psychiatric Press.

Arbolego-Florez, J. (1985), 'Amok', in R. C. Simmons and C. H. Hughes (eds.), *The Culture-bound Syndromes*, Boston: D. Reidel Publishing Co.

Averill, J. R. (1982), *Anger and Aggression*, New York: Springer-Verlag.

Bandem, I. M. (1990), *The State and Development of Balinese Art*, Denpasar: Sikola Tinggi Serri Indonesia.

Bandem, I. M. and deBoer, F. E. (1981), *Kaja and Kelod: Balinese Dance in Transition*, New York: Oxford University Press.

Barnouw, V. (1973), *Culture and Personality*, Homewood, Ill.: Dorsey Press.

—— (1985), 'Margaret Mead's from the South Seas', in *Culture and Personality*, 4th edn., Homewood, Ill.: Dorsey Press, pp. 94–127.

Bateson, G. (1936), *Naven*, Cambridge: Cambridge University Press.

—— (1949), 'Bali: The Value System of a Study State', in M. Fortes (ed.), *Social Structure*, Oxford: Clarendon Press; reprinted in G. Bateson, *Steps to an Ecology of Mind: Collected Essays in Anthropology, Psychiatry, Evolution, and Epistemology*, New York: Ballantine, 1972.

—— (1987), *Steps to an Ecology of Mind: Collected Essays in Anthropology, Psychiatry, Evolution, and Epistemology*, Northvale: Aronson.

Bateson, G. and Mead, M. (1942), *Balinese Character: A Photographic Analysis*, Vol. II, New York: New York Academy of Sciences.

Belo, J. (1935), 'The Balinese Temper', *Character and Personality*, 4: 120–46.

—— (1953), *Bali Temple Festival*, Seattle: University of Washington Press.

—— (1960), *Trance in Bali*, New York: Columbia University Press.

Benedict, R. (1934), *Patterns of Culture*, Boston: Houghton Mifflin.

Bernstein, E. A. and Putnam, F. W. (1986), 'Development, Reliability, and Validity of a Dissociation Scale', *Journal of Nervous and Mental Disorders*, 174: 727–35.

Bliss, E. L. (1984), 'Spontaneous Self Hypnosis in Multiple Personality Disorder', *Psychiatric Clinics of North America*, 7: 135–48.

Bock, P. K. (1988), *Rethinking Psychological Anthropology*, New York: W. H. Freeman & Co.

Bond, M. H. (1986), *The Psychology of the Chinese People*, Hong Kong: Oxford University Press.

Boon, J. A. (1977), *The Anthropological Romance of Bali, 1597–1972*, Cambridge: Cambridge University Press.

Bourguignon, E. (1973), 'Introduction: A Framework for the Comparative Study of Altered States of Consciousness', in E. Bourguignon (ed.), *Religion, Altered States of Consciousness and Social Change*, Columbus: Ohio State University Press, pp. 3–38.

Bowlby, J. (1973), *Attachment and Loss*, Vol. II, *Separation, Anxiety and Anger*, New York: Basic Books, Inc.

Brady, I. (ed.) (1985), 'Speaking in the Name of the Real: Freeman and Mead on Samoa', *American Anthropologist*, 85: 908–47.

Brown, D. P. and Fromm, E. (1986), *Hypnotherapy and Hypnoanalysis*, Hillsdale: Lawrence Erlbaum Associates, Publishers.

Brill, A. A. and Bleuler, E. (1924), *Textbook of Psychiatry*, New York: Macmillan.

Caudill, W. (1962), 'Patterns of Emotion in Modern Japan', in R. J. Smith and R. K. Beardsley (eds.), *Japanese Culture: Its Development and Characteristics*, New York: Werner-Gren Foundation.

Cerf, B. J. (1981), 'Ascaris and Malnutrition in a Balinese Village: A Conditional Relationship', *Tropical and Geographic Medicine*, 33: 367–73.

Chapman, L. F.; Goodell, H.; and Wolff, H. G. (1959), 'Changes in Tissue Vulnerability Induced during Hypnotic Suggestion', *Journal of Psychosomatic Research*, 4: 99–105.

Connor, L. H. (1982), 'Ships of Fools and Vessels of the Divine: Mental Hospital and Madness. A Case Study', *Social Science Medicine*, 16: 783–94.

——— (1984), 'The Unbounded Self: Balinese Therapy in Theory and Practice', in A. J. Marcella and G. M. White (eds.), *Cultural Conceptions of Mental Health and Therapy*, Dordrecht: D. Reidel Publishing Company, pp. 251–67.

Covarrubias, M. (1937), *Island of Bali*, New York: Alfred A. Knopf Co.

Crowley, G. (1987), *Newsweek* (Pacific Edition), 12 March, p. 48.

Devos, G. (1962), 'Developmental Social Change: A Psychological Evaluation of Trends in Japanese Delinquency and Suicide', in R. J. Smith and R. K. Beardsley (eds.), *Japanese Culture: Its Development and Characteristics*, New York: Werner-Gren Foundation.

de Zoete, B. and Spies, W. (1938), *Dance and Drama in Bali*, London: Faber & Faber.

Djelantik, A. A. M. (1986), *Balinese Paintings*, Singapore: Oxford University Press.

Doi, L. T. (1962), '"Amae": A Key Concept for Understanding Japanese Personality Structure', in R. J. Smith and R. K. Beardsley (eds.), *Japanese Culture: Its Development and Characteristics*, New York: Werner-Gren Foundation.

DSM-III-R (1987), *Diagnostic and Statistical Manual of Mental Disorders*, Washington, DC: American Psychiatric Association.

Eiseman, F. B., Jr. (1989), *Bali, Sekala and Niskala, Vol. I, Essays on Religion, Ritual, and Art*, Berkeley: Puriplus Editions.

Eissler, K. (1944), 'Balinese Character: A Critical Comment', *Psychiatry*, 7: 139–44.

Engle, D. L. (1977), 'The Need for a New Medical Model: A Challenge for Biomedicine, *Science*, 196: 129–36.

Erikson, E. H. (1940), 'Problems of Infancy and Early Childhood', in *Encyclopedia of Medicine, Surgery and Specialities*, Philadelphia: F. A. Davis Co., pp. 715–30.

———— (1950), *Childhood and Society*, New York: Norton & Co.

Estabrook, M. (1942), 'Hatred Is Healthy, Balinese Studies Show Repressed Emotions in Youth Produce Abnormal Adults with Schizoid Personality', *Science News Letters*, 102: 106–8.

Favazza, A. R. and Oman, M. (1980), 'Anthropology and Psychiatry', in H. I. Kaplan, A. M. Freedman, and B. J. Saddock (eds.), *Comprehensive Textbook of Psychiatry*, 3rd edn., Baltimore: Williams & Wilkins.

Feinberg, R. (1988), 'Margaret Mead and Samoa: Coming of Age in Fact and Fiction', *American Anthropologist*, 90: 656–63.

Fink, P. J. (1988), 'Response to the Presidential Address: Is "Biopsychosocial" the Pychiatric Shibboleth?', *American Journal of Psychiatry*, 145: 1061–7.

Freeman, D. (1983), *Margaret Mead and Samoa, The Making and Unmaking of an Anthropological Myth*, Cambridge: Harvard University Press.

Freud, S. (1953), *A General Introduction of Psychoanalysis*, Garden City: Permabooks.

Geertz, C. (1966), *Person, Time and Conduct in Bali: An Essay in Cultural Analyses*, New Haven: Yale Southeast Asia Studies.

———— (1973), *The Interpretation of Cultures, Selected Essays*, New York: Basic Books.

———— (1980), *Nagara: The Theatre State in Nineteenth Century Bali*, Princeton: Princeton University Press.

Geertz, H. and Geertz, C. (1975), *Kinship in Bali*, Chicago: University of Chicago Press.

Gill, M. M. and Brenman, M. (1961), *Hypnosis and Related States*, New York: International University Press.

Gorer, G. (1943), 'Themes in Japanese Culture', *Transactions of the New York Academy of Sciences*, Series II, Vol. 5, New York: New York Academy of Sciences, pp. 106–24.

Hinde, R. A. (1974), *Biological Basis of Human Social Behavior*, New York: McGraw-Hill.

Hite, S. (1976), *The Hite Report*, New York: Dell Publishing Co.

Hobart, M. (1985), 'Is God Evil?', in D. Parkin (ed.), *The Anthropology of Evil*, Oxford: Blackwell, pp. 165–93.

Hoffenberg, R. (1986), 'Primary Hypothyroidism', in S. H. Ingbar and L. E. Braverman (eds.), *The Thyroid*, 5th edn., Philadelphia: J. B. Lippincott.

Holt, C. and Bateson, G. (1970), 'Form and Function of the Dance in Bali', in J. Belo (ed.), *Traditional Balinese Culture*, New York: Columbia University Press.

Hooykaas, C. (1973), *Religion in Bali*, Leiden: E. J. Brill.

_____ (1977), *A Balinese Temple Festival*, The Hague: Martinus-Nijhoff.

Howard, A. (1984), *Margaret Mead: A Life*, New York: Simon & Schuster.

Inkles, A. (1953), 'Some Sociological Observations on Culture and Personality Studies', in C. Kluckholm, H. A. Murray, and O. N. Schneider (eds.), *Personality, Nature, Society and Culture*, New York: Alfred A. Knopf, pp. 577–92.

_____ (1979), 'Continuity and Change in the American National Character', in S. M. Lipset (ed.), *The Third Century: America as a Post-industrial Society*, Stanford: Hoover Institution Press, pp. 390–454.

_____ (1989), 'National Character Revisited', in *Kultur und Gesellschaft*, Frankfurt: Campus Verlang, pp. 98–112.

Inkles, A.; Hanfmann, E.; and Beier, H. (1958), 'Modal Personality and Adjustment to the Soviet Socio-political System', *Human Relations*, 11: 3–22.

Inkles, A. and Levinson, T. J. (1969), 'National Character: The Study of Modal Personality and Socio-cultural Systems', in G. Lindzey and E. Aronson (eds.), *The Handbook of Social Psychology*, 2nd edn., Vol. 4, Reading, Mass: Addison-Wesley, pp. 418–506.

Jensen, G. D. (1980), 'Cross-cultural Animal Studies of Sex', in H. I. Kaplan, A. M. Freedman, and B. J. Saddock (eds.), *Comprehensive Textbook of Psychiatry*, 3rd edn., Baltimore: Williams & Wilkins, pp. 1723–34.

Kaplan, H. I.; Freedman, A. M.; and Saddock, B. J. (eds.) (1980), *Comprehensive Textbook of Psychiatry*, 3rd edn., Baltimore: Williams & Wilkins.

Kaplan, H. I. and Saddock, B. J. (1988), *Clinical Psychology*, Baltimore: Williams & Wilkins.

Ketter, T. (1983), 'Cultural Stylization and Mental Illness in Bali', *Transcultural Psychiatric Research Review*, 20: 87–105.

Kleinman, A. (1980), *Patients and Healers in the Context of Cultures*, Berkeley: University of California Press.

Krause, G. (1988), *Bali 1912*, Wellington: January Books.

Kroeber, A. L. (1948), *Anthropology*, New York: Harcourt & Brace.

Lebra, T. S. (1976), *Japanese Patterns of Behavior*, Honolulu: University Press of Hawaii.

Lebra, W. P. (ed.) (1976), *Culture-bound Syndromes, Ethnopsychiatry and Alternative Therapies*, Honolulu: University Press of Hawaii.

Leimena, S. L. and Thong, D. H. (1983), 'Pengobatan Tradisional di Bali: Suatu laporan', in Setyonegoro and W. M. Roan (eds.), *Traditional Healing Practices*, Jakarta: Directorate of Mental Health, pp. 160–206.

LeVine, R. A. (1932), *Culture, Behavior and Personality*, 2nd edn., New York: Aldine.

Lewin, B. D. (1945), 'Book Review of Balinese Character', in *The Psychanalytic Study of the Child*, Vol. 1, New York: International Universities Press, pp. 379–87.

Li, Y.; Yang, Y.; and Yang, K. S. (eds.) (1974), *The Character of the Chinese: An Interdisciplinary Approach*, Nankang, Taipei: Institute of Ethnology, Academia Sinica.

Lipset, D. (1980), *Gregory Bateson: The Legacy of a Scientist*, Englewood Cliffs: Prentice-Hall.

Ludwig, A. M. (1966), 'Altered States of Consciousness', *Archives of General Psychiatry*, 15: 225–34.

McPhee, C. (1946), *A House in Bali*, New York: J. D. Day Co.

―――― (1948), 'Dance in Bali', *Dance Index*, 7: 156–207.

―――― (1970), 'Children and Music in Bali', in J. Belo (ed.), *Traditional Balinese Culture*, New York: Columbia University Press.

Masters, W. H. and Johnson, V. E. (1966), *The Human Sexual Response*, Boston: Little, Brown & Co.

Mead, M. (1928), *Coming of Age in Samoa: A Psychological Study of Primitive Youth for Western Civilization*, New York: Wm. Morrow.

―――― (1930a), *Growing up in New Guinea*, New York: Wm. Morrow.

―――― (1930b), 'Social Organization of Manu'a', *Bernice P. Bishop Museum Bulletin*, 76, Honolulu, reissued 1969.

―――― (1939), 'The Strolling Players in the Mountains of Bali', *Natural History*, XLIII (1): 17–26.

―――― (1940), 'The Mountain Arapesh, II, Supernaturalism', *Anthropological Papers of the American Museum of Natural History*, 37 (Part 3): 319–451; reprinted in *The Mountain Arapesh II: Arts and Supernaturalism*, New York: Natural History Press.

_____ (1955), 'Children and Ritual in Bali', in M. Mead and M. Wolfstein (eds.), *Childhood in Contemporary Cultures*, University of Chicago Press; reprinted in *Traditional Balinese Culture*, Belo (ed.), Chicago/New York: Columbia University Press, 1970, pp. 198–211.

_____ (1959), *An Anthropologist at Work: Writings of Ruth Benedict*, Boston: Houghton Mifflin.

_____ (1972), *Blackberry Winter, My Earlier Years*, New York: Wm. Morrow.

_____ (1977), *Letters from the Field 1925–1975*, New York: Harper & Row.

Mead, M. and Macgregor, F. C. (1951), *Growth and Culture*, New York: G. D. Putnam & Sons.

Moerdowo, R. M. (1973), *Ceremonies in Bali*, Jakarta: Bhrataru.

Morgan, A. H. and Hilgard, J. R. (1978–9), 'The Stanford Hypnotic Clinical Scale for Children', *American Journal of Clinical Hypnosis*, 21: 148–55.

Mrazek, R. (1983), *Bali: The Spirit Gate to Heaven*, London: Arbis Publishing.

Myers, J. K.; Weissman, M. M.; and Tischler, G. L. et al. (1984),'Six-month Prevalence of Psychiatric Disorders in Three Communities', *Archives of General Psychiatry*, 41: 959–67.

Oesterreich, T. K. (1974), *Possession and Exorcism*, New York: Causeway Books.

Patience, A. and Smith, J. W. (1986), 'Derick Freeman and Samoa: The Making and Unmaking of a Biobehavioral Myth', *American Anthropologist*, 88: 157–67.

Poffenberger, M. and Zurbachen, M. S. (1978), 'The Economics of Village Bali, Three Perspectives, *Jakarta*: USAID/Indonesia Information Center, Unpublished report.

Powell, H. (1930), *The Last Paradise*, New York: Johnathan, Cape & Harrison Smith, Inc.

Ramseyer, U. (1986), *The Art and Culture of Bali*, Singapore: Oxford University Press.

Rappaport, T. (1986), 'Desecrating the Holy Women: Derick Freeman's Attack on Margaret Mead', *American Scholar*, 55(3): 313–47.

Ross, C. A.; John, S.; and Currie, R. (1990), 'Dissociative Experiences in the Normal Population', *American Journal of Psychiatry*, 147: 1547–52.

Rouget, G. (1985), *Music and Trance*, Chicago: University of Chicago Press.

Simons, R. C. and Hughes, C. C. (eds.) (1985), *The Culture-bound Syndromes*, Boston: D. Reidel Publishing Co.

Soskis, D. A. (1986), *Teaching Self-hypnosis: An Introductory Guide for Clinicians*, New York: W. W. Norton.

Song, W. (1985), 'A Preliminary Study of the Character Traits of the

Chinese', in D. Y. H. Wu and W. S. Tseng (eds.), *Chinese Culture and Mental Health*, Orlando: Academic Press.

Suryani, L. K. (1984), 'Culture and Mental Disorder: The Case of *Bebainan* in Bali', *Culture, Medicine and Psychiatry*, 8: 95–113.

—— (1988), 'Psikosis Akut pada Orang Bali yang Beragama Hindu di Bali: Suatu Studi Pendekatan Kliniko-sosiobudaya', Ph.D. dissertation, Erlangga University, Surabaya, Java.

Suryani, L. K.; Adnjana, T. A. K.; and Jensen, G. D. (1990), 'Palm Wine Drinking in a Balinese Village: Environmental Influences', *International Journal of Addictions*, 25: 911–20.

Suryani, L. K.; Adnjana, T. A. K.; Thong, D.; Mink, T. I. R.; Putra, I. D. K. W.; Widjana, W.; Tama, D. W.; and Jensen, G. D. (1988), 'The Physical and Mental Health of Elderly in a Balinese Village, *Journal of Cross-cultural Gerontology*, 3: 105–20.

Suryani, L. K. and Jensen, G. D. (1991), 'Psychiatrist, Traditional Healer and Culture Integrated in Medical Practice', *Medical Anthropology*, 13: 301–14.

Tart, C. T. (1986), *Waking up: Overcoming the Obstacles to Human Potential*, Boston: New Science Library.

Teok, J. and Tan, E. (1976), 'An Epidemic Outbreak of Hysteria in West Malaysia', in W. P. Lebra (ed.), *Culture-bound Syndromes, Ethnopsychiatry and Alternate Therapies*, Vol. IV, Honolulu: University of Hawaii Press.

Terkelson, K. G. (1983), 'Schizophrenia and the Family: Adverse Effects of Family Therapy', *Family Process*, 22: 191–200.

Thomas, A. and Chess, S. (1977), *Temperament and Development*, New York: Brunner/Mazel.

Toffler, A. (1971), *Culture Shock*, New York: Bantam.

—— (1980), *The Third Wave*, New York: Wm. Morrow.

Trevarthen, C. (1983), 'Interpersonal Abilities of Infants as Generators for Transmission of Language and Culture', in M. A. Oliverio and M. Zappella (eds.), *The Behavior of Human Infants*, London: Plenum.

Tseng, W. S.; Ebata, K.; Miguichi, M.; Egawa, M.; and McLaughlin, D. G. (1990), 'Transethnic Adaption and Personality Traits: A Lesson from Japanese Orphans Returned from China to Japan', *American Journal of Psychiatry*, 174: 330–5.

Van der Krann, A. (1980), *Lombok: Conquest, Colinization, and Under-development, 1870–1940*, Singapore: Heinemann Educational Books (Asia), Ltd.

Wallace, A. F. C. (1961), *Culture and Personality*, New York: Random House.

Webster (1965), *Webster's Seventh New Collegiate Dictionary*, Cambridge: Riverside Press.

Weck, W. (1937), *Pengetahuan tentang Penyembuhan dan Pekerti Rakyat di Bali*, Stuttgart: Ferdinand Enke.

Weizhan, S. (1985), 'A Preliminary Study of Character Traits of Chinese', in W. Tsing and D. Y. H. Wu (eds.), *Chinese Culture and Mental Health*, New York: Academic Press.

WHO (1979), *Schizophrenia: An International Follow-up Study*, New York: Wiley.

Wikan, U. (1987), 'Public Grace and Private Fears: Gaiety, Offense, and Sorcery in Northern Bali', *Ethos*, 15: 337–65.

_____ (1988), 'Bereavement and Loss in Two Muslim Communities: Egypt and Bali Compared', *Social Science and Medicine*, 27: 451–60.

_____ (1989a), 'Illness from Fright or Soul Loss: A North Balinese Culture-bound Syndrome?', *Culture, Medicine, and Psychiatry*, 13: 25–50.

_____ (1989b), 'Managing the Heart to Brighten Face and Soul: Emotions in Balinese Morality and Health Care', *American Ethnologist*, 16: 294–312.

Yang, K. S. (1986), 'Chinese Personality and its Change', in M. H. Bond (ed.), *The Psychology of the Chinese People*, Hong Kong: Oxford University Press.

Index

Cock-fights, 3, 37, 96, 106–8, 116n, pl. 51, 52

Connor, L. H.: on ceremonies, 28; on sibling spirits, 26; on traditional healers, 28

Covarrubias, M., 17, 20, 38, 53, 79, 83, 104n, 106, 110, 123, 154n

Cremation ceremony, 10, 18, 38, 95, 103, 135–6

DADIA, 15, 137, pl. 18, 19, 25, 27, 53

Dance, 21, 93, 103, 124, 144–5, pl. 24, 25; arja drama, 83; baris, 42; Calonarang, 79, 91n, 97, 112; and emotional expression, 112; kris, 56, 80, 81, 82–3, 94, 124; trance, 128, 144–5

Denpasar, 9, 12n, 13, 17, 79, 83, 100, 127, 144, 151, pl. 4

Desa, 14, 20, 22

Dewa, 26

Dissociation, 72, 74n; see also Trance; Possession

Djelantik, A. A. M.: on art, 134, 138

Dokar, 18

Dupa, 23

Dutch, 36, 47–48, 53, 58n, 66, 96; influence, 8, 123; translation by Kaler, 35

ELDERLY, 6, 116n

Emotions, 26, 27, 50, 61, 62, 68, 72, 73, 78, 80, 99, 100, 101, 103, 105; control of, 111–12; expression of, 105–9, 110, 111, 112, 113, 116n, 155n, pl. 1, 44, 55, 58; withholding of, 113

Erikson, E. H.: approach to character, 55; influence on Mead, 58n; theory of human development, 89–90, 101, 131, 138

Evil, 80, 81, 82–3

Evil spirits, 22, 24, 28, 29, 80, 85–8, 100, pl. 46

FEAR: basis of culture, 3, 75–91, 105; from leak, 86; managing, 88; from

parents, 77–9, 101; and orientation, 76–7, 105; and sleep, 85, 105; the witch plays, 79–85

Films, 31, 67, 68, 94; see also Karba: 'Karba's First Years'

Freeman, D., 45–6, 57n, 127, 152

GALUNGUN, 22, 23, pl. 20

Gamelan, 15, 24, 41, 97, 98, 104n, 112, 124, 134, pl. 24, 53

Geertz, C., 11n, 12n, 25, 61, 93, 95, 96, 97, 102, 106, 109, 135–6, 155n; on Balinese religion, 25; on climax, 93, 95, 96, 97, 109; on cock-fights, 106; on hierarchy, 136; and influence of Bateson and Mead, 109; on lek, 61

Geertz, H., 11n, 25, 43n, 53, 94; on Balinese language, 43n; on Balinese religion, 25; on Bateson and Mead collaboration, 11n; on climax in ritual, 94; on influences on Bateson and Mead, 53

Gods, see Balinese Hindu religion

Goitre, see Illness

Gumicik, 56, pl. 3

HENING, 109

Hindu–Dharma beliefs, 25–6; see also Balinese Hindu religion

Hobart, M.: on misinterpretation of culture, 3, 131

Holy water, 23, pl. 19

Homosexuality: interrogation about, 12n, 124

Howard, A.: Margaret Mead: A Life, 7, 12n, 35, 53, 55; and homosexual interrogation, 124; on Kaler, 66

Hypnosis, 146–7, self-hypnosis, 72; see also Trance

Hypothyroidism, 33, 35–6, 43

ILLNESS, 26, 157–62; at Bayung Gede, 35–6, 44n, pl. 37; bebainan, 31, 32n, 105, 113–45, 157–62; concepts of, 27–31; goitre, 35–6, 58n; by leak, 86